THE TRANSFORMERS

FORMERS

REGENERATION ONE

VOLUME 2

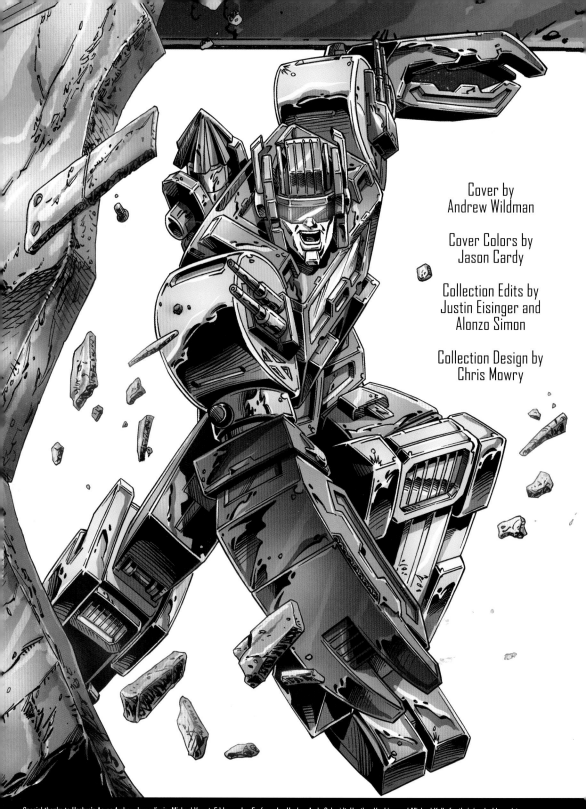

Cover by
Andrew Wildman

Cover Colors by
Jason Cardy

Collection Edits by
Justin Eisinger and
Alonzo Simon

Collection Design by
Chris Mowry

Special thanks to Hasbro's Aaron Archer, Jerry Jivoin, Michael Verret, Ed Lane, Joe Furfaro, Jos Huxley, Andy Schmidt, Heather Hopkins, and Michael Kelly for their invaluable assistance.

IDW founded by Ted Adams, Alex Garner, Kris Oprisko, and Robbie Robbins |

ISBN: 978-1-61377-642-1   16 15 14 13   1 2 3 4

Licensed By:

Ted Adams, CEO & Publisher
Greg Goldstein, President & COO
Robbie Robbins, EVP/Sr. Graphic Artist
Chris Ryall, Chief Creative Officer/Editor-in-Chief
Matthew Ruzicka, CPA, Chief Financial Officer
Alan Payne, VP of Sales
Dirk Wood, VP of Marketing
Lorelei Bunjes, VP of Digital Services

Become our fan on Facebook **facebook.com/idwpublishing**
Follow us on Twitter **@idwpublishing**
Check us out on YouTube **youtube.com/idwpublishing**
www.IDWPUBLISHING.com

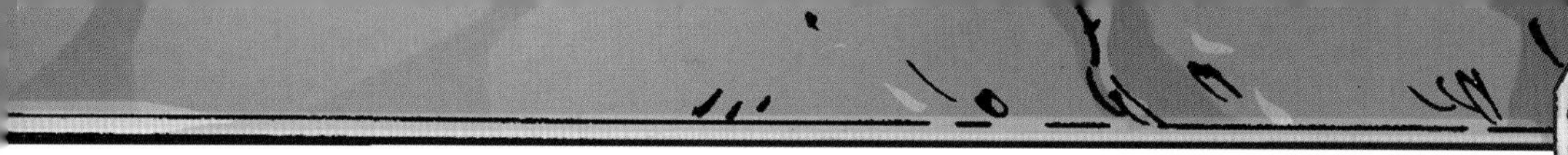

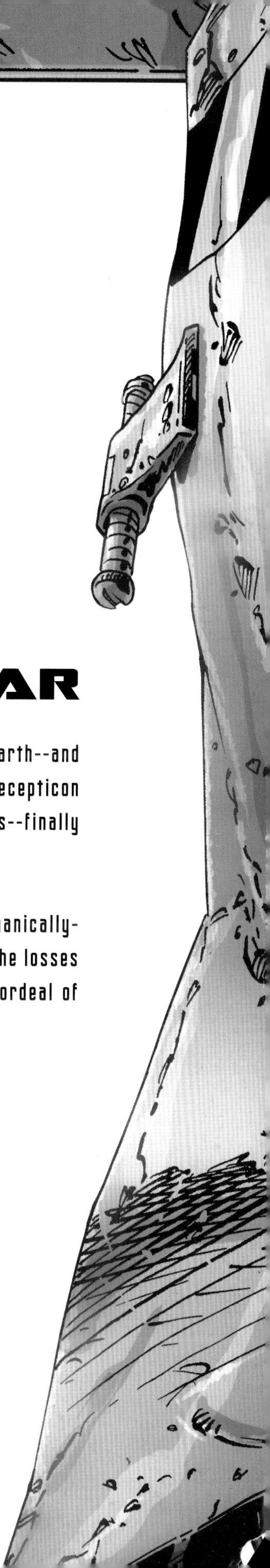

THE STORY SO FAR

After a decades-long absence, the Autobots have returned to Earth--and find a world in ruins, devastated by Megatron and his zombie Decepticon hordes. Optimus Prime returns and confronts his old nemesis--finally killing Megatron in battle.

As Autobots and their human teammates--including a bio-mechanically-enhanced Spike Witwicky--survey the damage to the planet and the losses they have both felt, the Dinobot leader Grimlock undergoes an ordeal of his own...

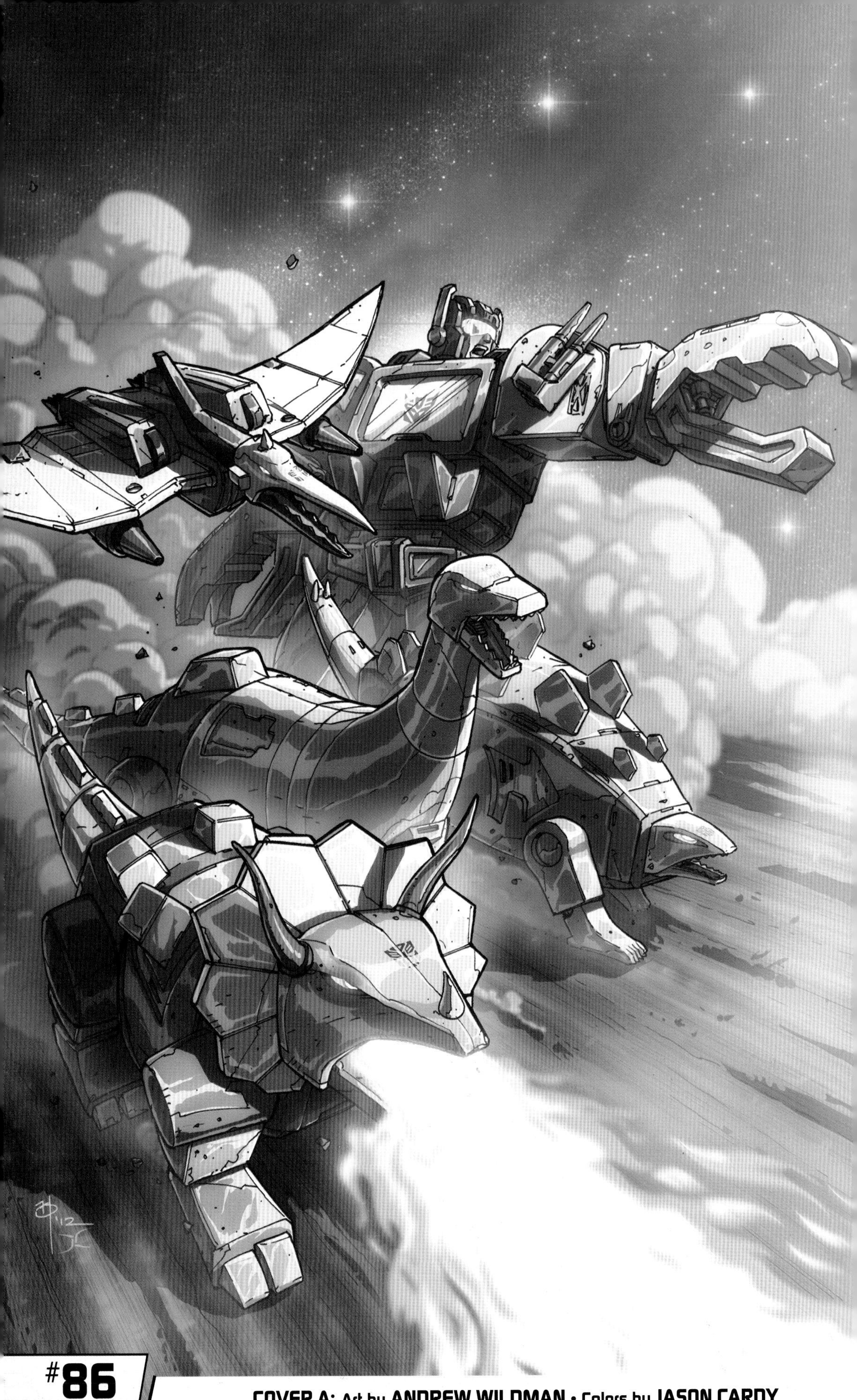

#86 **COVER A:** Art by **ANDREW WILDMAN** • Colors by **JASON CARDY**

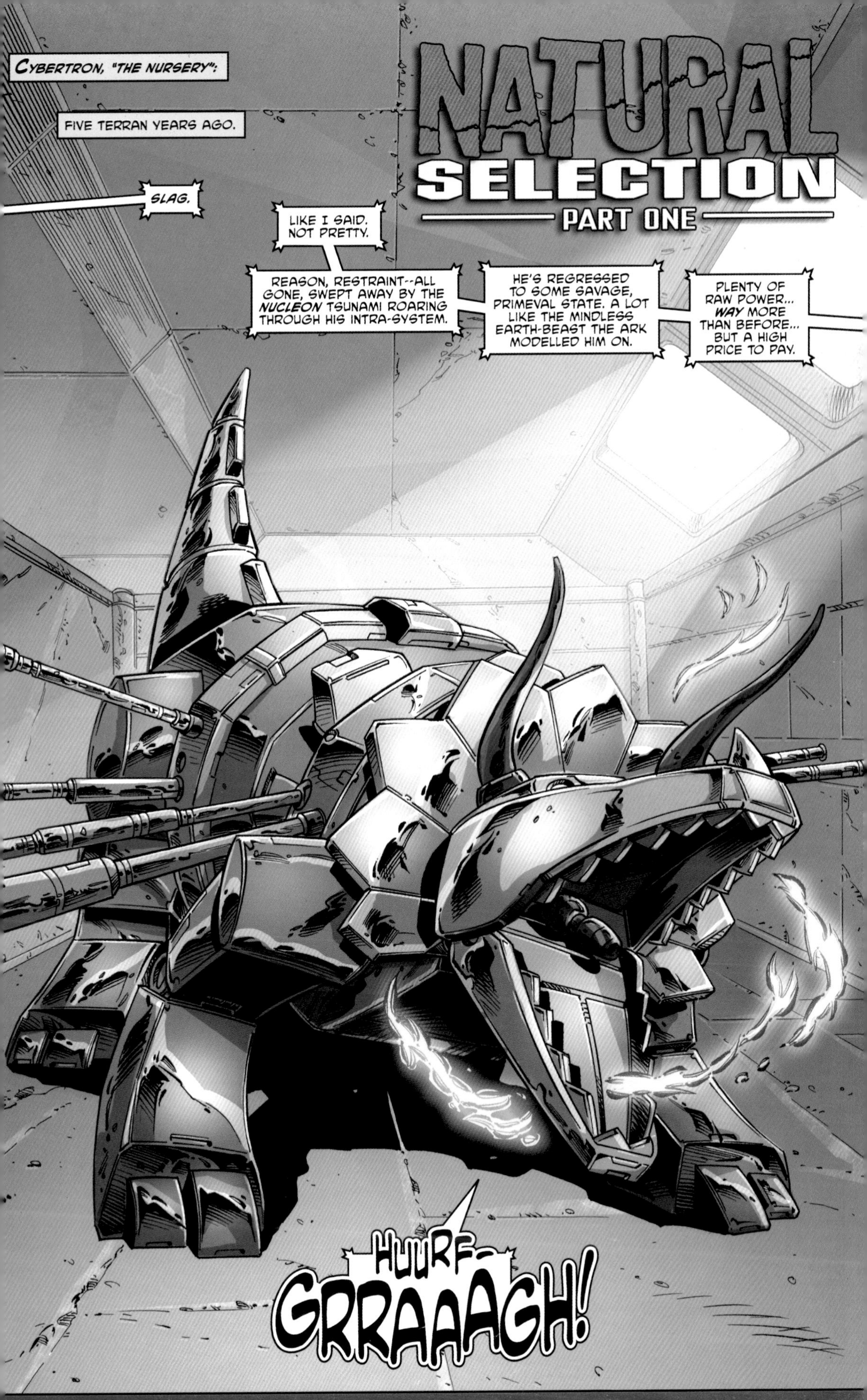
CYBERTRON, "THE NURSERY":
FIVE TERRAN YEARS AGO.
NATURAL SELECTION
PART ONE
SLAG.
LIKE I SAID. NOT PRETTY.
REASON, RESTRAINT--ALL GONE, SWEPT AWAY BY THE ***NUCLEON*** TSUNAMI ROARING THROUGH HIS INTRA-SYSTEM.
HE'S REGRESSED TO SOME SAVAGE, PRIMEVAL STATE. A LOT LIKE THE MINDLESS EARTH-BEAST THE ARK MODELLED HIM ON.
PLENTY OF RAW POWER... ***WAY*** MORE THAN BEFORE... BUT A HIGH PRICE TO PAY.
HUURF-GRRAAAGH!

WRITER IMON FURMAN | PENCILER ANDREW WILDMAN | INKER STEPHEN BASKERVILLE | COLORIST JOHN-PAUL BOVE | LETTERER CHRIS MOWRY | EDITOR JOHN BARBER | EDITOR-IN-CHIEF CHRIS RYALL

GRIMLOCK.
SLUDGE.
WOULDN'T YOU SAY?
SWOOP.
SNARL.
YES. HIGH PRICE.
AND YOU DID IT TO HIM.
AND THEM!
BLASTER.
INFERNO.
SILVERBOLT.
HUFFER.

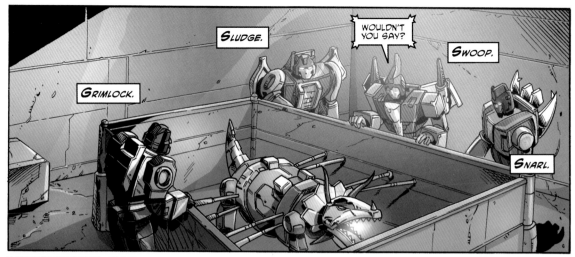

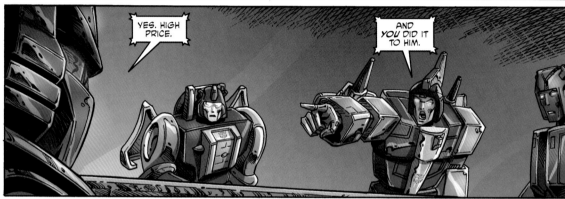

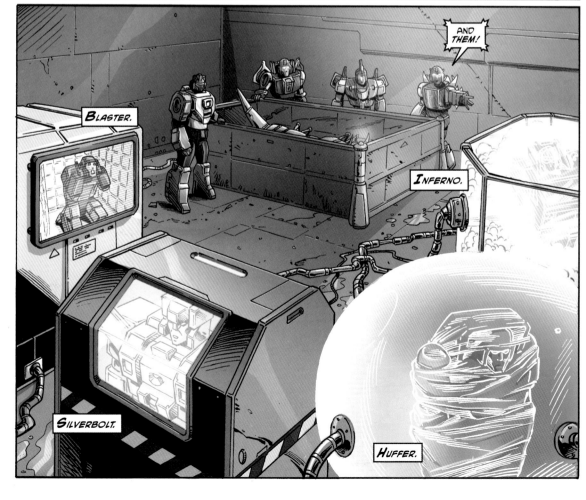

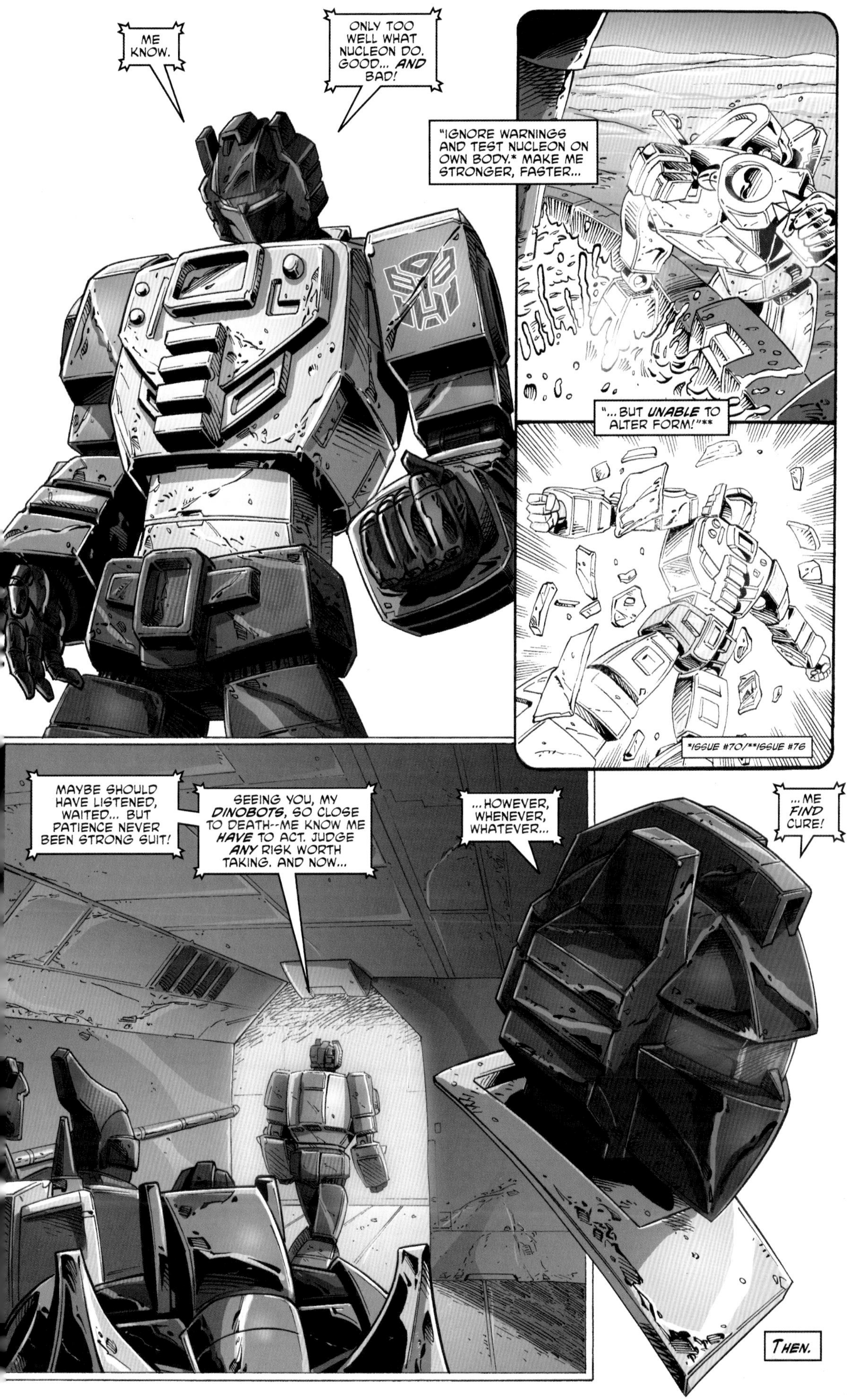
ME KNOW.
ONLY TOO WELL WHAT NUCLEON DO. GOOD... AND BAD!
"IGNORE WARNINGS AND TEST NUCLEON ON OWN BODY.* MAKE ME STRONGER, FASTER...
"...BUT UNABLE TO ALTER FORM!"**
*ISSUE #70/**ISSUE #76
MAYBE SHOULD HAVE LISTENED, WAITED... BUT PATIENCE NEVER BEEN STRONG SUIT!
SEEING YOU, MY DINOBOTS, SO CLOSE TO DEATH--ME KNOW ME HAVE TO ACT. JUDGE ANY RISK WORTH TAKING. AND NOW...
...HOWEVER, WHENEVER, WHATEVER...
...ME FIND CURE!
THEN.

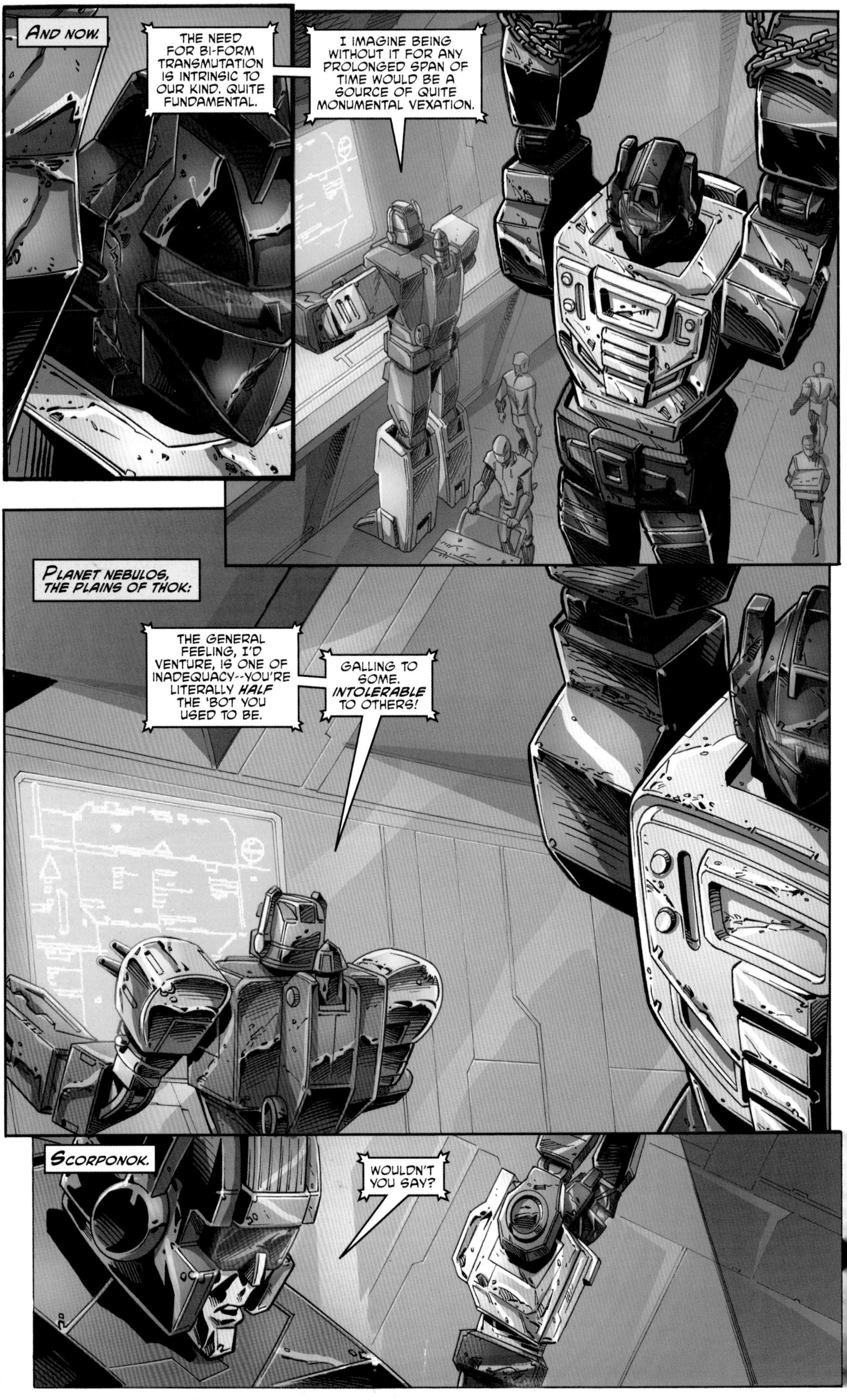
AND NOW.
THE NEED FOR BI-FORM TRANSMUTATION IS INTRINSIC TO OUR KIND. QUITE FUNDAMENTAL.
I IMAGINE BEING WITHOUT IT FOR ANY PROLONGED SPAN OF TIME WOULD BE A SOURCE OF QUITE MONUMENTAL VEXATION.
PLANET NEBULOS, THE PLAINS OF THOK:
THE GENERAL FEELING, I'D VENTURE, IS ONE OF INADEQUACY--YOU'RE LITERALLY HALF THE 'BOT YOU USED TO BE.
GALLING TO SOME. INTOLERABLE TO OTHERS!
SCORPONOK.
WOULDN'T YOU SAY?

FASCINATING STUFF, NUCLEON. I'D HEARD RUMORS, OF COURSE, BUT THE CHANCE TO STUDY IT UP CLOSE IS A *RARE* PRIVILEGE.

FAR FROM CONFINING ITSELF TO YOUR INTRA-SYSTEM, IT HAS PERMEATED THE FUNDAMENTAL BUILDING BLOCKS OF YOUR GENETIC STRUCTURE--AND REASSEMBLED THEM.

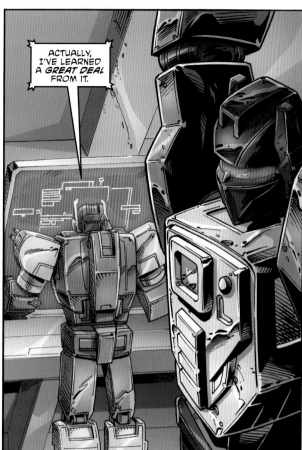

ACTUALLY, I'VE LEARNED A *GREAT DEAL* FROM IT.

ONE THING ME NOT UNDERSTAND.

OH? JUST ONE?

ME--YOU, MEET BEFORE. LONG AGO... IN BATTLE! NO TALK THEN. ONLY COMBAT. LANGUAGE OF *WAR!*

WHAT CHANGE?

FINALLY! AFTER SIXTEEN NEBULAN SOLAR REVOLUTIONS YOU POSE A REASONED, RELEVANT QUESTION.

THE SIMPLE ANSWER IS, *I* HAVE CHANGED! IMMEASURABLY!

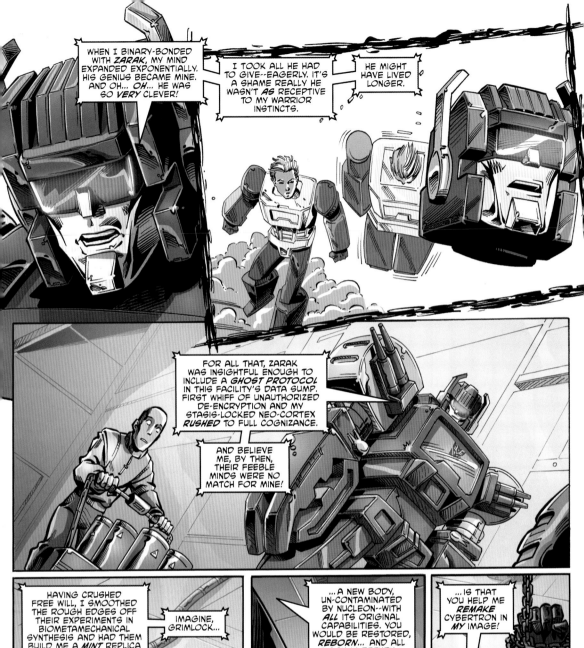

WHEN I BINARY-BONDED WITH *ZARAK*, MY MIND EXPANDED EXPONENTIALLY. HIS GENIUS BECAME MINE. AND OH... *OH...* HE WAS SO *VERY* CLEVER!

I TOOK ALL HE HAD TO GIVE--EAGERLY. IT'S A SHAME REALLY HE WASN'T *AS* RECEPTIVE TO MY WARRIOR INSTINCTS.

HE MIGHT HAVE LIVED LONGER.

FOR ALL THAT, ZARAK WAS INSIGHTFUL ENOUGH TO INCLUDE A *GHOST PROTOCOL* IN THIS FACILITY'S DATA SUMP. FIRST WHIFF OF UNAUTHORIZED DE-ENCRYPTION AND MY STASIS-LOCKED NEO-CORTEX *RUSHED* TO FULL COGNIZANCE.

AND BELIEVE ME, BY THEN, THEIR FEEBLE MINDS WERE NO MATCH FOR MINE!

HAVING CRUSHED FREE WILL, I SMOOTHED THE ROUGH EDGES OFF THEIR EXPERIMENTS IN BIOMETAMECHANICAL SYNTHESIS AND HAD THEM BUILD ME A *MINT* REPLICA OF MY ORIGINAL BODY.

IMAGINE, GRIMLOCK...

... A NEW BODY, UN-CONTAMINATED BY NUCLEON--WITH *ALL* ITS ORIGINAL CAPABILITIES. YOU WOULD BE RESTORED, *REBORN*... AND ALL I ASK IN RETURN...

... IS THAT YOU HELP ME *REMAKE* CYBERTRON IN *MY* IMAGE!

NO? WE SHALL SEE. WE SHALL SEE...

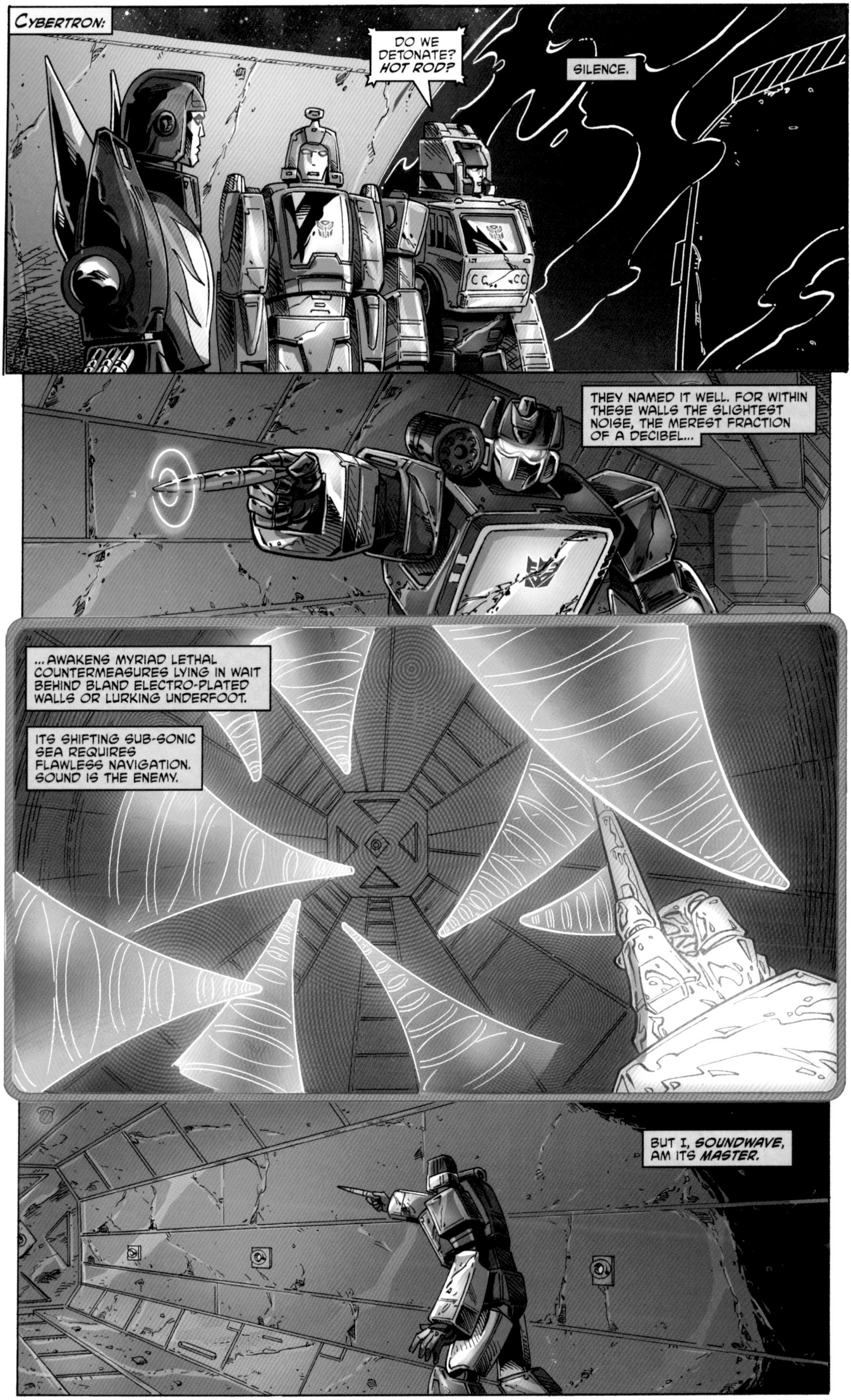
CYBERTRON:
DO WE DETONATE? HOT ROD?
SILENCE.
THEY NAMED IT WELL. FOR WITHIN THESE WALLS THE SLIGHTEST NOISE, THE MEREST FRACTION OF A DECIBEL...
...AWAKENS MYRIAD LETHAL COUNTERMEASURES LYING IN WAIT BEHIND BLAND ELECTRO-PLATED WALLS OR LURKING UNDERFOOT.
ITS SHIFTING SUB-SONIC SEA REQUIRES FLAWLESS NAVIGATION. SOUND IS THE ENEMY.
BUT I, SOUNDWAVE, AM ITS MASTER.

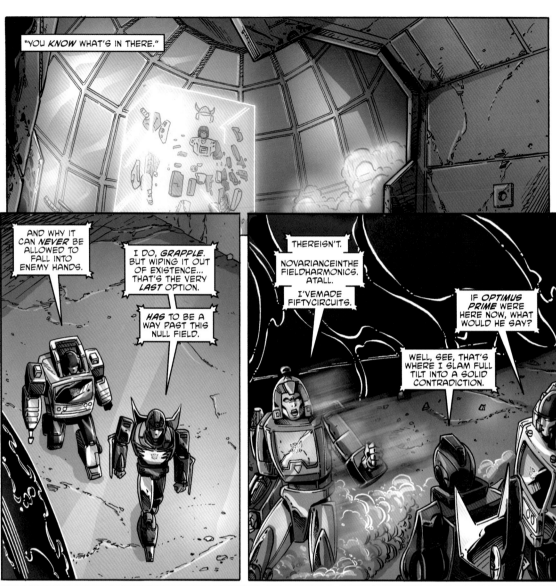

"YOU *KNOW* WHAT'S IN THERE."

AND WHY IT CAN *NEVER* BE ALLOWED TO FALL INTO ENEMY HANDS.

I DO, *GRAPPLE.* BUT WIPING IT OUT OF EXISTENCE... THAT'S THE VERY *LAST* OPTION.

HAS TO BE A WAY PAST THIS NULL FIELD.

THEREISN'T.

NOVARIANCEINTHE FIELDHARMONICS. ATALL.

I'VEMADE FIFTYCIRCUITS.

IF *OPTIMUS PRIME* WERE HERE NOW, WHAT WOULD HE SAY?

WELL, SEE, THAT'S WHERE I SLAM FULL TILT INTO A SOLID CONTRADICTION.

PRIME WOULD SAY, FOLLOW YOUR INSTINCTS. BUT IN THIS CASE, MINE FLY FULLY IN THE FACE OF *HIS* EDICT.

BECAUSE EVEN *IF* WHAT'S IN THERE WAS ONCE *THUNDERWING,* AND IS STILL TAINTED BY PURE EVIL, IT'S ALSO ALL THAT'S LEFT OF THE *CREATION MATRIX!* THE LAST TANGIBLE LINK TO OUR CREATOR, *PRIMUS!*

LOOK, I DESIGNED AND BUILT THE *HALL OF SILENCE,* THE LAST THING I WANT IS TO BLOW IT TO KINGDOM COME... BUT IT *HAS* TO BE DONE!

EVERYTHING NOW DEPENDS ON HOT ROD, ON HIS FOLLOWING PROTOCOL--TO THE LETTER.

HIS LACK OF COMMAND EXPERIENCE, HIS INABILITY--OR RELUCTANCE--TO MAKE A PURELY INTUITIVE JUDGMENT CALL...

...IS *MY* EXIT STRATEGY.

FOR IN THE EVENT OF A BREACH OF SECURITY AT THE HALL OF SILENCE, IF ALL EFFORTS TO SECURE THE SCENE FAIL...

≥SIGH≤

THIS IS HOT ROD. COMMAND AUTHORITY: CEPHEUS-AURIGA-PAVO-NINE.

DETONATE THE CHARGES.

VVERP

DHOOOOOOOM

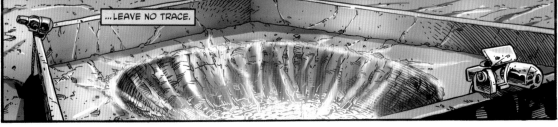

...LEAVE NO TRACE.

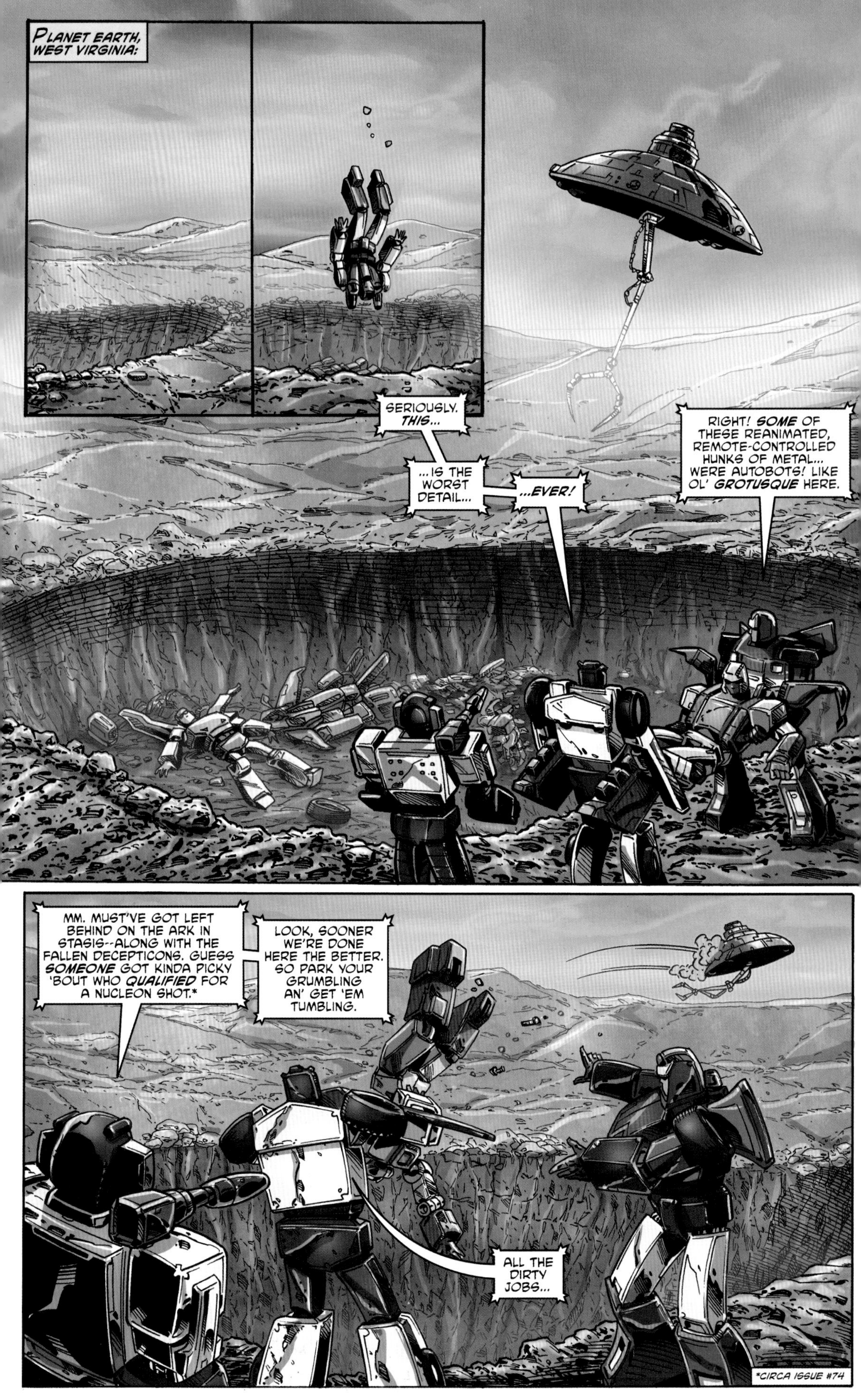
PLANET EARTH, WEST VIRGINIA:
SERIOUSLY. THIS...
...IS THE WORST DETAIL...
...EVER!
RIGHT! SOME OF THESE REANIMATED, REMOTE-CONTROLLED HUNKS OF METAL... WERE AUTOBOTS! LIKE OL' GROTUSQUE HERE.
MM. MUST'VE GOT LEFT BEHIND ON THE ARK IN STASIS--ALONG WITH THE FALLEN DECEPTICONS. GUESS SOMEONE GOT KINDA PICKY 'BOUT WHO QUALIFIED FOR A NUCLEON SHOT.*
LOOK, SOONER WE'RE DONE HERE THE BETTER. SO PARK YOUR GRUMBLING AN' GET 'EM TUMBLING.
ALL THE DIRTY JOBS...
*CIRCA ISSUE #74

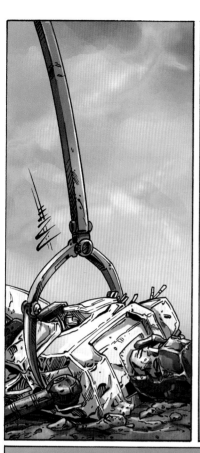

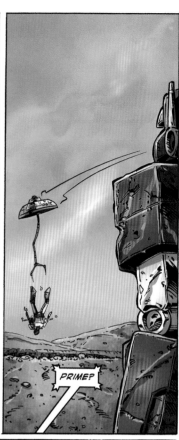

PRIME?

YOU, AH, ASKED FOR A STATUS REPORT.

YES. GO AHEAD, *FIRST AID.*

UM, WE'VE FOUR ON THE CRITICAL LIST--*LEADFOOT, MIRAGE, BRAWN,* AND *BROADSIDE.* THE REST ARE MOSTLY BUMPS, BURNS, AND SCRAPES.

TWO FATALITIES-- *SPRINGER...* AND *RATCHET.* THOUGH, WITH RATCHET, I'M NOT ENTIRELY SURE HE QUALIFIED AS ALIVE, EVEN BEFORE KUP, WELL...

EXECUTED HIM.

AS *I* EXECUTED *MEGATRON.*

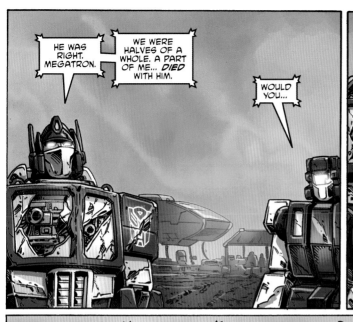

HE WAS RIGHT. MEGATRON.

WE WERE HALVES OF A WHOLE. A PART OF ME... *DIED* WITH HIM.

WOULD YOU...

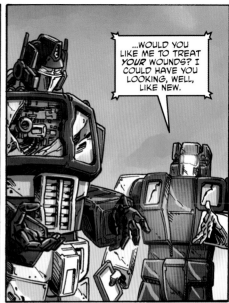

...WOULD YOU LIKE ME TO TREAT *YOUR* WOUNDS? I COULD HAVE YOU LOOKING, WELL, LIKE NEW.

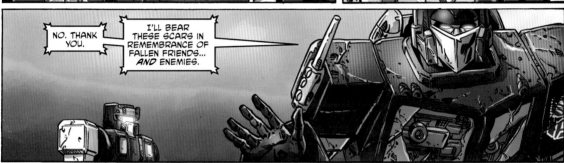

NO. THANK YOU.

I'LL BEAR THESE SCARS IN REMEMBRANCE OF FALLEN FRIENDS... *AND* ENEMIES.

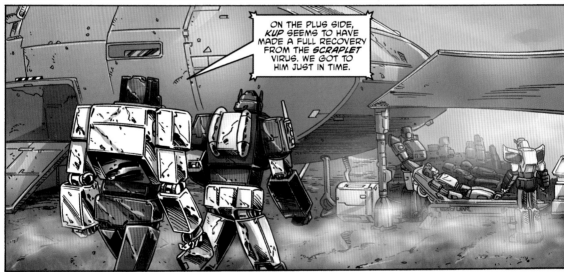

ON THE PLUS SIDE, *KUP* SEEMS TO HAVE MADE A FULL RECOVERY FROM THE *SCRAPLET* VIRUS. WE GOT TO HIM JUST IN TIME.

KUP?

PRIME.

I--

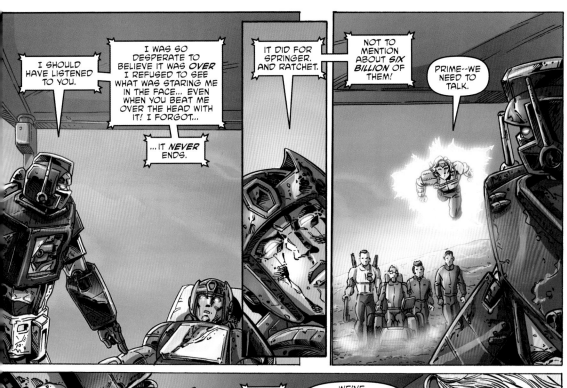

I SHOULD HAVE LISTENED TO YOU.

I WAS SO DESPERATE TO BELIEVE IT WAS *OVER* I REFUSED TO SEE WHAT WAS STARING ME IN THE FACE... EVEN WHEN YOU BEAT ME OVER THE HEAD WITH IT! I FORGOT...

...IT *NEVER* ENDS.

IT DID FOR SPRINGER. AND RATCHET.

NOT TO MENTION ABOUT *SIX BILLION* OF THEM!

PRIME--WE NEED TO TALK.

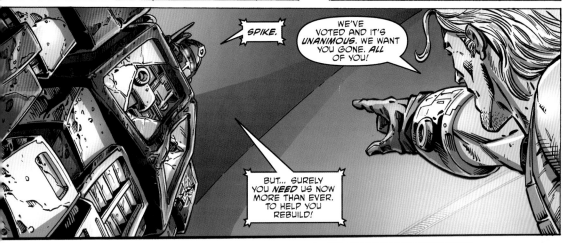

SPIKE.

WE'VE VOTED AND IT'S *UNANIMOUS.* WE WANT YOU GONE. *ALL* OF YOU!

BUT... SURELY YOU *NEED* US NOW MORE THAN EVER. TO HELP YOU REBUILD!

REBUILD? IT'S WAY, *WAY* BEYOND THAT. IT'S STARTING OVER FROM SCRATCH, AND YOU'RE TO HAVE NO PART IN IT!

IT WAS YOUR PRESENCE, AND SUBSEQUENT NEGLECT... THAT LED TO ALL THIS!

DON'T...

...MAKE US ASK TWICE.

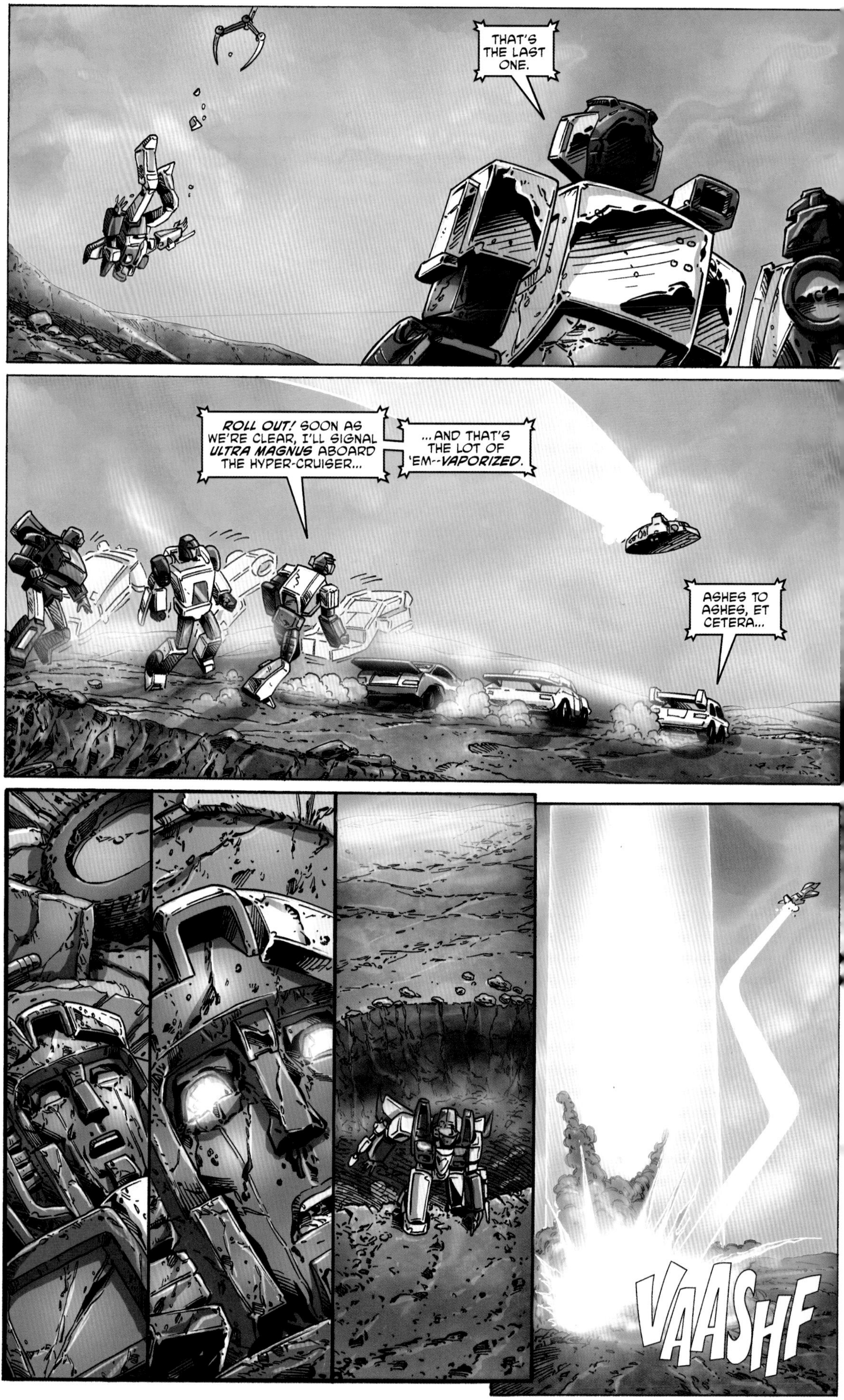
THAT'S THE LAST ONE.
ROLL OUT! SOON AS WE'RE CLEAR, I'LL SIGNAL ULTRA MAGNUS ABOARD THE HYPER-CRUISER...
...AND THAT'S THE LOT OF 'EM--VAPORIZED.
ASHES TO ASHES, ET CETERA...
VAASHF

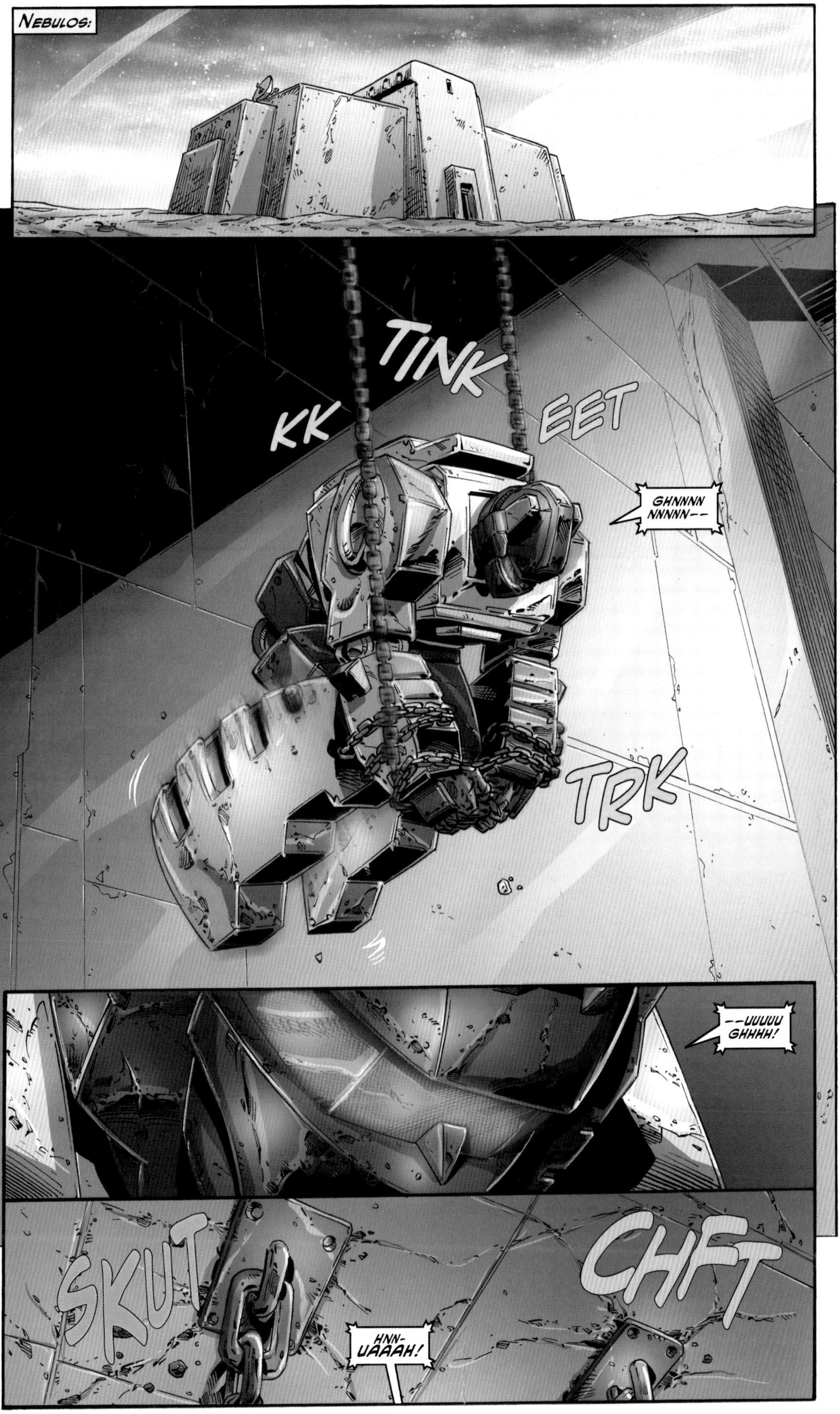
NEBULOS:
TINK
KK
EET
GHNNNN NNNNN--
TRK
--UUUUU GHHHH!
SKUT
CHFT
HNN- UAAAH!

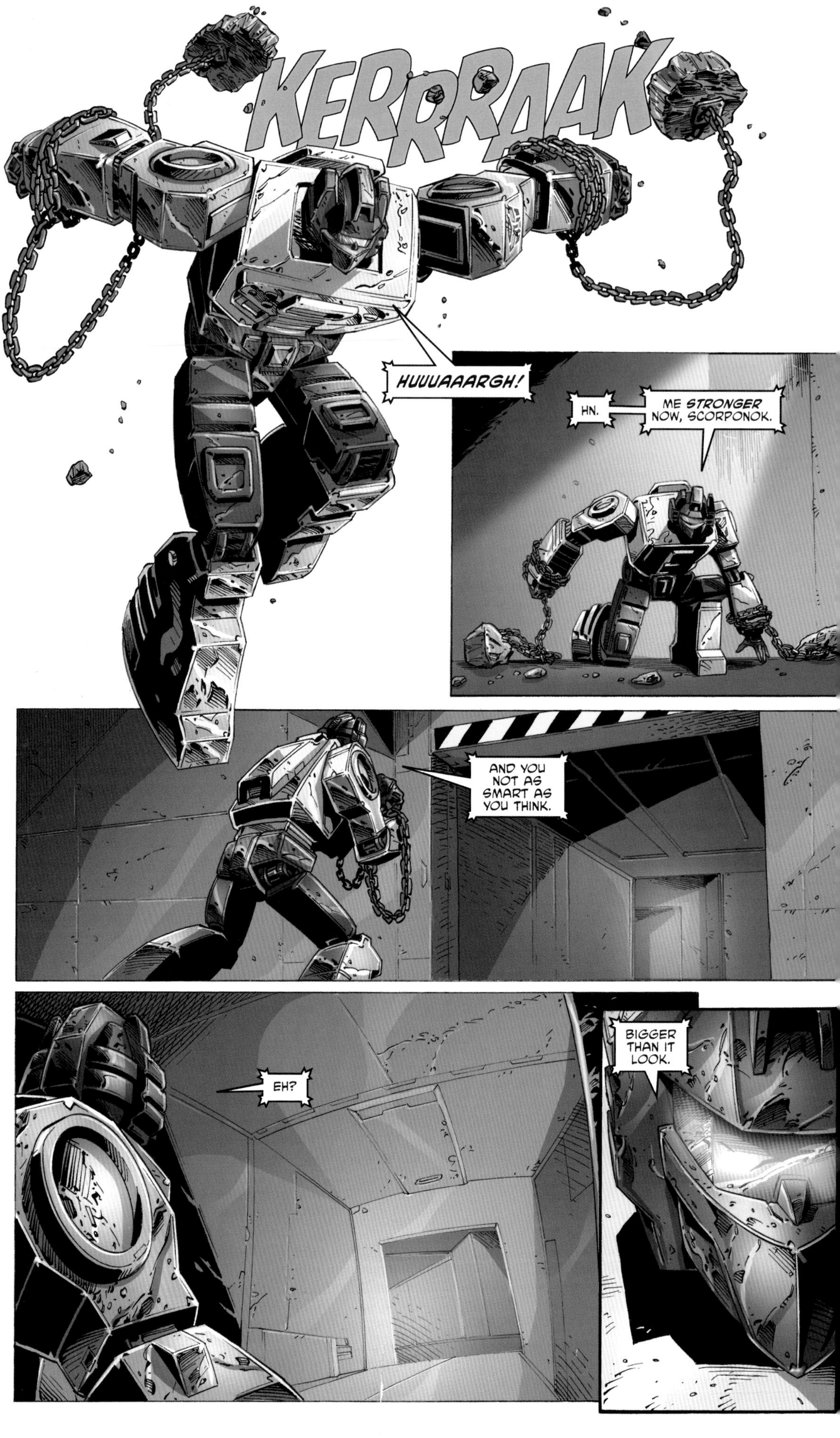
KERRRAAK
HUUUAAARGH!
HN.
ME STRONGER NOW, SCORPONOK.
AND YOU NOT AS SMART AS YOU THINK.
EH?
BIGGER THAN IT LOOK.

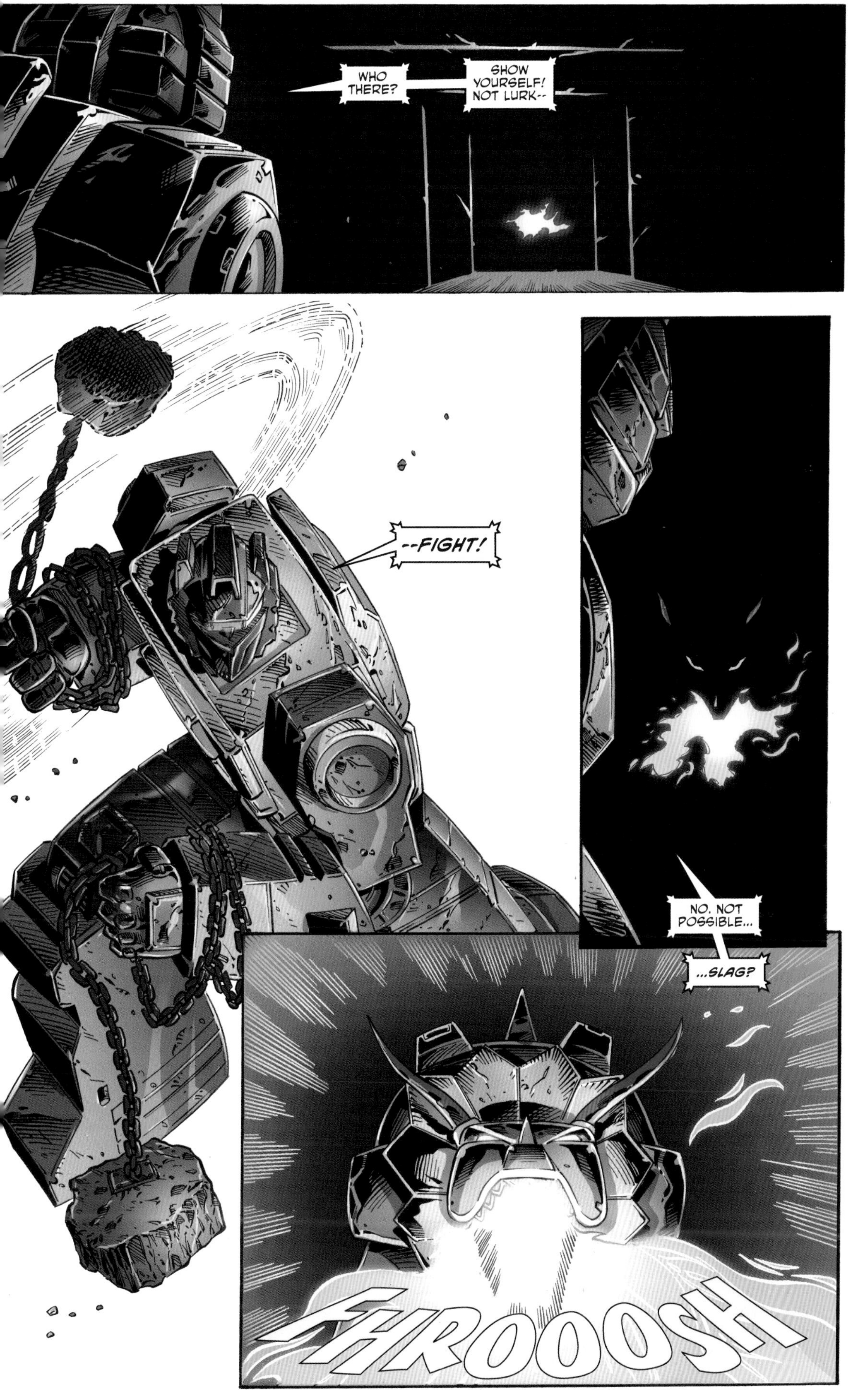
WHO THERE?
SHOW YOURSELF! NOT LURK--
--FIGHT!
NO. NOT POSSIBLE...
...SLAG?
FHROOOSH

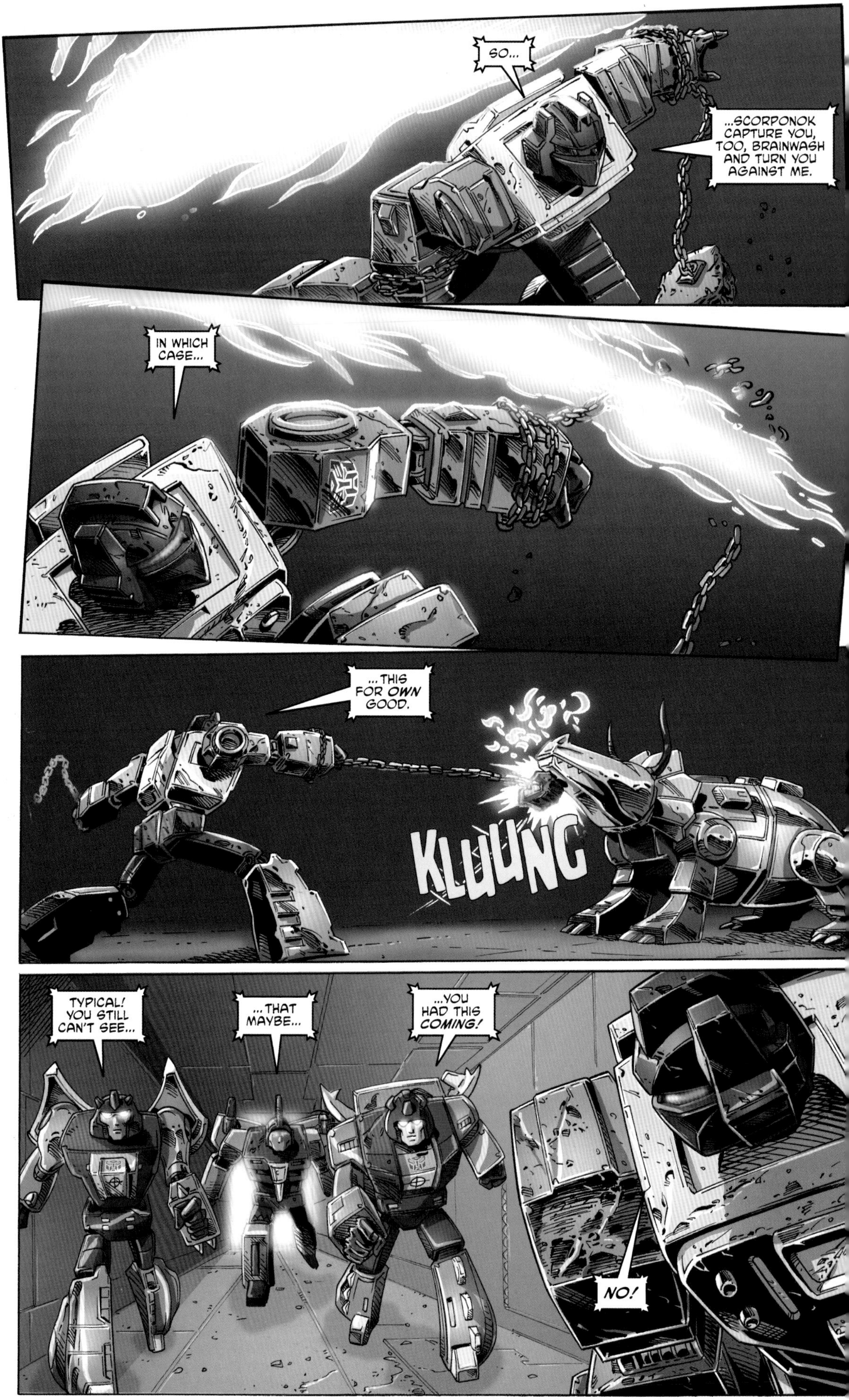
SO...
...SCORPONOK CAPTURE YOU, TOO, BRAINWASH AND TURN YOU AGAINST ME.
IN WHICH CASE...
...THIS FOR *OWN* GOOD.
KLUUNG
TYPICAL! YOU STILL CAN'T SEE...
...THAT MAYBE...
...YOU HAD THIS *COMING!*
NO!

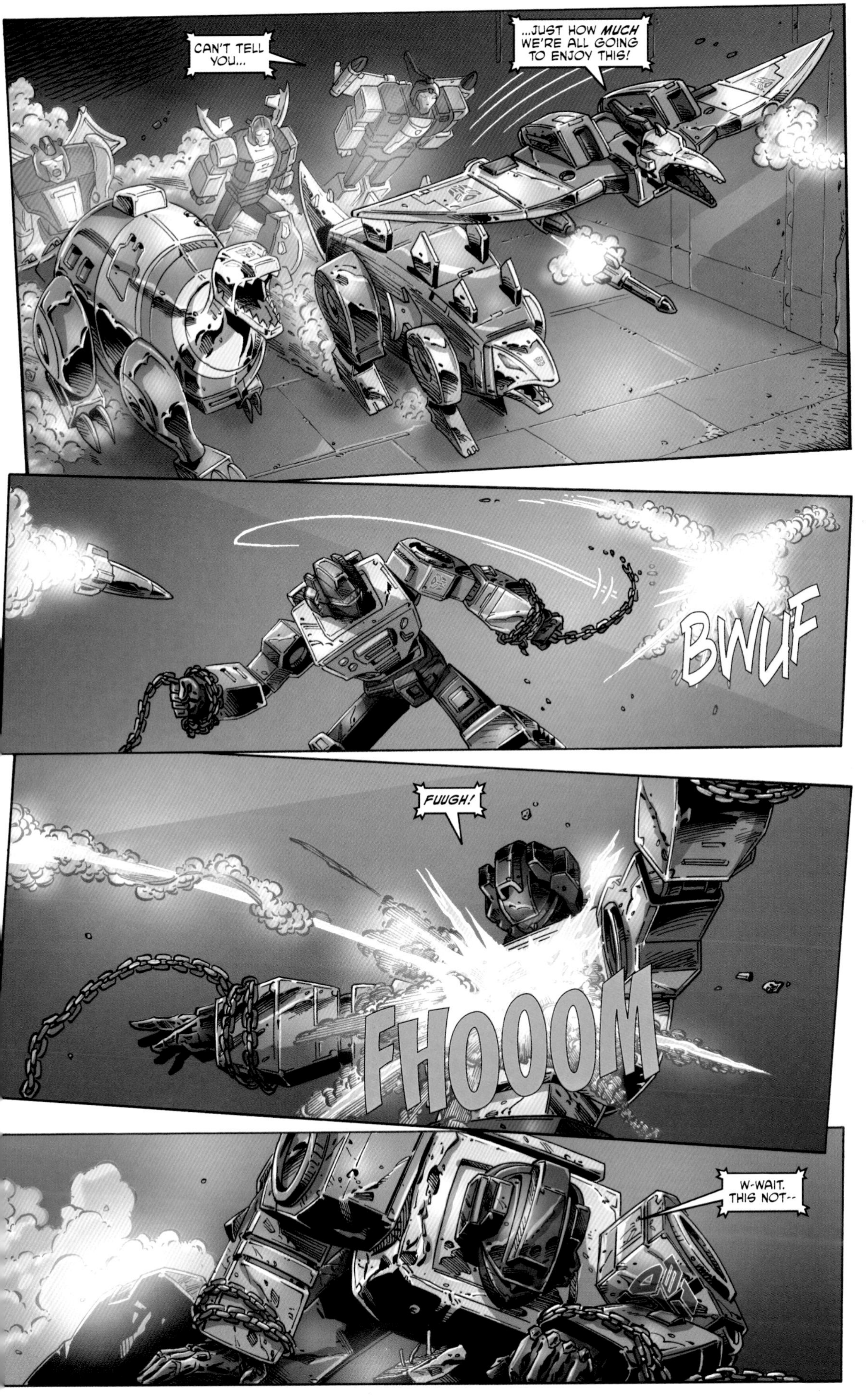
CAN'T TELL YOU...
...JUST HOW MUCH WE'RE ALL GOING TO ENJOY THIS!
BWUF
FUUGH!
FHOOOM
W-WAIT. THIS NOT--

FLANNG
NUHH!
YOU GAMBLED WITH OUR LIVES, OUR SANITY...
AND HANG THE CONSEQUENCES!
NOW--IT'S *JUDGMENT* DAY!
GUILTY!
GUILTY!
GUILTY!
GUILTY!
WHATEVER YOU ARE NOW, YOU'RE *NOT* ONE OF US! PAINFUL TRUTH IS...
KRUMMP
"...YOU'RE BETTER OFF DEAD!"

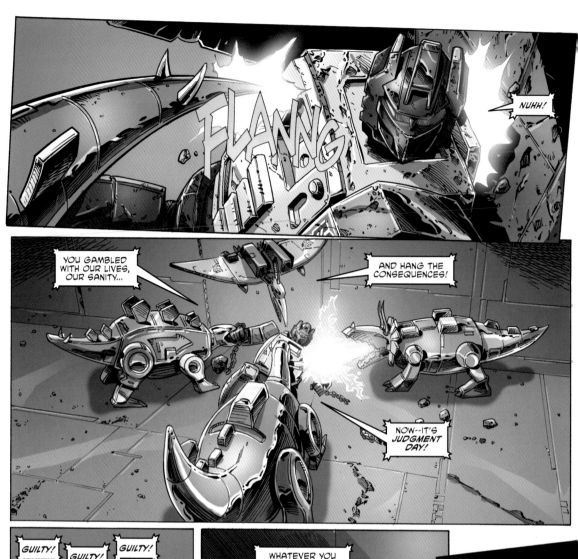

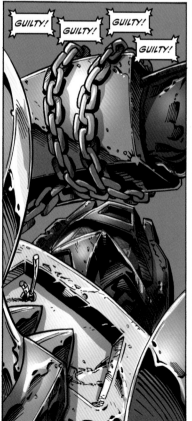

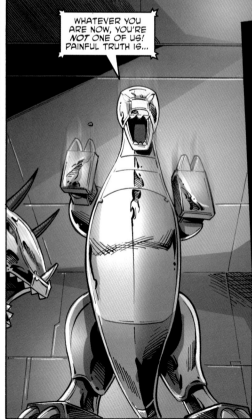

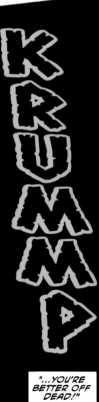

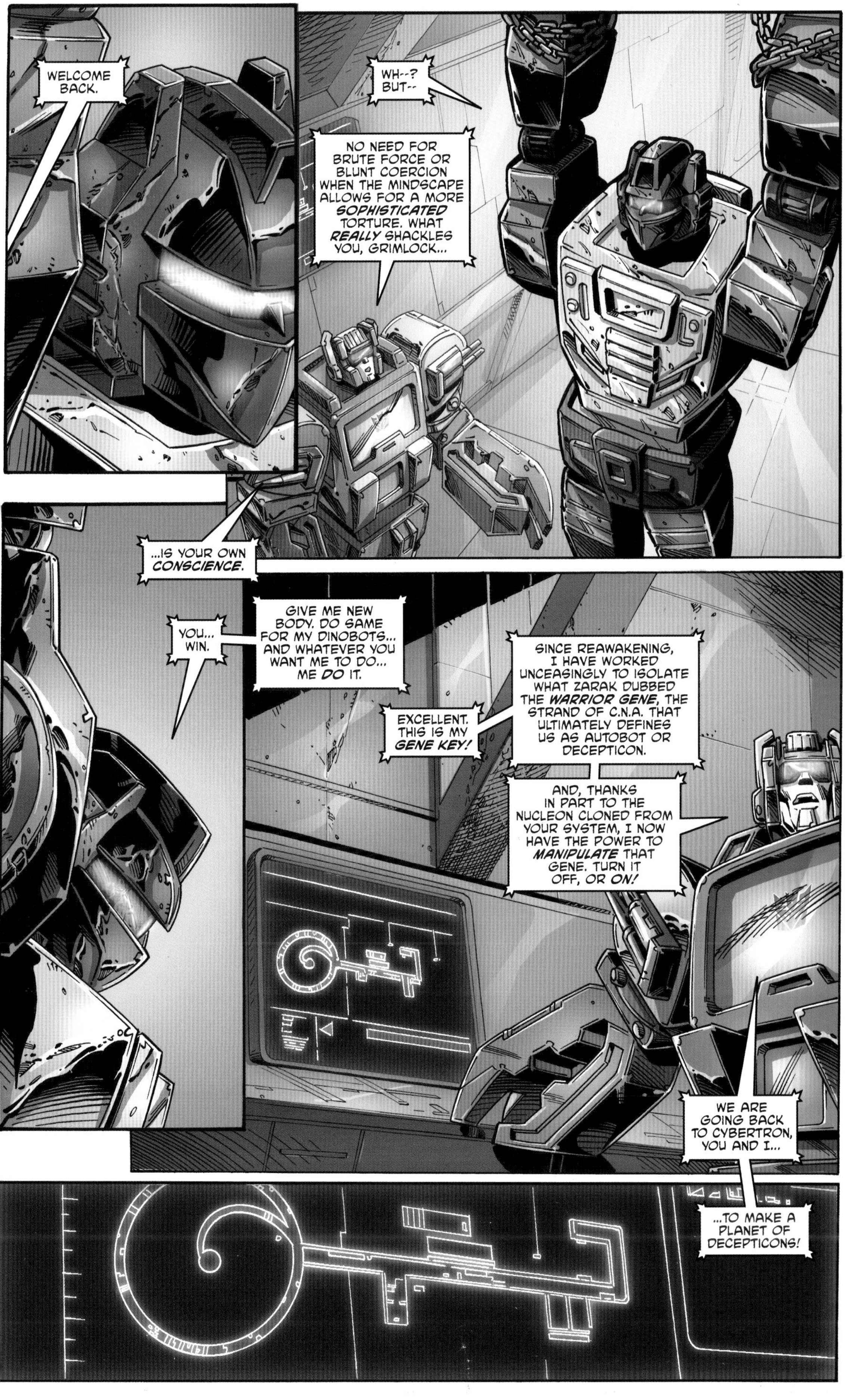

WELCOME BACK.
WH--? BUT--
NO NEED FOR BRUTE FORCE OR BLUNT COERCION WHEN THE MINDSCAPE ALLOWS FOR A MORE *SOPHISTICATED* TORTURE. WHAT *REALLY* SHACKLES YOU, GRIMLOCK...
...IS YOUR OWN *CONSCIENCE*.
YOU... WIN.
GIVE ME NEW BODY. DO SAME FOR MY DINOBOTS... AND WHATEVER YOU WANT ME TO DO... ME *DO* IT.
EXCELLENT. THIS IS MY *GENE KEY!*
SINCE REAWAKENING, I HAVE WORKED UNCEASINGLY TO ISOLATE WHAT ZARAK DUBBED THE *WARRIOR GENE*, THE STRAND OF C.N.A. THAT ULTIMATELY DEFINES US AS AUTOBOT OR DECEPTICON.
AND, THANKS IN PART TO THE NUCLEON CLONED FROM YOUR SYSTEM, I NOW HAVE THE POWER TO *MANIPULATE* THAT GENE. TURN IT OFF, OR *ON!*
WE ARE GOING BACK TO CYBERTRON, YOU AND I...
...TO MAKE A PLANET OF DECEPTICONS!

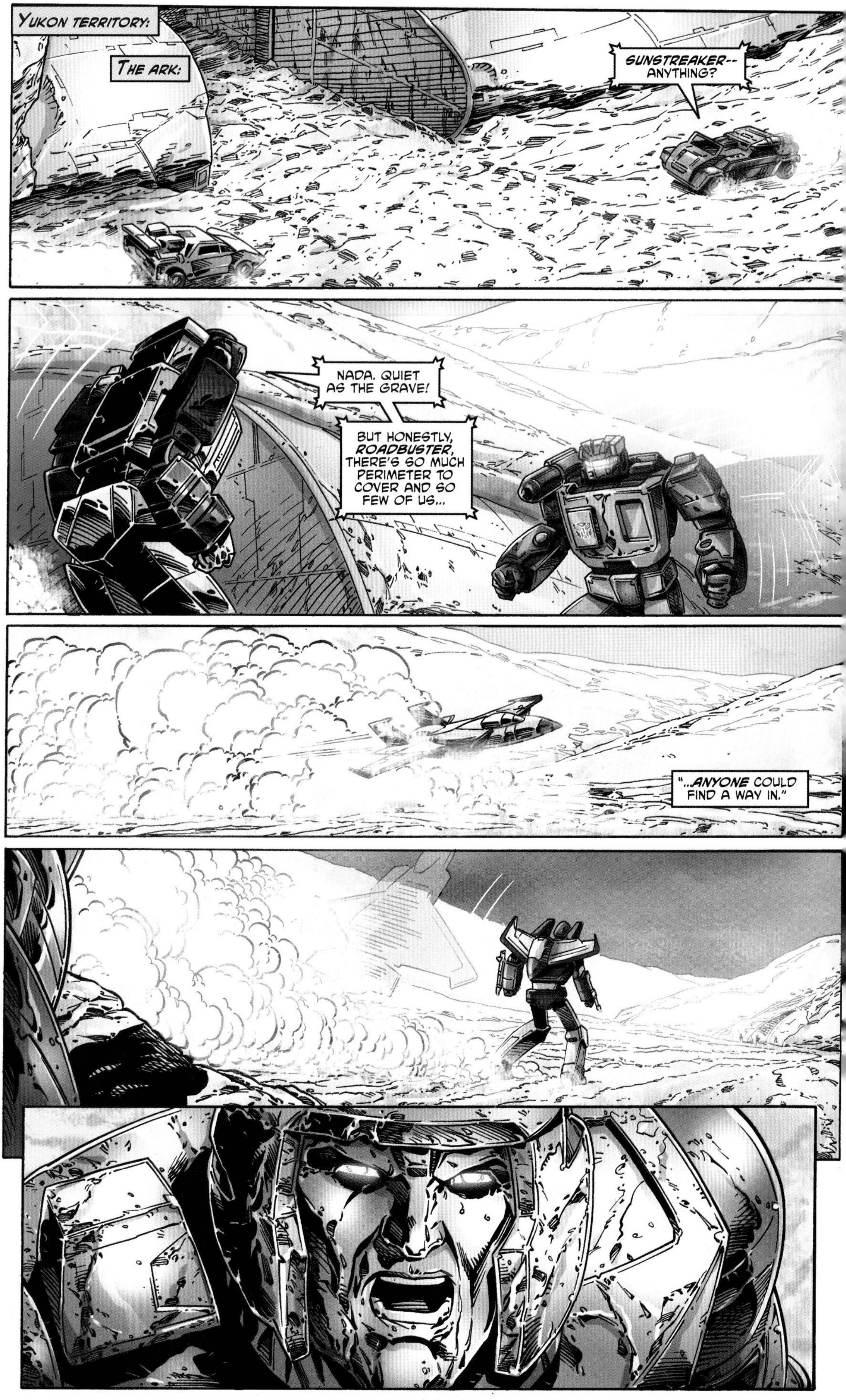

YUKON TERRITORY:
THE ARK:
SUNSTREAKER-- ANYTHING?
NADA. QUIET AS THE GRAVE!
BUT HONESTLY, ROADBUSTER, THERE'S SO MUCH PERIMETER TO COVER AND SO FEW OF US...
"...ANYONE COULD FIND A WAY IN."

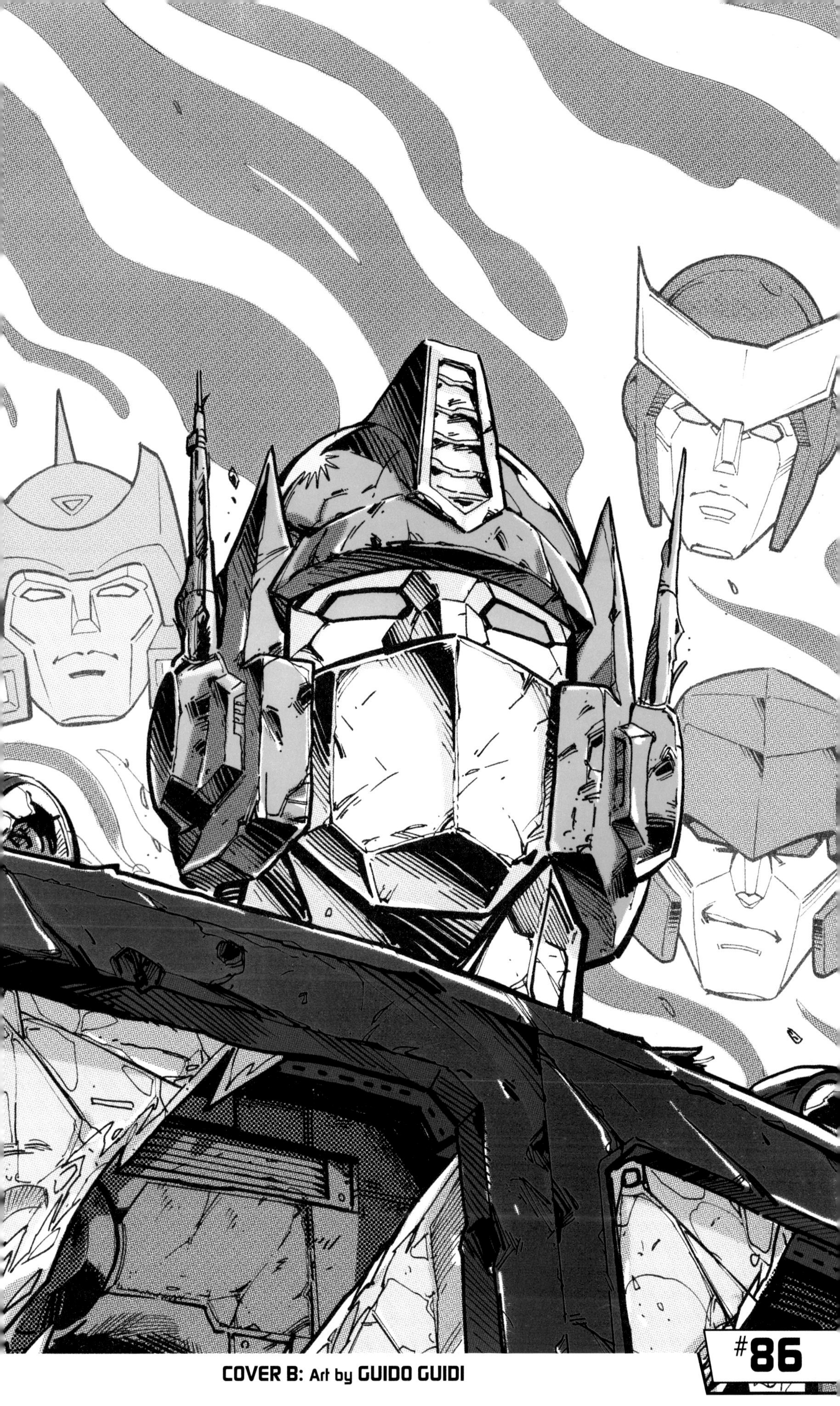
#86
COVER B: Art by GUIDO GUIDI

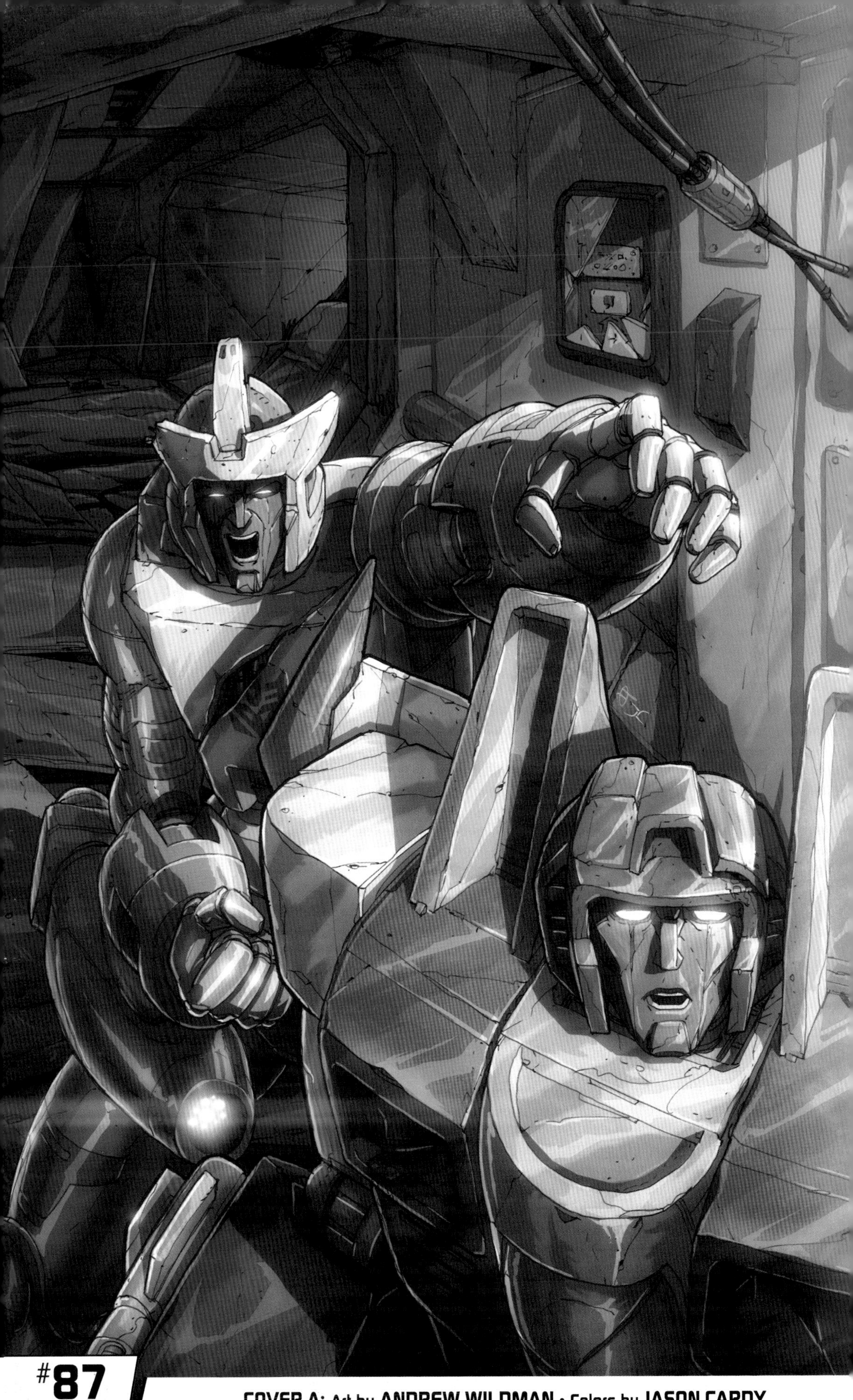

#87

COVER A: Art by ANDREW WILDMAN • Colors by JASON CARDY

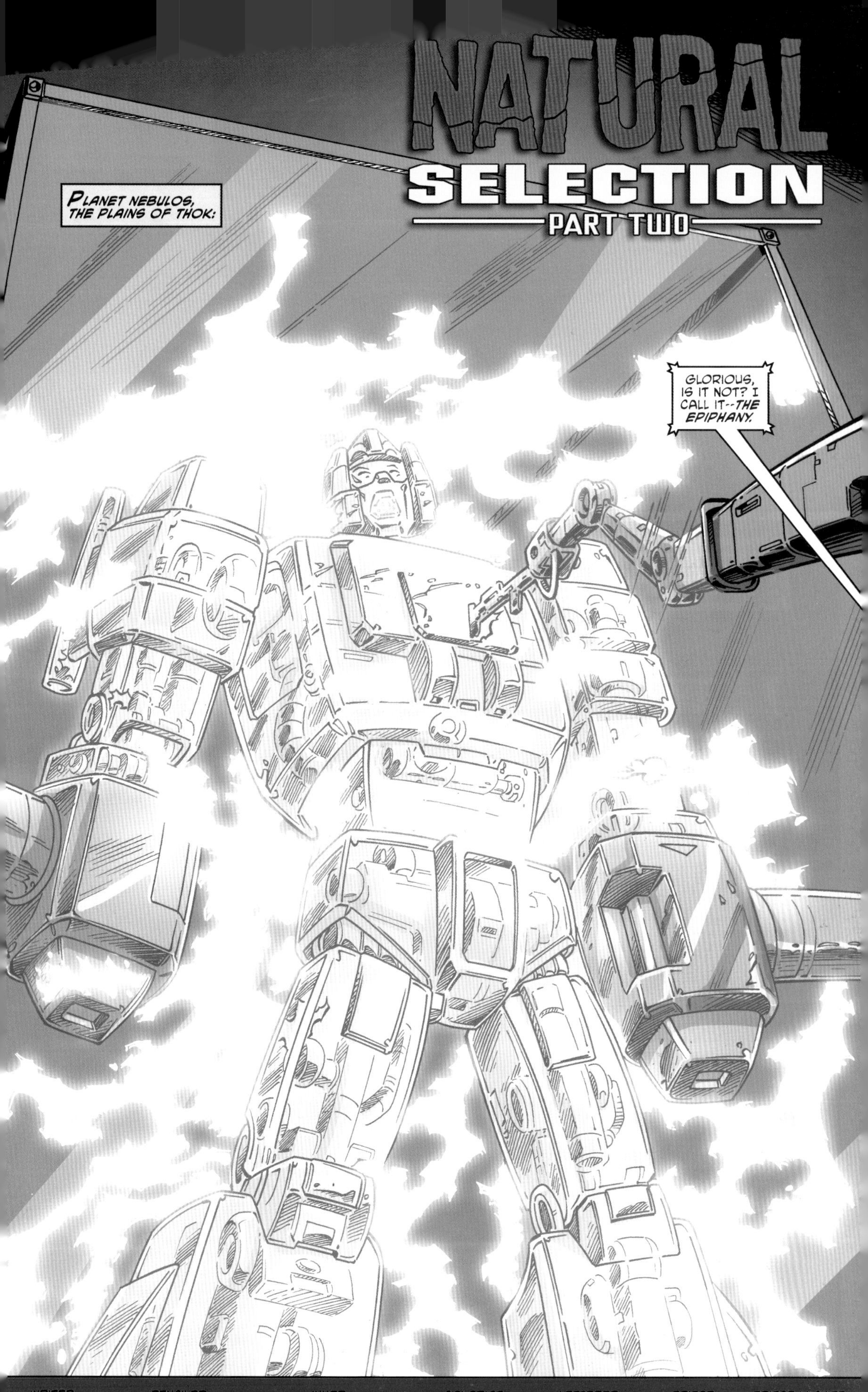
NATURAL SELECTION
PART TWO
PLANET NEBULOS, THE PLAINS OF THOK:
GLORIOUS, IS IT NOT? I CALL IT--THE EPIPHANY.

WRITER SIMON FURMAN · PENCILER ANDREW WILDMAN · INKER STEPHEN BASKERVILLE · COLORIST JOHN-PAUL BOVE · LETTERER CHRIS MOWRY · EDITOR JOHN BARBER · EDITOR-IN-CHIEF CHRIS RYALL

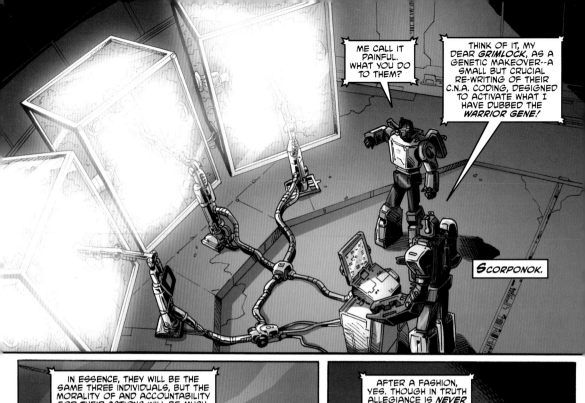

ME CALL IT PAINFUL. WHAT YOU DO TO THEM?

THINK OF IT, MY DEAR *GRIMLOCK*, AS A GENETIC MAKEOVER--A SMALL BUT CRUCIAL RE-WRITING OF THEIR C.N.A. CODING, DESIGNED TO ACTIVATE WHAT I HAVE DUBBED THE *WARRIOR GENE!*

SCORPONOK.

IN ESSENCE, THEY WILL BE THE SAME THREE INDIVIDUALS, BUT THE MORALITY OF AND ACCOUNTABILITY FOR THEIR ACTIONS WILL BE MUCH, MUCH LESS OF AN *ISSUE* TO THEM.

TRANSLATION: *DECEPTICONS!*

AFTER A FASHION, YES. THOUGH IN TRUTH ALLEGIANCE IS *NEVER* QUITE THAT CUT AND DRIED OR BLACK OR WHITE. BUT...

...THEY'LL CERTAINLY BE MORE MOTIVATIONALLY INCLINED TO THE MAYHEM I HAVE IN MIND.

OBSERVE. *HIGHBROW, BRAINSTORM, HARDHEAD*--

--STEP FORWARD AND EMBRACE *EVOLUTION!*

I FEEL... DIFFERENT. ENLIGHTENED! LIBERATED! LIKE I CAN DO... ANYTHING!

A VARIETY OF POSSIBLE SCENARIOS PRESENT THEMSELVES, ALL DELICIOUSLY ENTICING.

SUCH AS... PUTTIN' THE HURT ON THIS *THROWBACK* HERE!

THROW... BACK?

WE DON'T MUCH CARE FOR SHARING THIS AMOUNT OF SPACE WITH A WEAK-SOCKETED AUTOBOT SYMPATHIZER LIKE YOU.

AND WE ARE SIMPLY TEEMING WITH IDEAS ON HOW TO *REMEDY* THAT SITUATION.

ME KNOW YOU NOT YOURSELF-S... SO ME FEEL *BAD* ABOUT THIS.

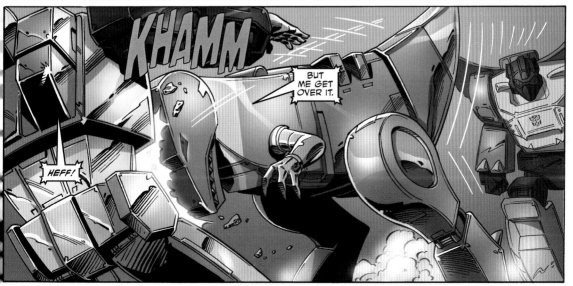

KHAMM

BUT ME GET OVER IT.

HEFF!

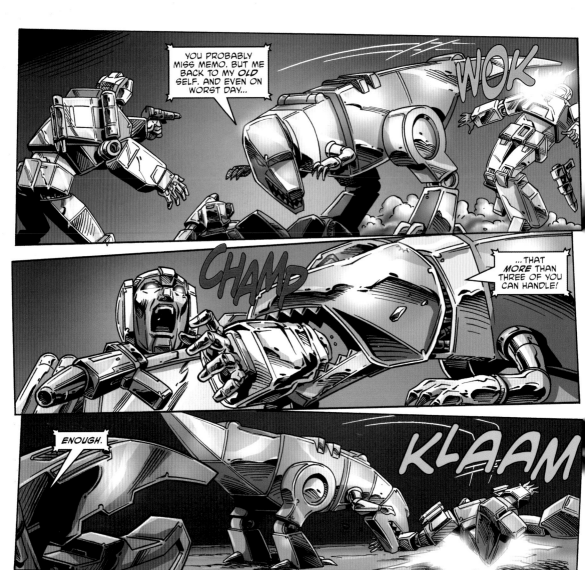

YOU PROBABLY MISS MEMO. BUT ME BACK TO MY *OLD* SELF. AND EVEN ON WORST DAY...

WOK

CHAMP

...THAT *MORE* THAN THREE OF YOU CAN HANDLE!

ENOUGH.

KLAAM

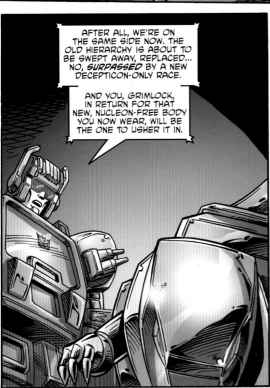

AFTER ALL, WE'RE ON THE SAME SIDE NOW. THE OLD HIERARCHY IS ABOUT TO BE SWEPT AWAY, REPLACED... NO, *SURPASSED* BY A NEW DECEPTICON-ONLY RACE.

AND YOU, GRIMLOCK, IN RETURN FOR THAT NEW, NUCLEON-FREE BODY YOU NOW WEAR, WILL BE THE ONE TO USHER IT IN.

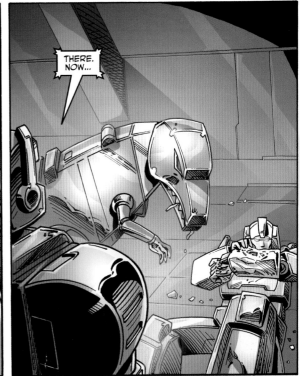

THERE. NOW...

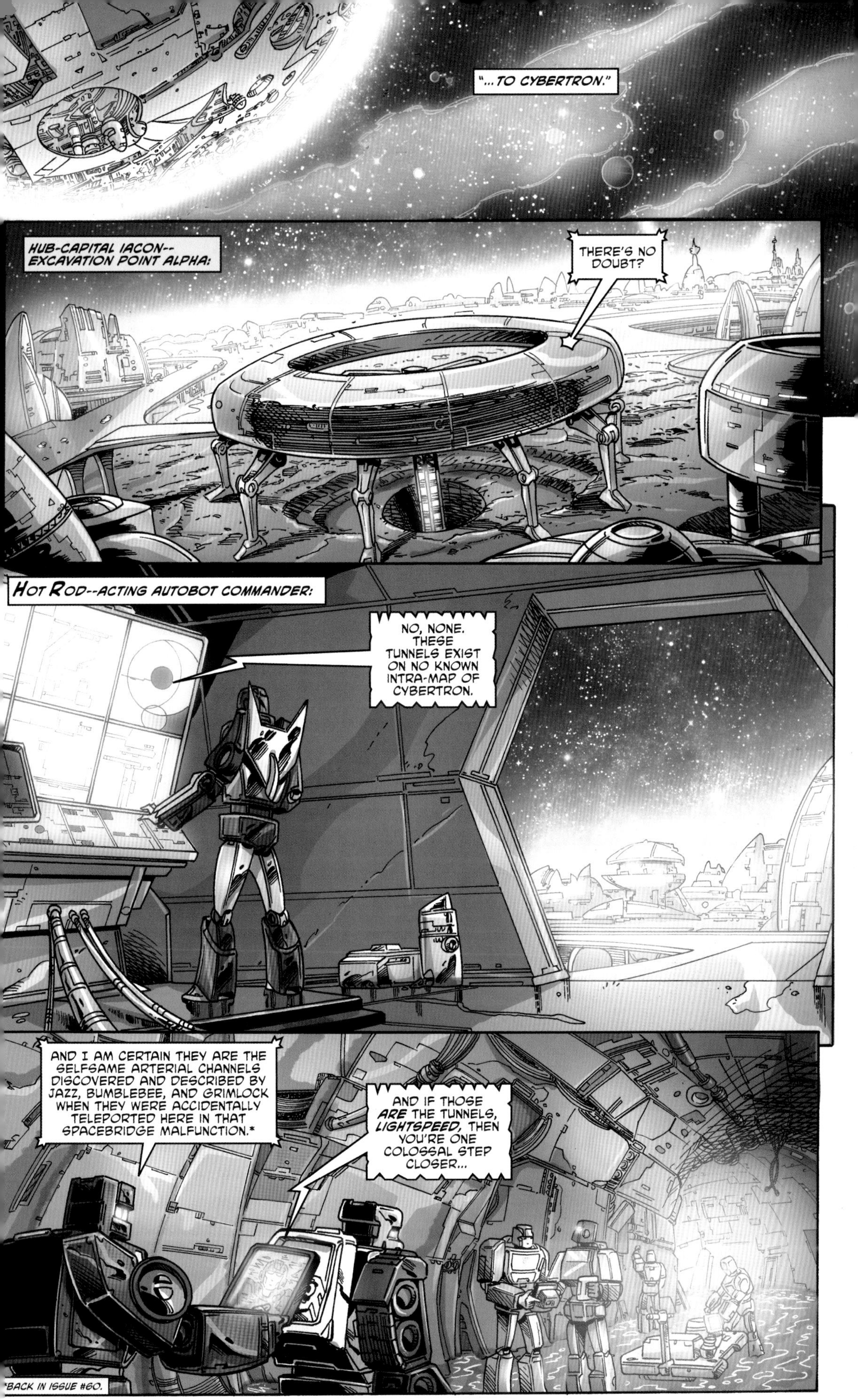
"...TO CYBERTRON."
HUB-CAPITAL IACON--
EXCAVATION POINT ALPHA:
THERE'S NO DOUBT?
HOT ROD--ACTING AUTOBOT COMMANDER:
NO, NONE. THESE TUNNELS EXIST ON NO KNOWN INTRA-MAP OF CYBERTRON.
AND I AM CERTAIN THEY ARE THE SELFSAME ARTERIAL CHANNELS DISCOVERED AND DESCRIBED BY JAZZ, BUMBLEBEE, AND GRIMLOCK WHEN THEY WERE ACCIDENTALLY TELEPORTED HERE IN THAT SPACEBRIDGE MALFUNCTION.*
AND IF THOSE ***ARE*** THE TUNNELS, ***LIGHTSPEED,*** THEN YOU'RE ONE COLOSSAL STEP CLOSER...
*BACK IN ISSUE #60.

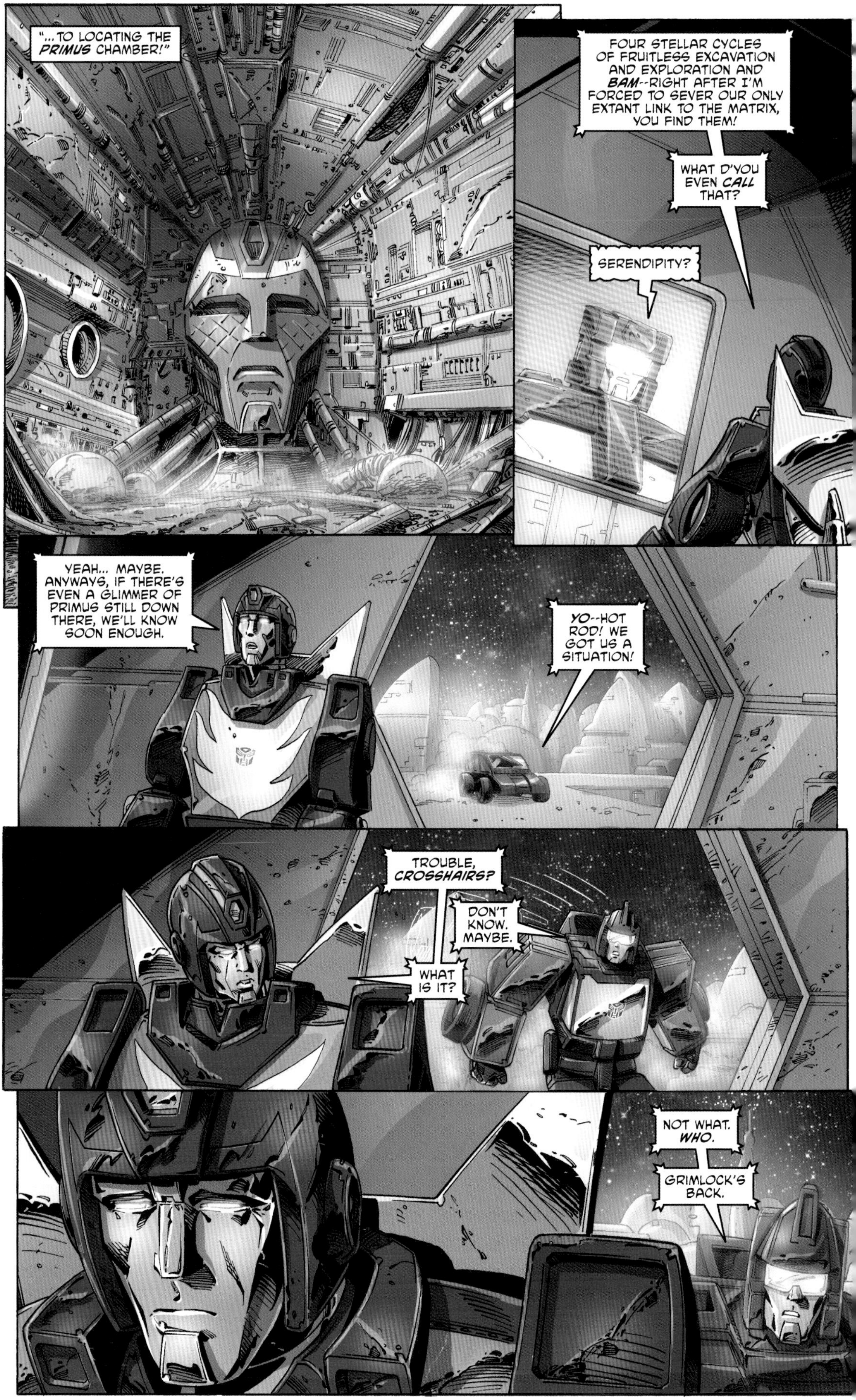
"...TO LOCATING THE *PRIMUS* CHAMBER!"
FOUR STELLAR CYCLES OF FRUITLESS EXCAVATION AND EXPLORATION AND *BAM*--RIGHT AFTER I'M FORCED TO SEVER OUR ONLY EXTANT LINK TO THE MATRIX, YOU FIND THEM!
WHAT D'YOU EVEN *CALL* THAT?
SERENDIPITY?
YEAH... MAYBE. ANYWAYS, IF THERE'S EVEN A GLIMMER OF PRIMUS STILL DOWN THERE, WE'LL KNOW SOON ENOUGH.
YO--HOT ROD! WE GOT US A SITUATION!
TROUBLE, *CROSSHAIRS?*
DON'T KNOW. MAYBE.
WHAT IS IT?
NOT WHAT. *WHO*.
GRIMLOCK'S BACK.

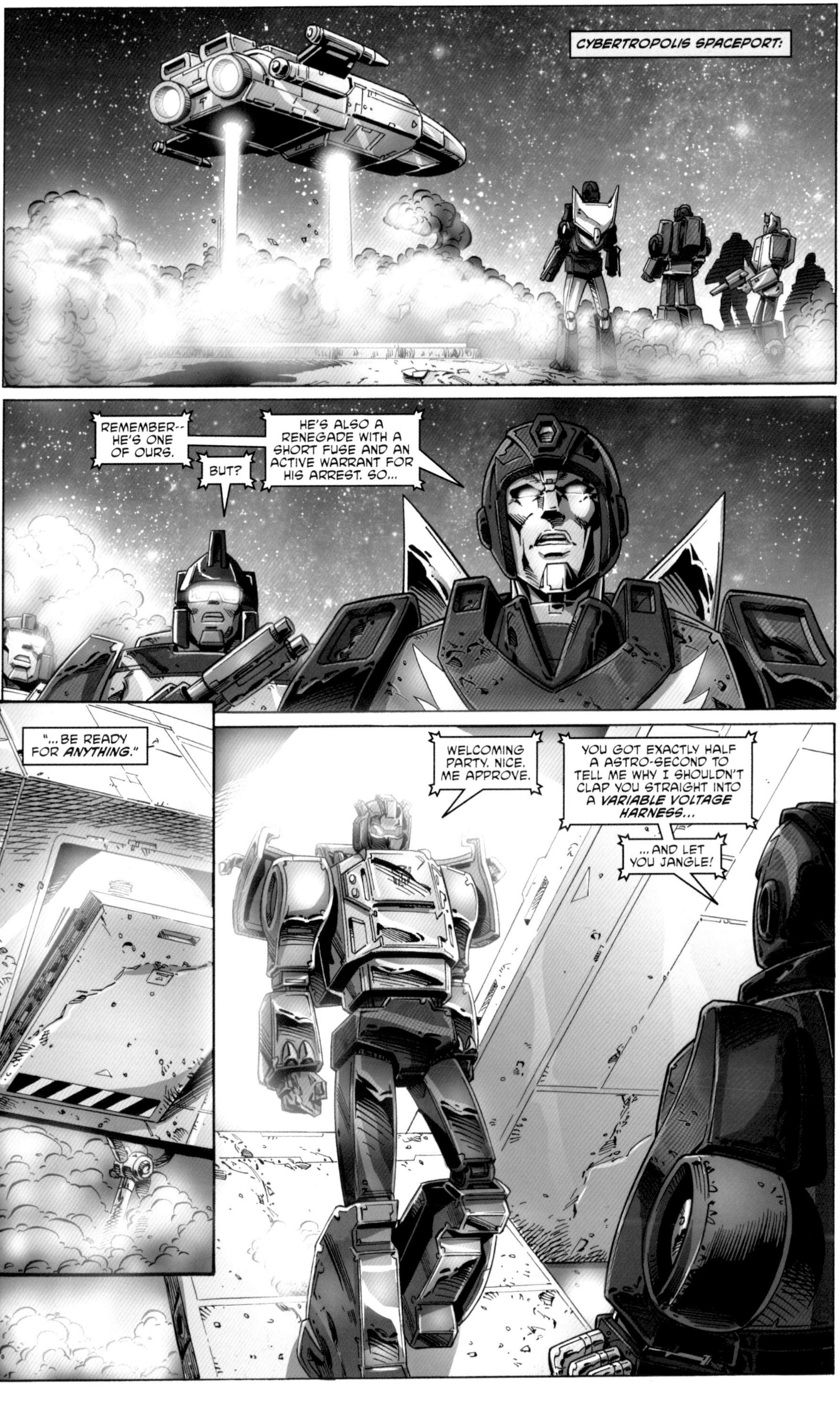
CYBERTROPOLIS SPACEPORT:
REMEMBER-- HE'S ONE OF OURS.
BUT?
HE'S ALSO A RENEGADE WITH A SHORT FUSE AND AN ACTIVE WARRANT FOR HIS ARREST. SO...
"...BE READY FOR ANYTHING."
WELCOMING PARTY. NICE. ME APPROVE.
YOU GOT EXACTLY HALF A ASTRO-SECOND TO TELL ME WHY I SHOULDN'T CLAP YOU STRAIGHT INTO A VARIABLE VOLTAGE HARNESS...
...AND LET YOU JANGLE!

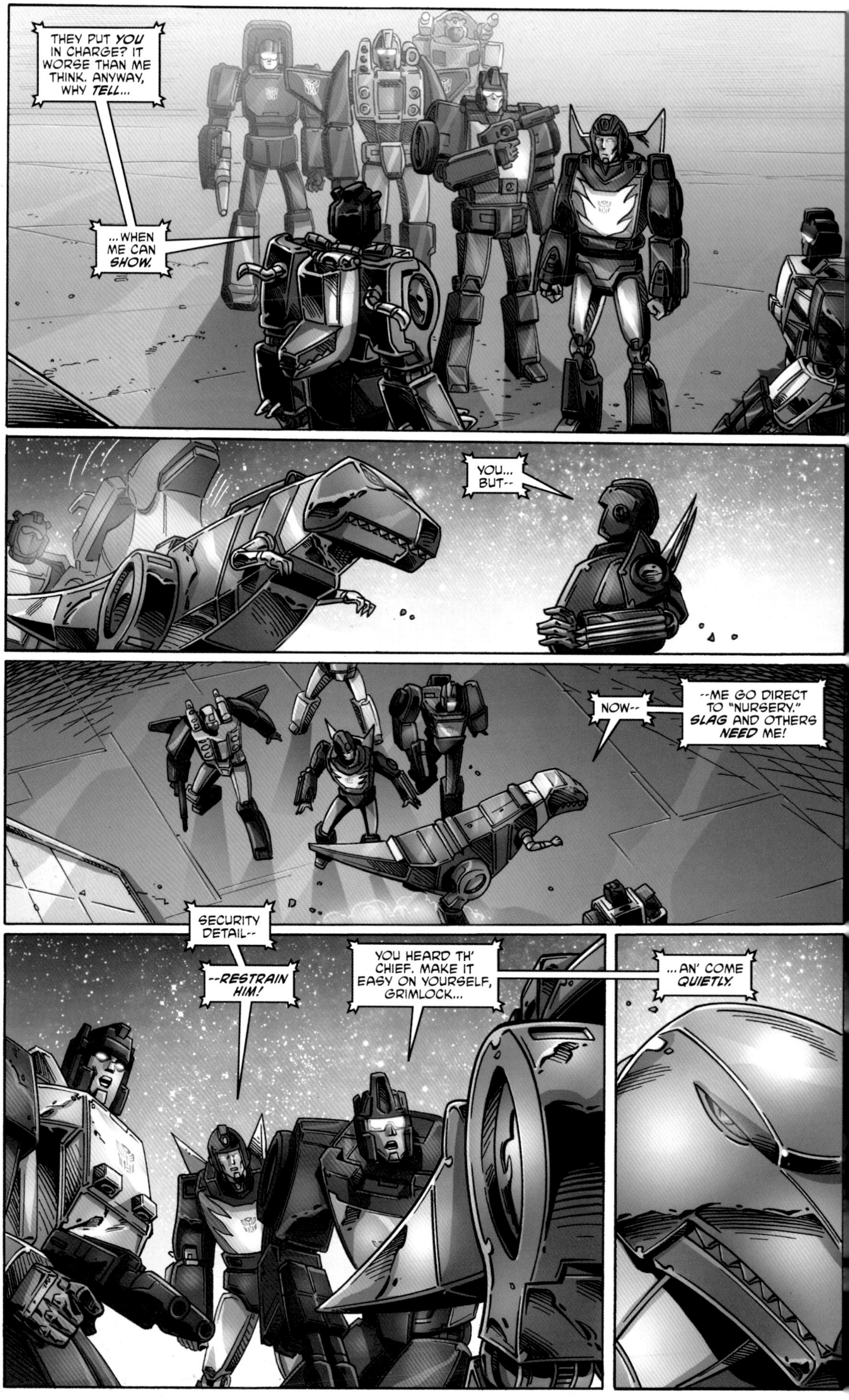
THEY PUT *YOU* IN CHARGE? IT WORSE THAN ME THINK. ANYWAY, WHY *TELL*...
...WHEN ME CAN *SHOW.*
YOU... BUT--
NOW--
--ME GO DIRECT TO "NURSERY." *SLAG* AND OTHERS *NEED* ME!
SECURITY DETAIL--
--RESTRAIN HIM!
YOU HEARD TH' CHIEF. MAKE IT EASY ON YOURSELF, GRIMLOCK...
...AN' COME *QUIETLY.*

HH--

GEH--

HH-UH--

HE'S IN!

BASTION-FIVE LOCK-UP:

PHHH... ACTIVATE CONTAINMENT GRID!

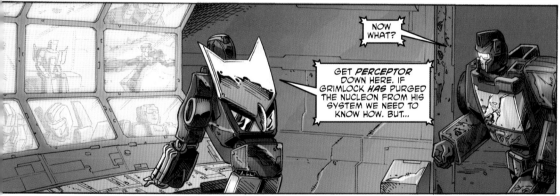

NOW WHAT?

GET *PERCEPTOR* DOWN HERE. IF GRIMLOCK *HAS* PURGED THE NUCLEON FROM HIS SYSTEM WE NEED TO KNOW HOW. BUT...

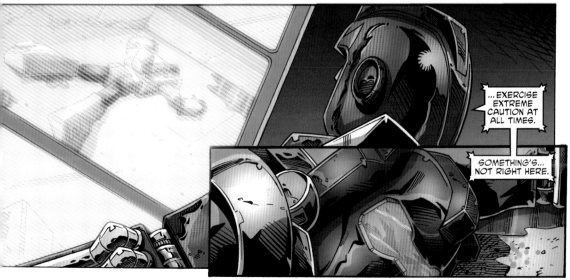

... EXERCISE EXTREME CAUTION AT ALL TIMES.

SOMETHING'S... NOT RIGHT HERE.

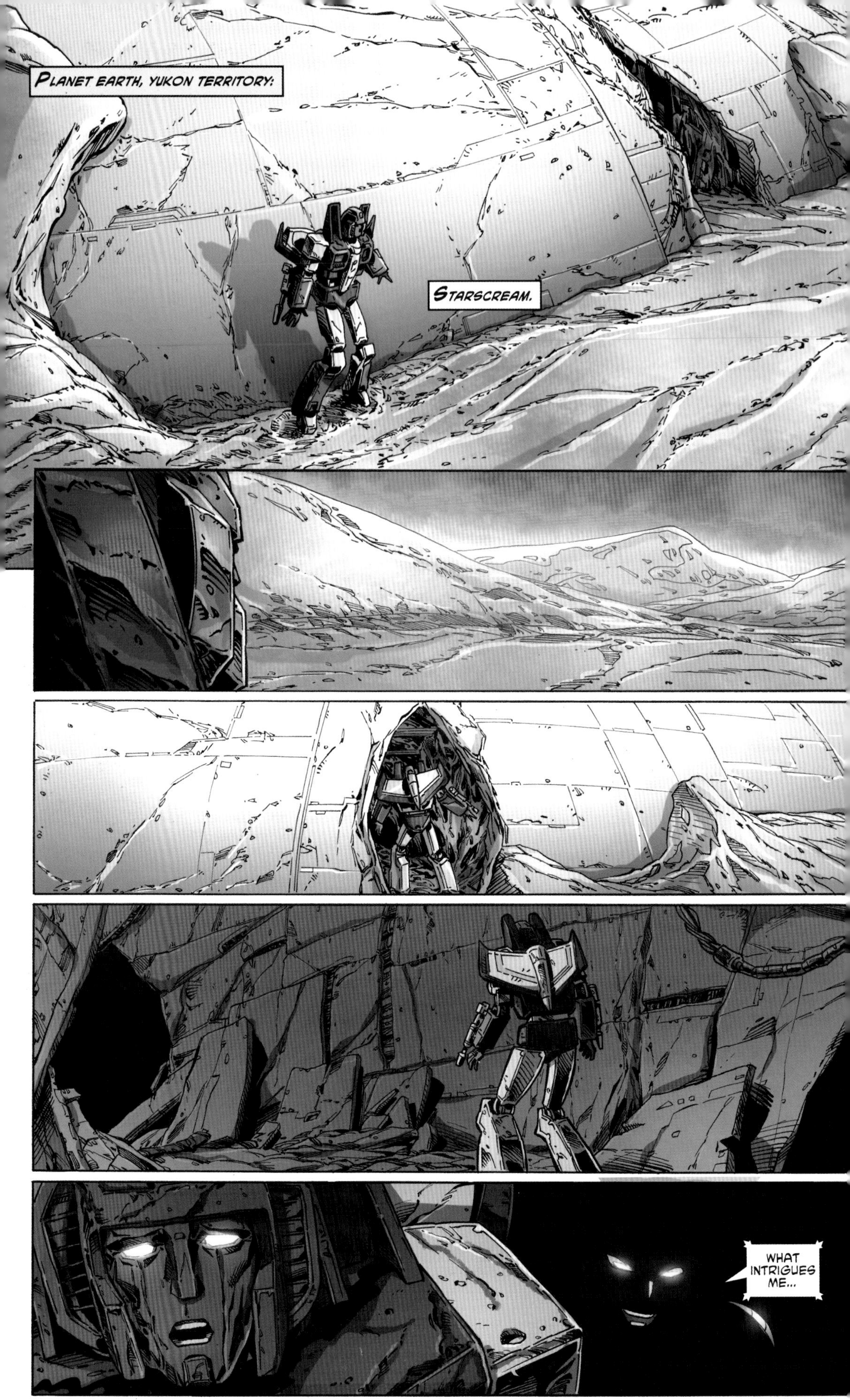
PLANET EARTH, YUKON TERRITORY:
STARSCREAM.
WHAT INTRIGUES ME...

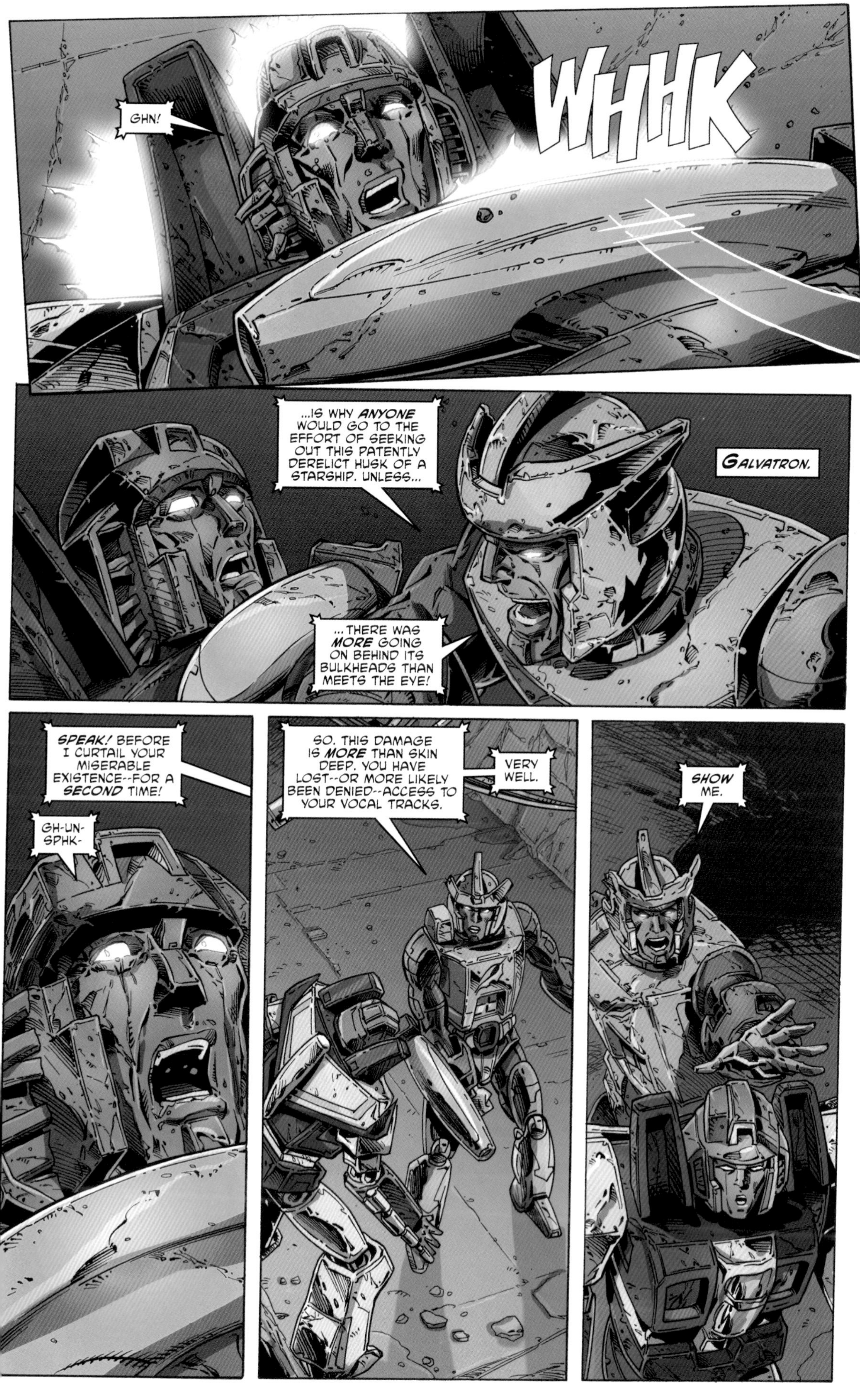
GHN!
WHHK
...IS WHY *ANYONE* WOULD GO TO THE EFFORT OF SEEKING OUT THIS PATENTLY DERELICT HUSK OF A STARSHIP. UNLESS...
GALVATRON.
...THERE WAS *MORE* GOING ON BEHIND ITS BULKHEADS THAN MEETS THE EYE!
SPEAK! BEFORE I CURTAIL YOUR MISERABLE EXISTENCE--FOR A *SECOND* TIME!
GH-UN-SPHK-
SO. THIS DAMAGE IS *MORE* THAN SKIN DEEP. YOU HAVE LOST--OR MORE LIKELY BEEN DENIED--ACCESS TO YOUR VOCAL TRACKS.
VERY WELL.
SHOW ME.

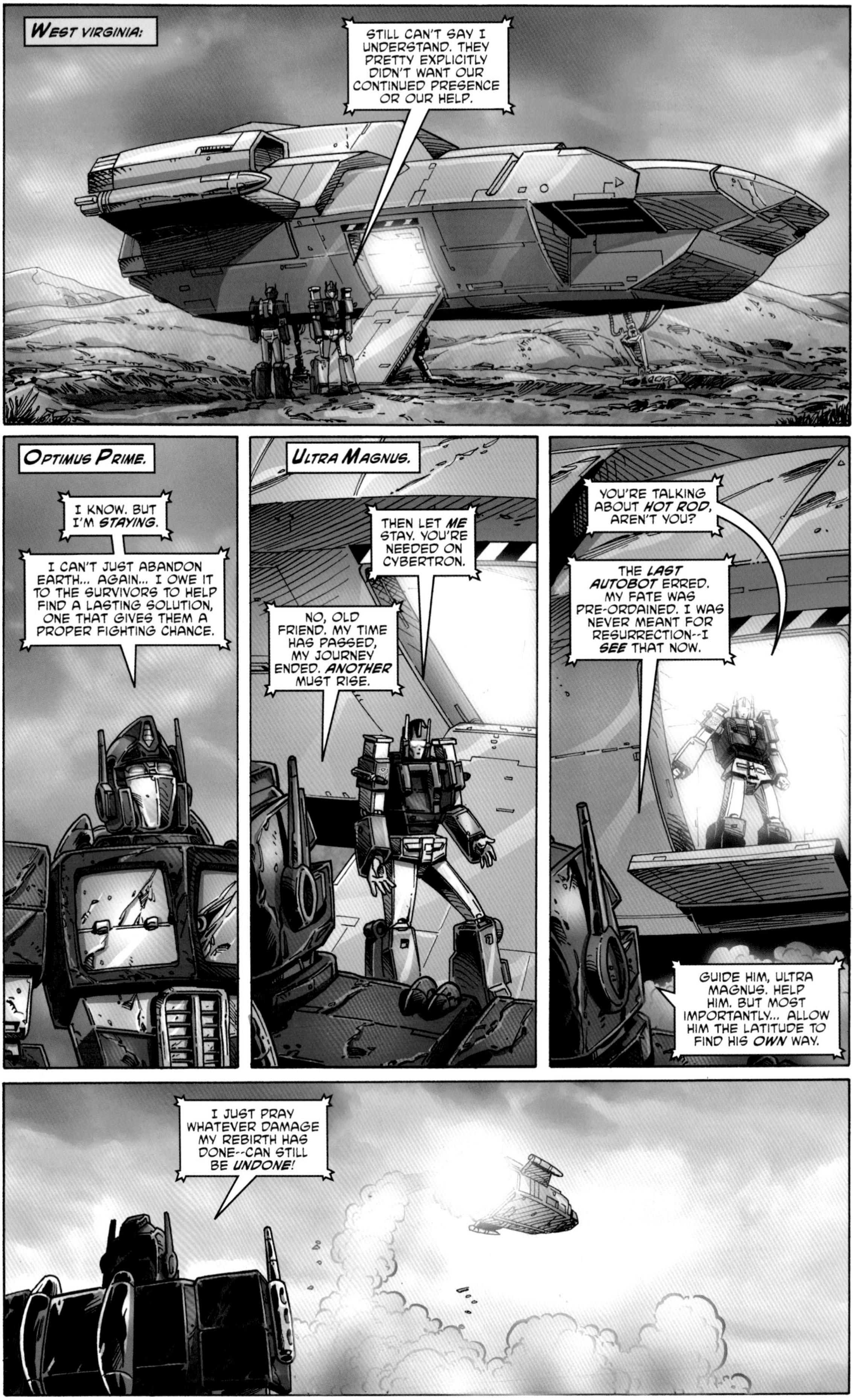
WEST VIRGINIA:
STILL CAN'T SAY I UNDERSTAND. THEY PRETTY EXPLICITLY DIDN'T WANT OUR CONTINUED PRESENCE OR OUR HELP.
OPTIMUS PRIME.
I KNOW. BUT I'M *STAYING*.
I CAN'T JUST ABANDON EARTH... AGAIN... I OWE IT TO THE SURVIVORS TO HELP FIND A LASTING SOLUTION, ONE THAT GIVES THEM A PROPER FIGHTING CHANCE.
ULTRA MAGNUS.
THEN LET *ME* STAY. YOU'RE NEEDED ON CYBERTRON.
NO, OLD FRIEND. MY TIME HAS PASSED, MY JOURNEY ENDED. *ANOTHER* MUST RISE.
YOU'RE TALKING ABOUT *HOT ROD*, AREN'T YOU?
THE *LAST AUTOBOT* ERRED. MY FATE WAS PRE-ORDAINED. I WAS NEVER MEANT FOR RESURRECTION--I *SEE* THAT NOW.
GUIDE HIM, ULTRA MAGNUS. HELP HIM. BUT MOST IMPORTANTLY... ALLOW HIM THE LATITUDE TO FIND HIS *OWN* WAY.
I JUST PRAY WHATEVER DAMAGE MY REBIRTH HAS DONE--CAN STILL BE *UNDONE*!

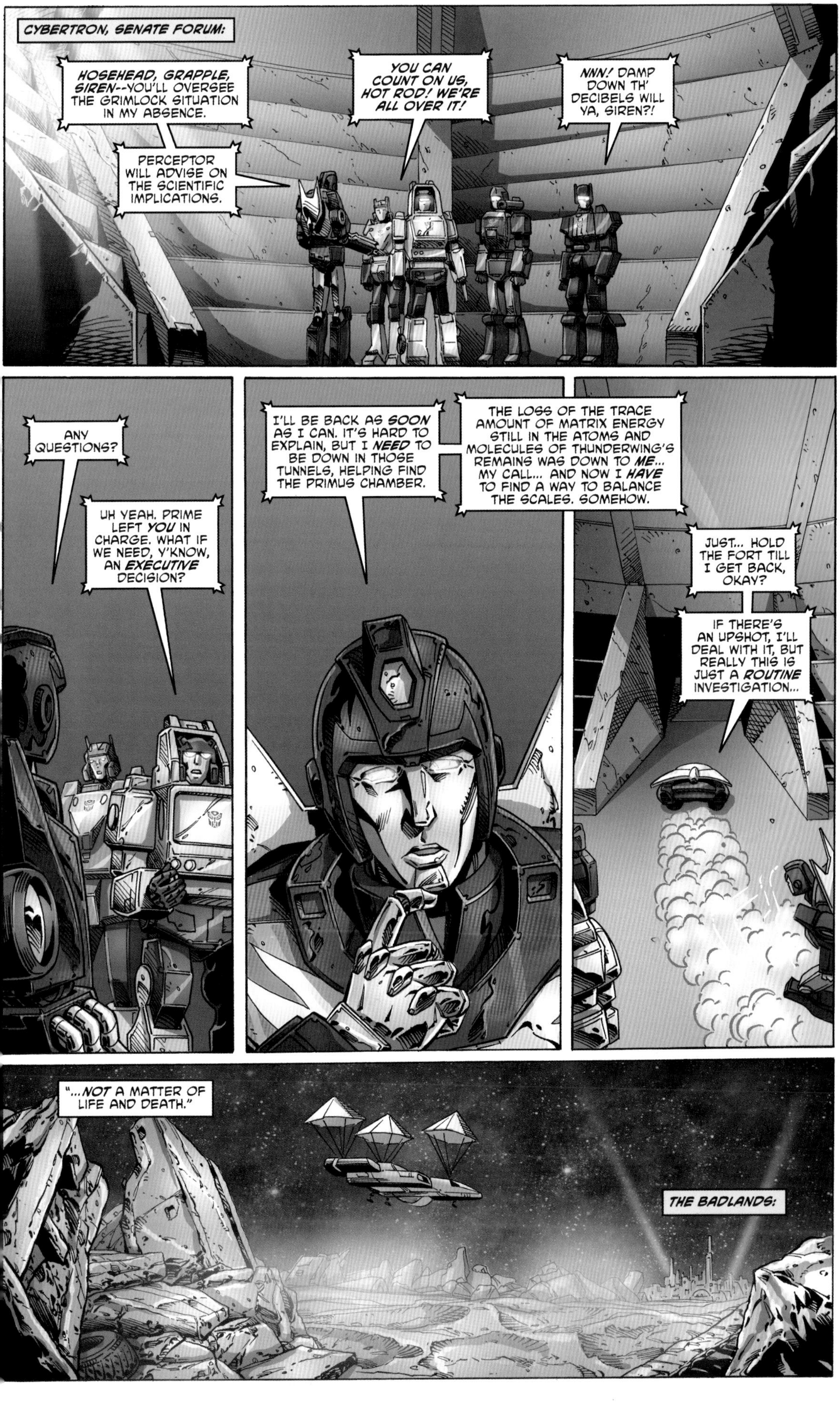
CYBERTRON, SENATE FORUM:
HOSEHEAD, GRAPPLE, SIREN--YOU'LL OVERSEE THE GRIMLOCK SITUATION IN MY ABSENCE.
PERCEPTOR WILL ADVISE ON THE SCIENTIFIC IMPLICATIONS.
YOU CAN COUNT ON US, HOT ROD! WE'RE ALL OVER IT!
NNN! DAMP DOWN TH' DECIBELS WILL YA, SIREN?!
ANY QUESTIONS?
UH YEAH. PRIME LEFT YOU IN CHARGE. WHAT IF WE NEED, Y'KNOW, AN EXECUTIVE DECISION?
I'LL BE BACK AS SOON AS I CAN. IT'S HARD TO EXPLAIN, BUT I NEED TO BE DOWN IN THOSE TUNNELS, HELPING FIND THE PRIMUS CHAMBER.
THE LOSS OF THE TRACE AMOUNT OF MATRIX ENERGY STILL IN THE ATOMS AND MOLECULES OF THUNDERWING'S REMAINS WAS DOWN TO ME... MY CALL... AND NOW I HAVE TO FIND A WAY TO BALANCE THE SCALES. SOMEHOW.
JUST... HOLD THE FORT TILL I GET BACK, OKAY?
IF THERE'S AN UPSHOT, I'LL DEAL WITH IT, BUT REALLY THIS IS JUST A ROUTINE INVESTIGATION...
"...NOT A MATTER OF LIFE AND DEATH."
THE BADLANDS:

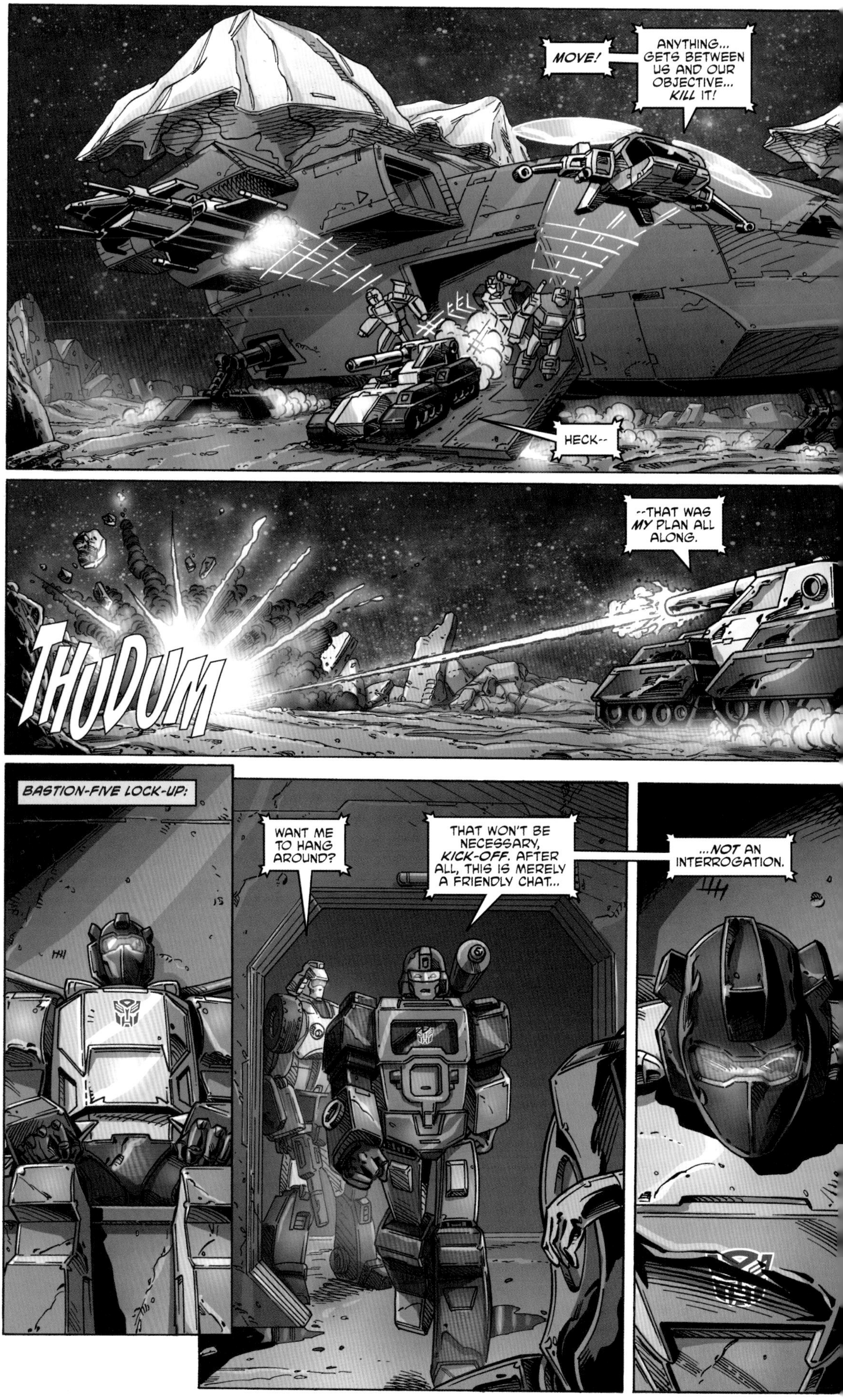
MOVE!
ANYTHING... GETS BETWEEN US AND OUR OBJECTIVE... KILL IT!
HECK--
--THAT WAS MY PLAN ALL ALONG.
THUDUM
BASTION-FIVE LOCK-UP:
WANT ME TO HANG AROUND?
THAT WON'T BE NECESSARY, KICK-OFF. AFTER ALL, THIS IS MERELY A FRIENDLY CHAT...
...NOT AN INTERROGATION.

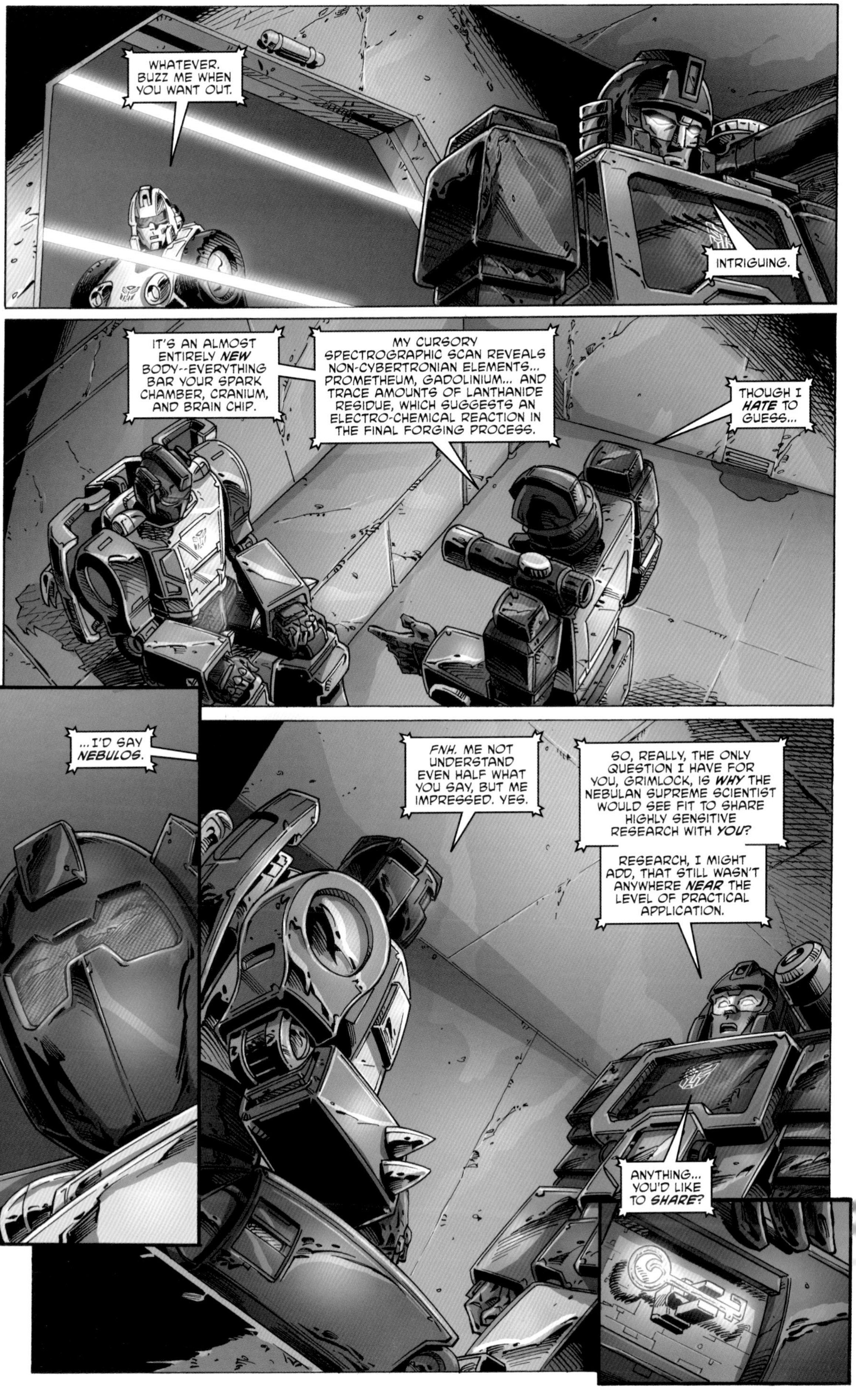
WHATEVER. BUZZ ME WHEN YOU WANT OUT.
INTRIGUING.
IT'S AN ALMOST ENTIRELY *NEW* BODY--EVERYTHING BAR YOUR SPARK CHAMBER, CRANIUM, AND BRAIN CHIP.
MY CURSORY SPECTROGRAPHIC SCAN REVEALS NON-CYBERTRONIAN ELEMENTS... PROMETHEUM, GADOLINIUM... AND TRACE AMOUNTS OF LANTHANIDE RESIDUE, WHICH SUGGESTS AN ELECTRO-CHEMICAL REACTION IN THE FINAL FORGING PROCESS.
THOUGH I *HATE* TO GUESS...
...I'D SAY *NEBULOS*.
FNH. ME NOT UNDERSTAND EVEN HALF WHAT YOU SAY, BUT ME IMPRESSED. YES.
SO, REALLY, THE ONLY QUESTION I HAVE FOR YOU, GRIMLOCK, IS *WHY* THE NEBULAN SUPREME SCIENTIST WOULD SEE FIT TO SHARE HIGHLY SENSITIVE RESEARCH WITH *YOU*?
RESEARCH, I MIGHT ADD, THAT STILL WASN'T ANYWHERE *NEAR* THE LEVEL OF PRACTICAL APPLICATION.
ANYTHING... YOU'D LIKE TO *SHARE*?

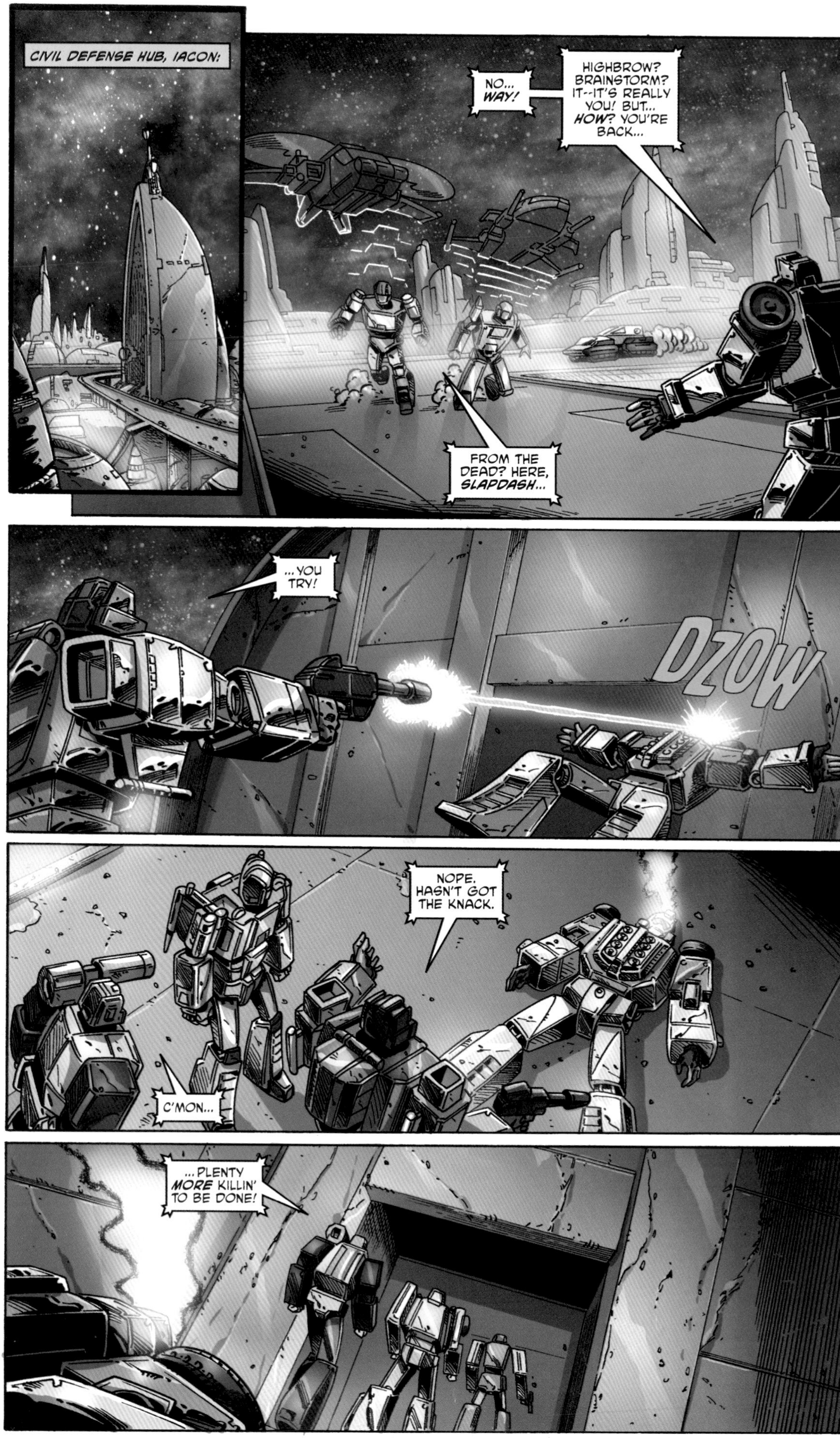
CIVIL DEFENSE HUB, IACON:
NO... WAY!
HIGHBROW? BRAINSTORM? IT--IT'S REALLY YOU! BUT... HOW? YOU'RE BACK...
FROM THE DEAD? HERE, SLAPDASH...
...YOU TRY!
DZOW
NOPE. HASN'T GOT THE KNACK.
C'MON...
...PLENTY MORE KILLIN' TO BE DONE!

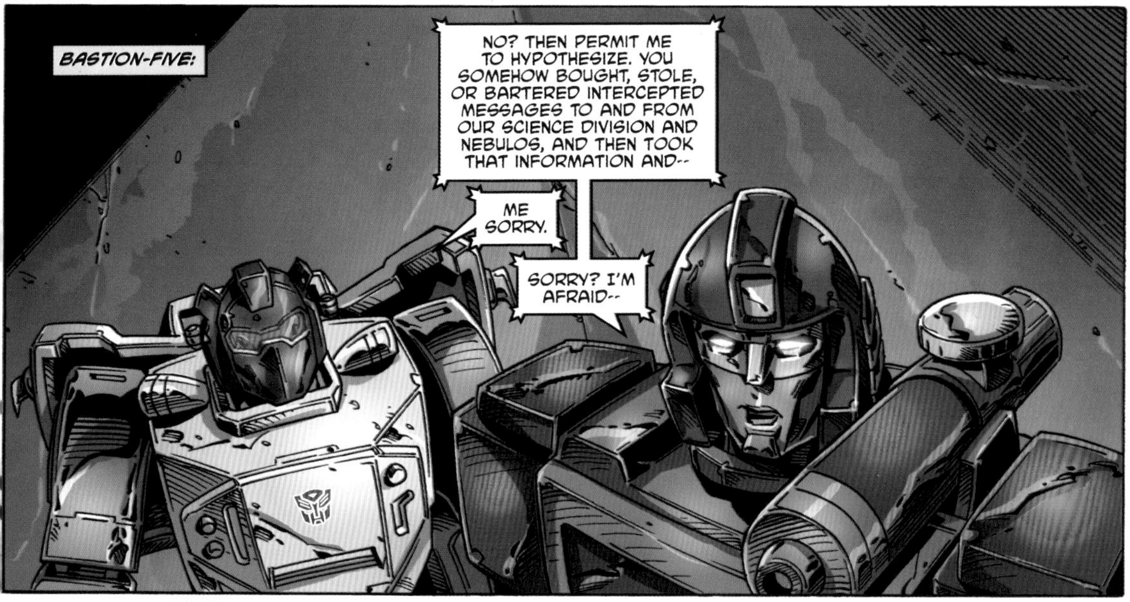
BASTION-FIVE:
NO? THEN PERMIT ME TO HYPOTHESIZE. YOU SOMEHOW BOUGHT, STOLE, OR BARTERED INTERCEPTED MESSAGES TO AND FROM OUR SCIENCE DIVISION AND NEBULOS, AND THEN TOOK THAT INFORMATION AND--
ME SORRY.
SORRY? I'M AFRAID--
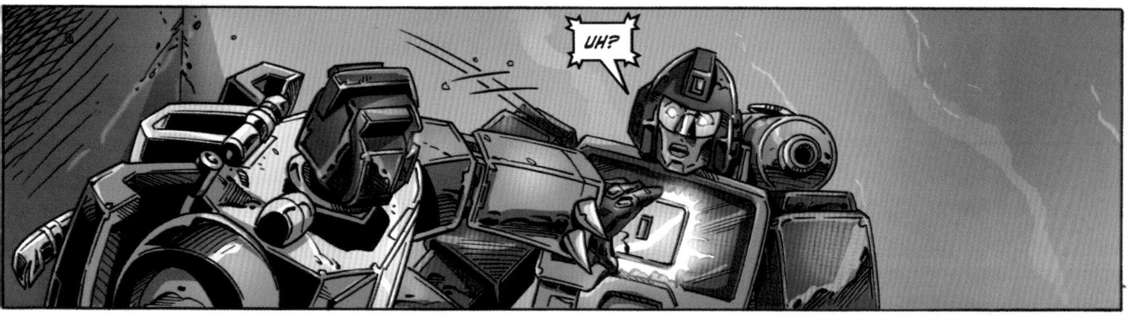
UH?
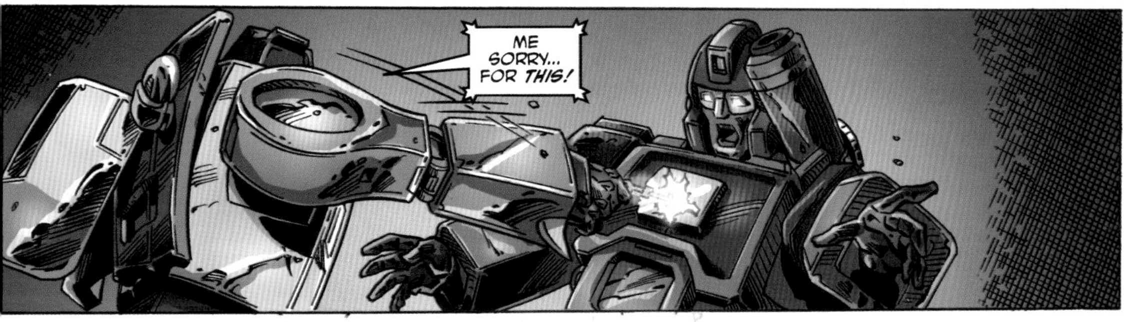
ME SORRY... FOR *THIS!*
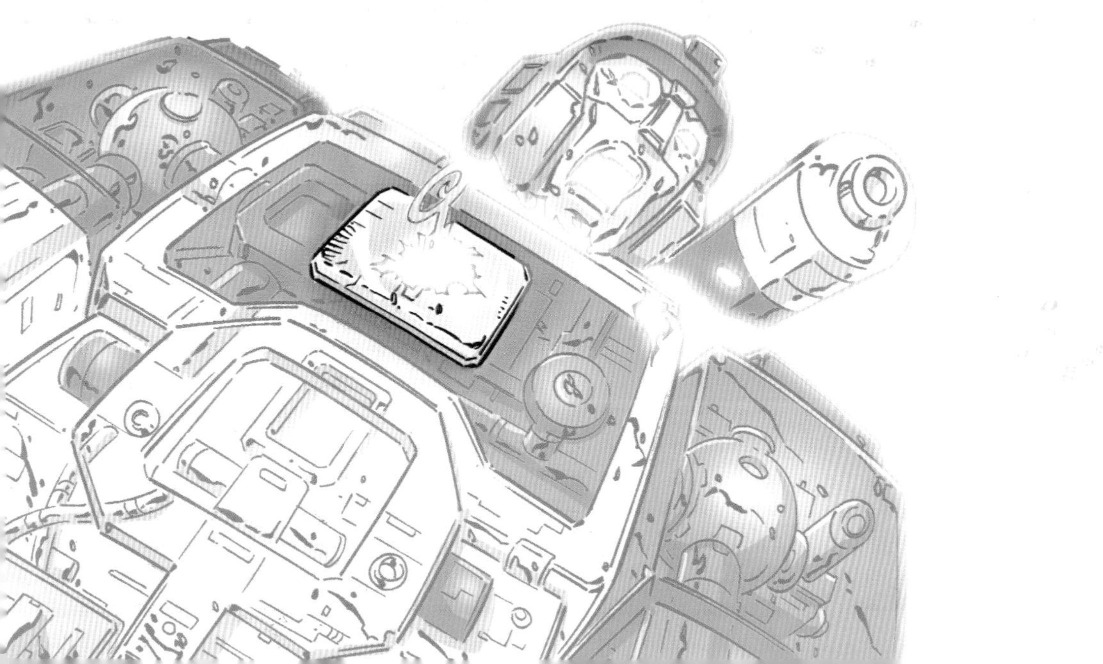

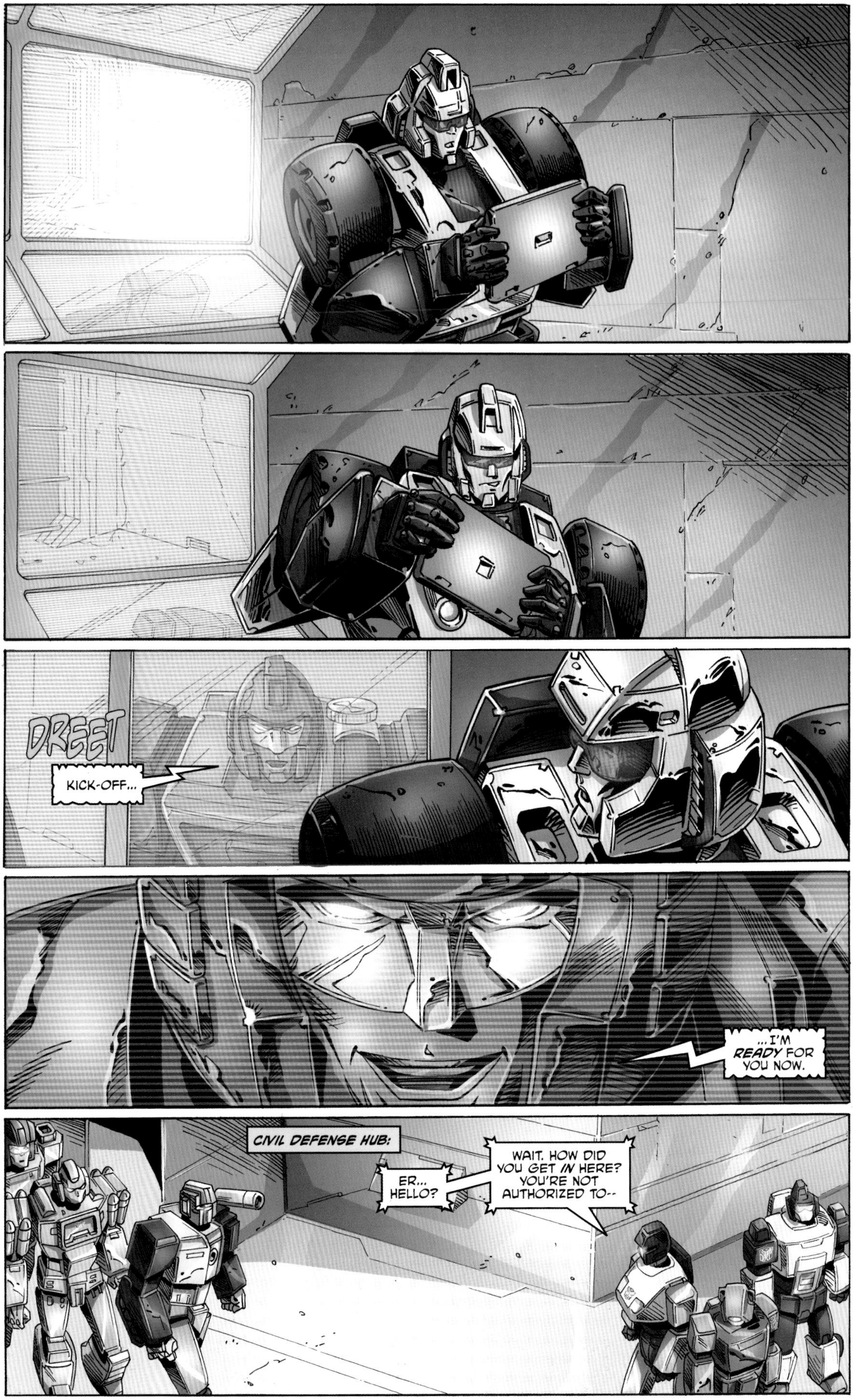
DREEET
KICK-OFF...
...I'M READY FOR YOU NOW.
CIVIL DEFENSE HUB:
ER... HELLO?
WAIT. HOW DID YOU GET IN HERE? YOU'RE NOT AUTHORIZED TO--

PWUM

VAARK

ZWAH

MMM-MUST--

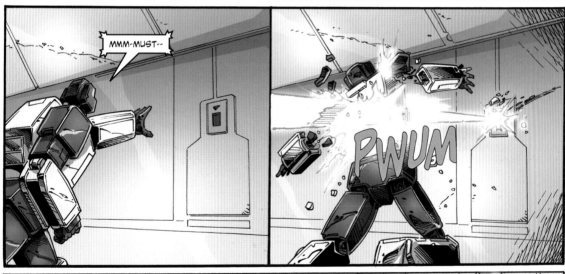

PWUM

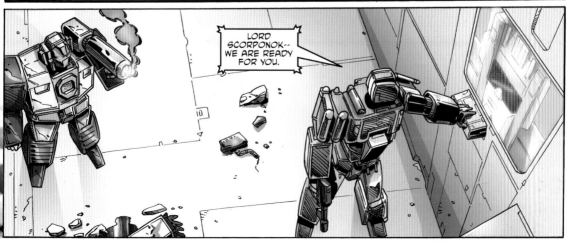

LORD SCORPONOK-- WE ARE READY FOR YOU.

EXCAVATION POINT ALPHA:

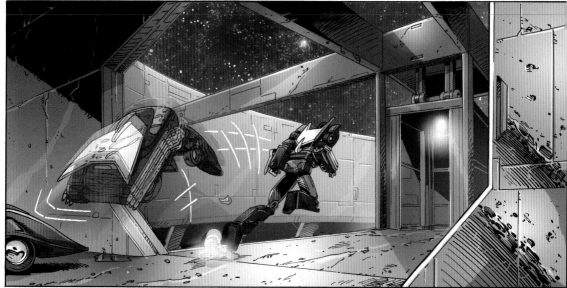

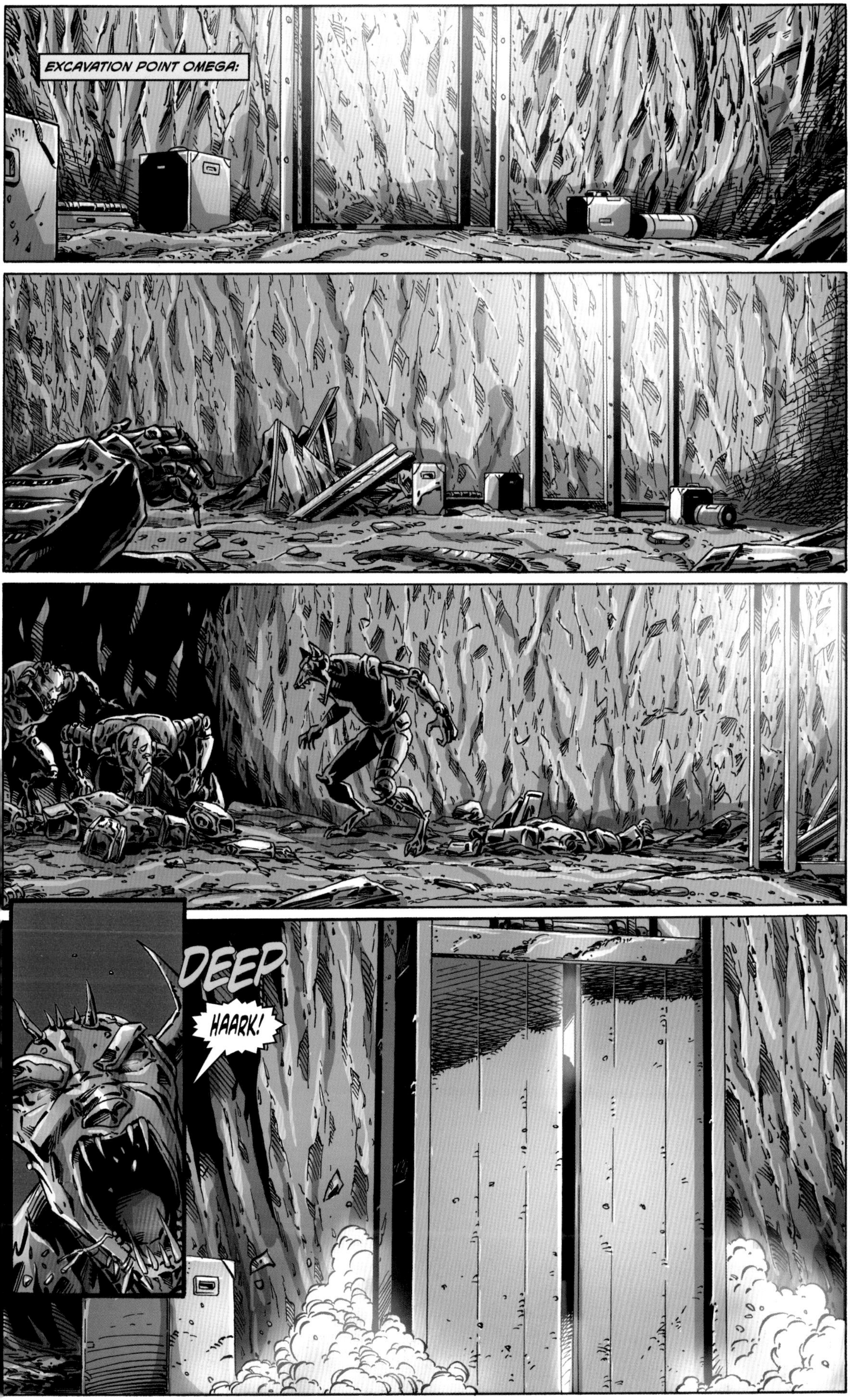
EXCAVATION POINT OMEGA:
DEEP
HAARK!

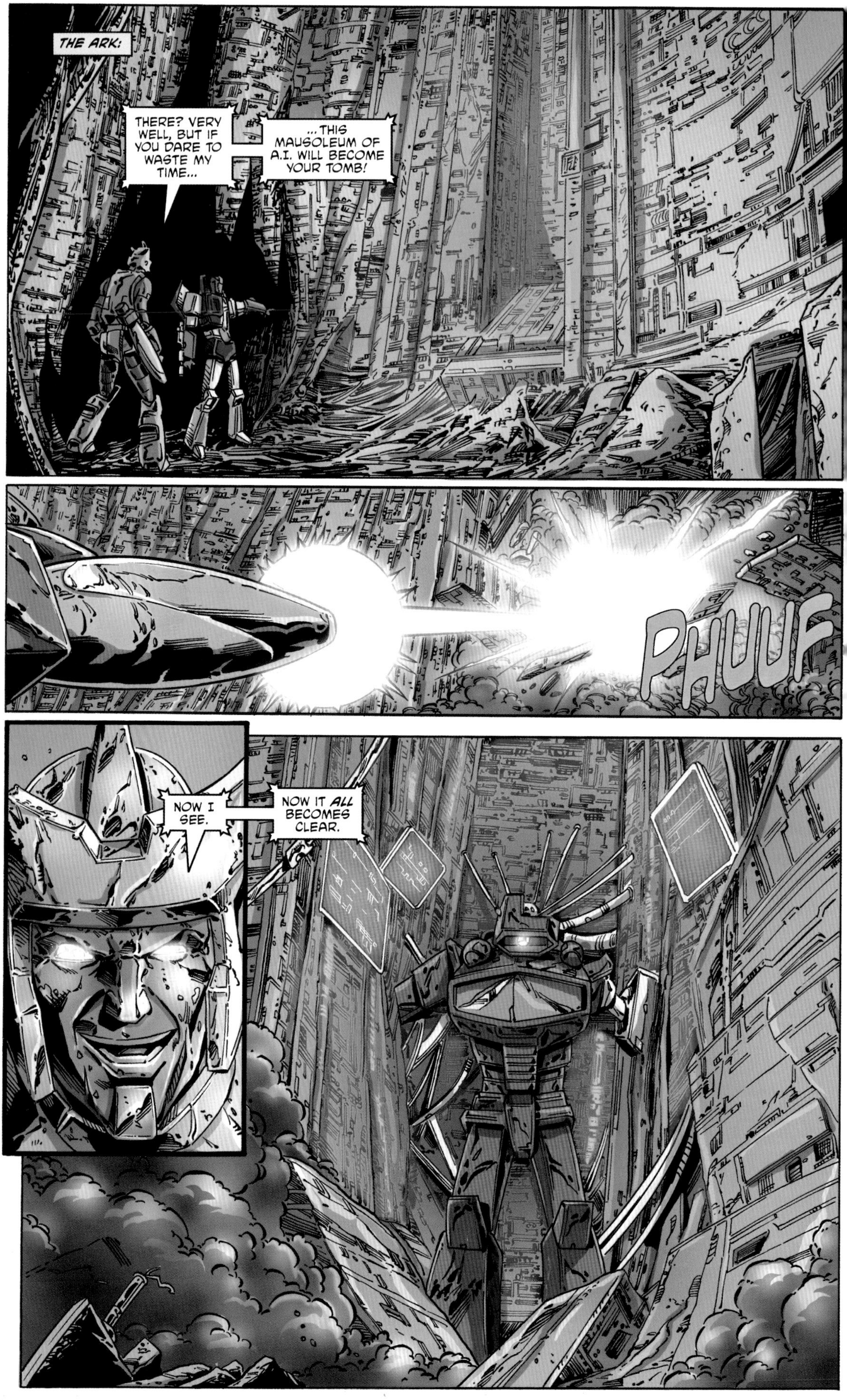
THE ARK:
THERE? VERY WELL, BUT IF YOU DARE TO WASTE MY TIME...
...THIS MAUSOLEUM OF A.I. WILL BECOME YOUR TOMB!
PHUUF
NOW I SEE.
NOW IT ALL BECOMES CLEAR.

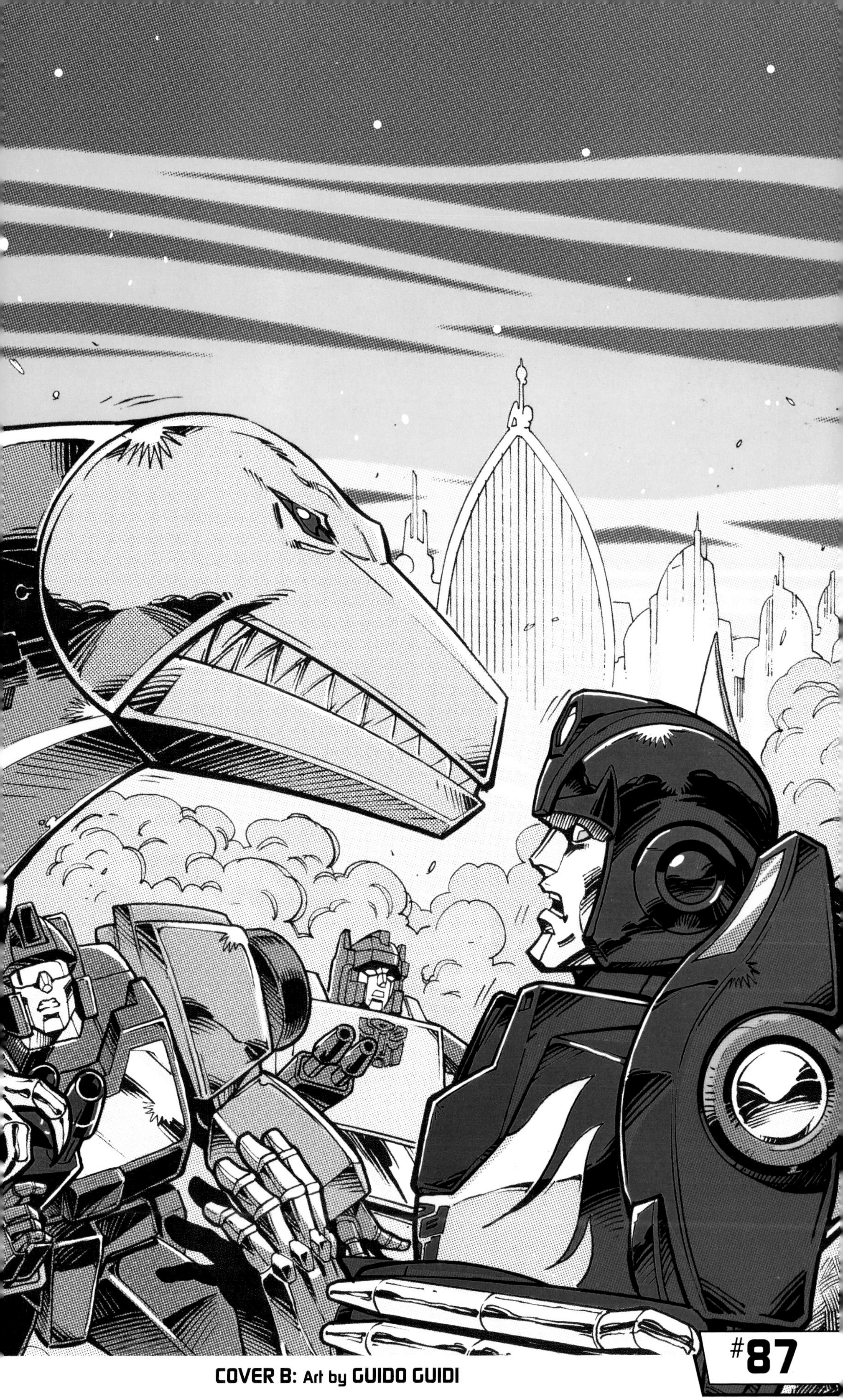
#87

COVER B: Art by GUIDO GUIDI

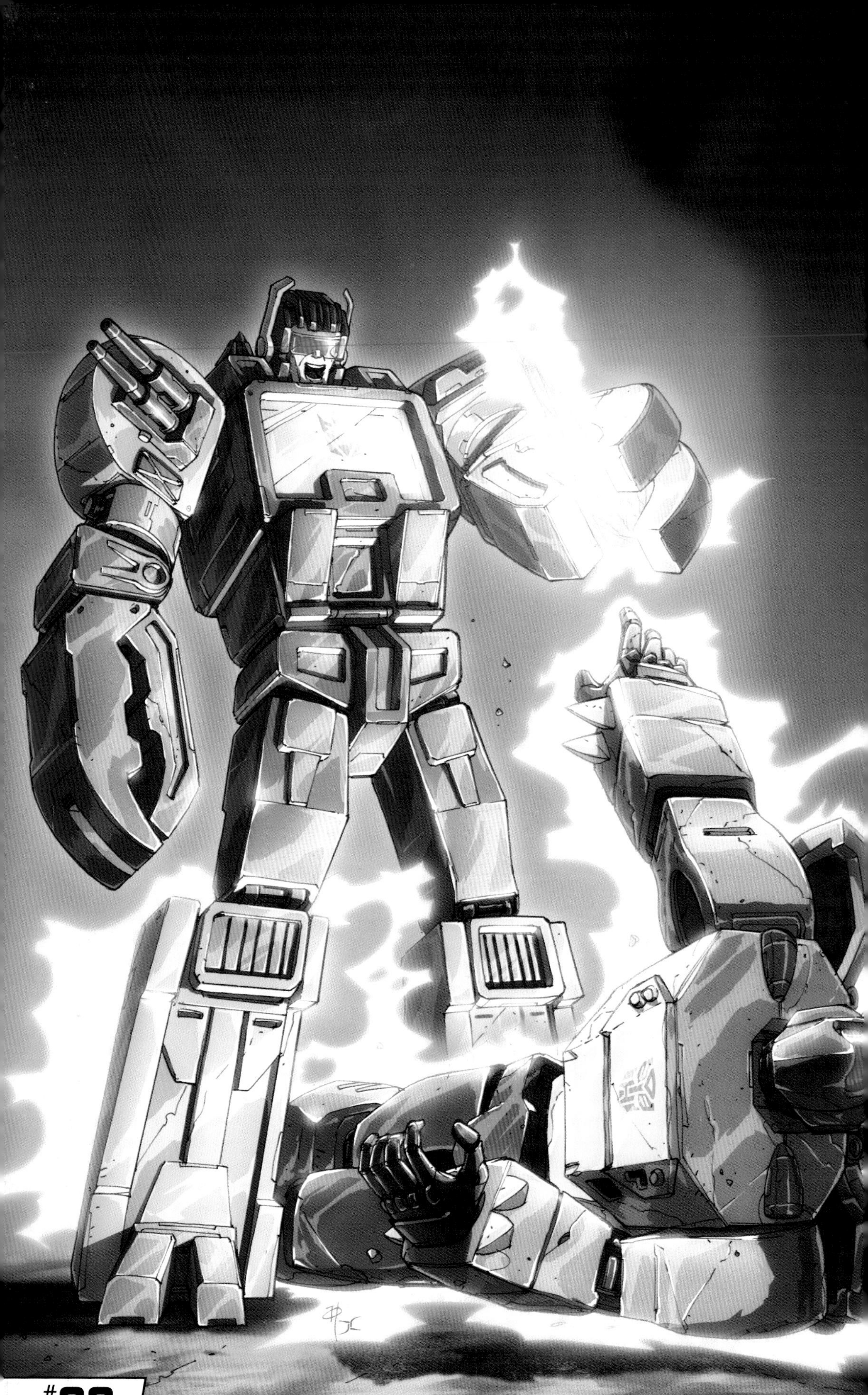

#88

COVER A: Art by ANDREW WILDMAN • Colors by JASON CARDY

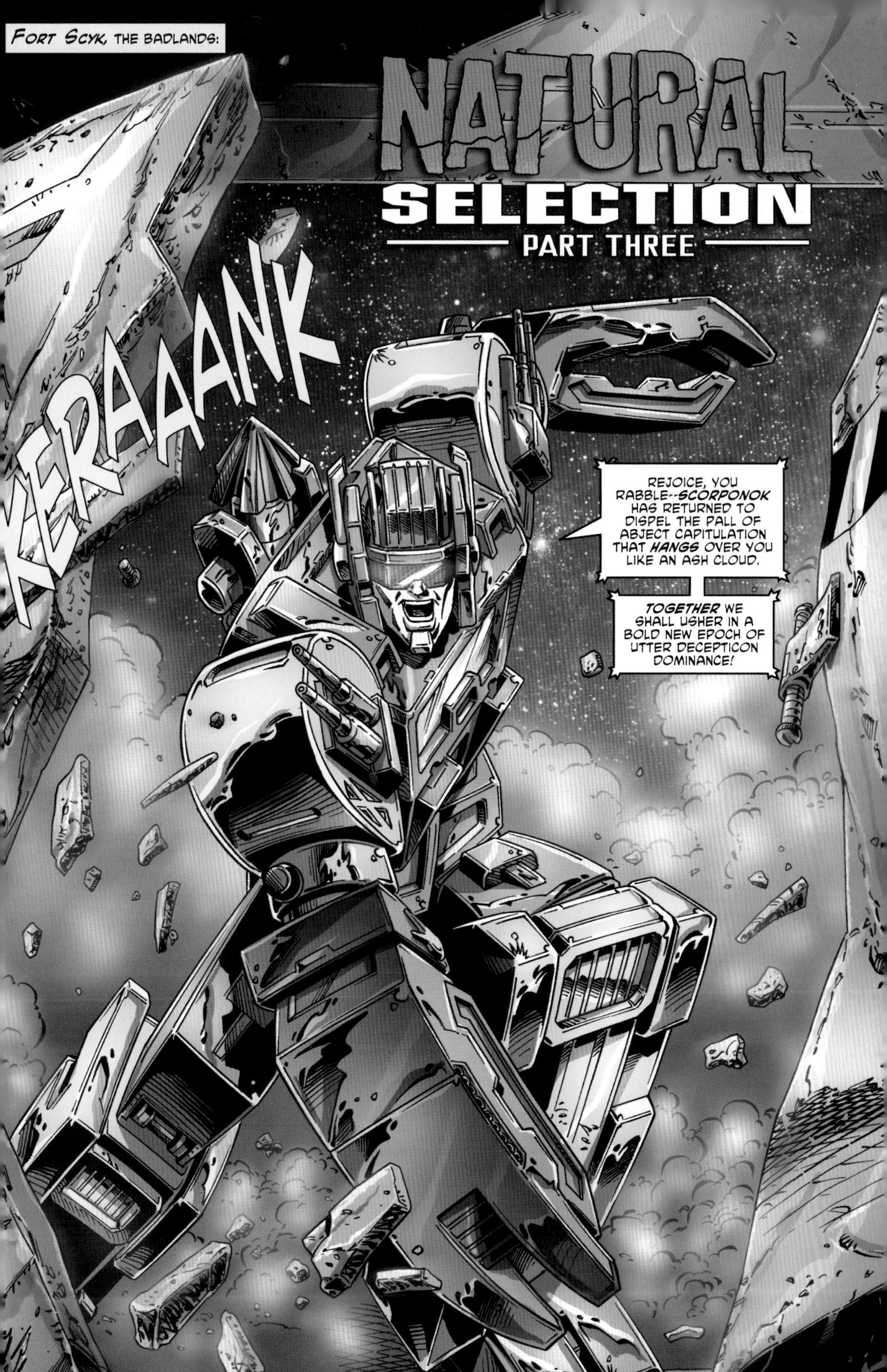
FORT SCYK, THE BADLANDS:
NATURAL SELECTION
PART THREE
KERAAANK
REJOICE, YOU RABBLE--SCORPONOK HAS RETURNED TO DISPEL THE PALL OF ABJECT CAPITULATION THAT HANGS OVER YOU LIKE AN ASH CLOUD.
TOGETHER WE SHALL USHER IN A BOLD NEW EPOCH OF UTTER DECEPTICON DOMINANCE!

WRITER MON FURMAN
PENCILER ANDREW WILDMAN
INKER STEPHEN BASKERVILLE
COLORIST JOHN-PAUL BOVE
LETTERER CHRIS MOWRY
EDITOR JOHN BARBER
EDITOR-IN-CHIEF CHRIS RYALL

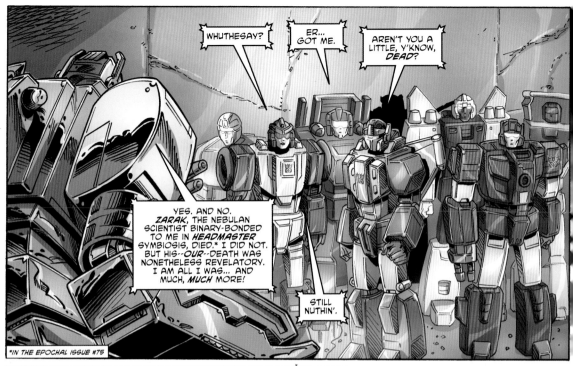

WHUTHESAY?

ER... GOT ME.

AREN'T YOU A LITTLE, Y'KNOW, DEAD?

YES. AND NO. ZARAK, THE NEBULAN SCIENTIST BINARY-BONDED TO ME IN HEADMASTER SYMBIOSIS, DIED.* I DID NOT. BUT HIS--OUR--DEATH WAS NONETHELESS REVELATORY. I AM ALL I WAS... AND MUCH, MUCH MORE!

STILL NUTHIN'.

*IN THE EPOCHAL ISSUE #75

IT IS TIME FOR YOU TO COME IN FROM THE WILDERNESS AND CLAW BACK WHAT IS RIGHTFULLY YOURS!

MY BATTLE STANDARD IS RAISED. MANY OTHERS--LIKE DREADWIND AND DARKWING HERE--HAVE ALREADY ANSWERED THE CALL TO ARMS. JOIN ME!

NO OFFENSE, BUT WE ALREADY GOT A THING OF OUR OWN GOING ON. SOUNDWAVE'S THE BOSS 'ROUND HERE!

OH. I BEG YOUR PARDON, MISFIRE.

KRRK

KUNCH

DID I MAKE THAT SOUND LIKE A REQUEST?

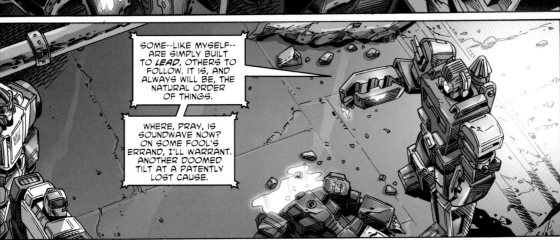

SOME--LIKE MYSELF-- ARE SIMPLY BUILT TO *LEAD*, OTHERS TO FOLLOW. IT IS, AND ALWAYS WILL BE, THE NATURAL ORDER OF THINGS.

WHERE, PRAY, IS SOUNDWAVE NOW? ON SOME FOOL'S ERRAND, I'LL WARRANT. ANOTHER DOOMED TILT AT A PATENTLY LOST CAUSE.

ASK YOURSELVES WHY, ALL THIS TIME AFTER REOCCUPATION, ARE YOU STILL COWERING IN THIS CRUMBLING RELIC OF A BYGONE WAR?

I OFFER YOU A BESPOKE CYBERTRON OF CERTAINTIES AND CLARITY, WHERE ONE UNIFIED, ABSOLUTE VISION HOLDS SWAY. A WORLD--

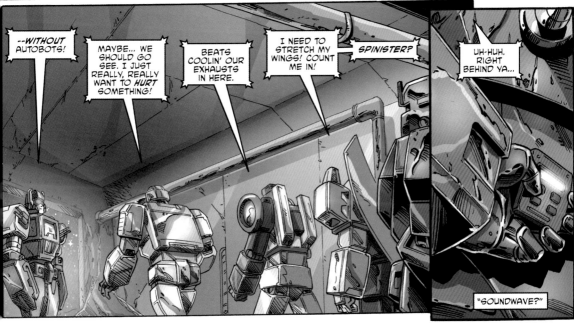

--WITHOUT AUTOBOTS!

MAYBE... WE SHOULD GO SEE. I JUST REALLY, REALLY WANT TO *HURT* SOMETHING!

BEATS COOLIN' OUR EXHAUSTS IN HERE.

I NEED TO STRETCH MY WINGS! COUNT ME IN!

SPINISTER?

UH-HUH. RIGHT BEHIND YA...

"SOUNDWAVE?"

PROBLEM?

NOTHING. NO. CONTINUE...

VERY WELL. ONCE THE MORTAL REMAINS OF *THUNDERWING* AND ITS MATRIX RESERVOIR ARE IN MY POSSESSION WE WILL BE READY TO MOUNT A CONCERTED AND DECIMATING ASSAULT ON CYBERTRON.

SO YOU SAY, *BLUDGEON*. BUT WHILE THIS *WARWORLD* IS CERTAINLY MIGHTY, ALONE IT CANNOT HOPE TO PREVAIL AGAINST CYBERTRON'S PLANETARY DEFENSES.

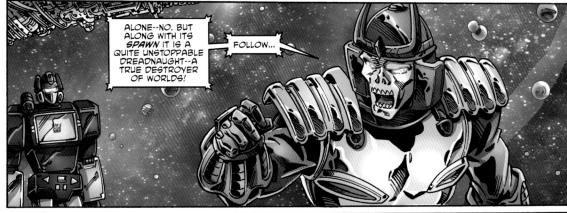

ALONE--NO. BUT ALONG WITH ITS *SPAWN* IT IS A QUITE UNSTOPPABLE DREADNAUGHT--A TRUE DESTROYER OF WORLDS!

FOLLOW...

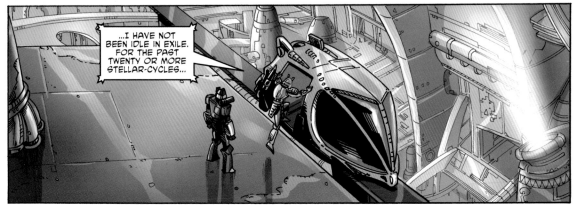

...I HAVE NOT BEEN IDLE IN EXILE. FOR THE PAST TWENTY OR MORE STELLAR-CYCLES...

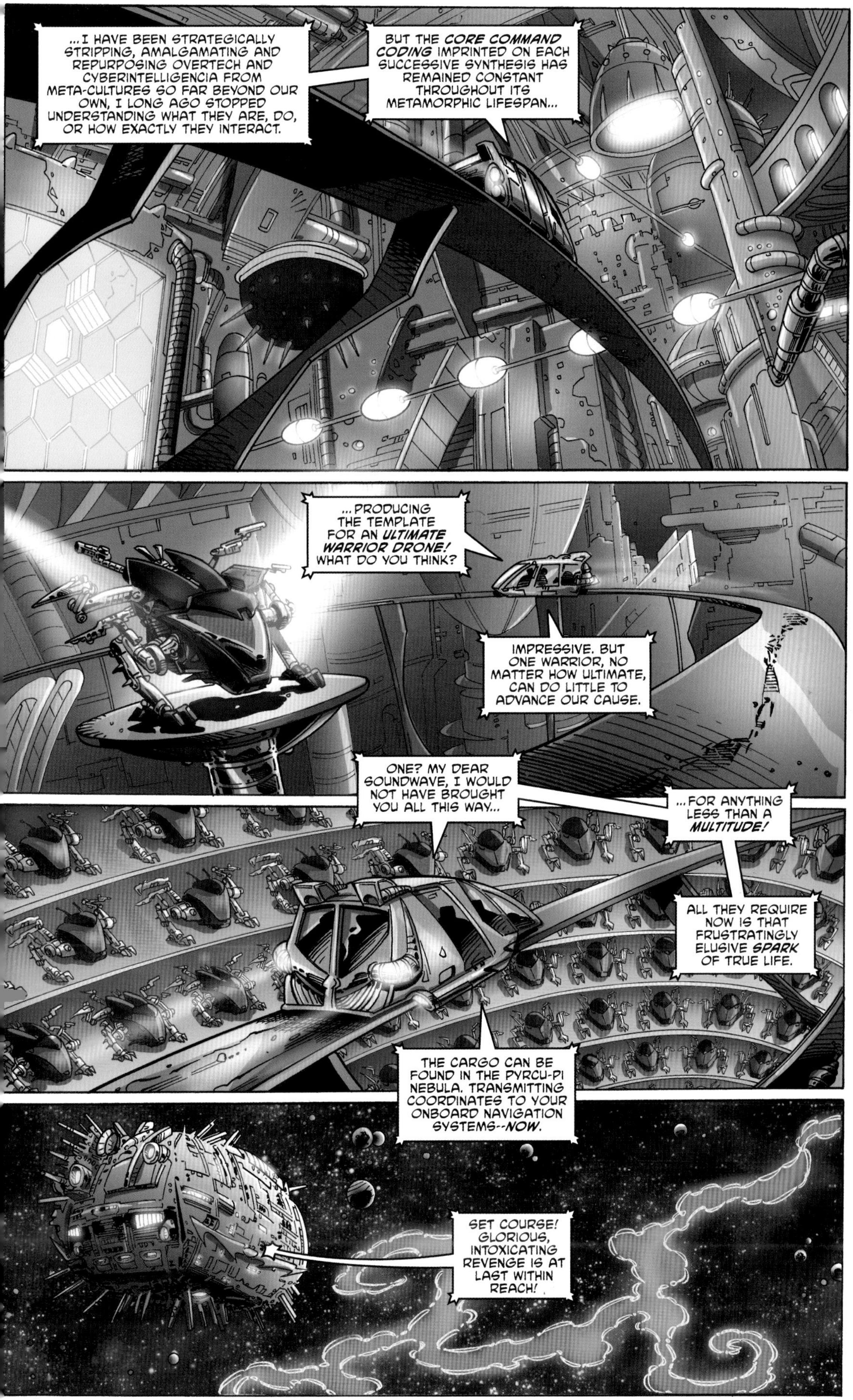
...I HAVE BEEN STRATEGICALLY STRIPPING, AMALGAMATING AND REPURPOSING OVERTECH AND CYBERINTELLIGENCIA FROM META-CULTURES SO FAR BEYOND OUR OWN, I LONG AGO STOPPED UNDERSTANDING WHAT THEY ARE, DO, OR HOW EXACTLY THEY INTERACT.
BUT THE *CORE COMMAND CODING* IMPRINTED ON EACH SUCCESSIVE SYNTHESIS HAS REMAINED CONSTANT THROUGHOUT ITS METAMORPHIC LIFESPAN...
...PRODUCING THE TEMPLATE FOR AN *ULTIMATE WARRIOR DRONE!* WHAT DO YOU THINK?
IMPRESSIVE. BUT ONE WARRIOR, NO MATTER HOW ULTIMATE, CAN DO LITTLE TO ADVANCE OUR CAUSE.
ONE? MY DEAR SOUNDWAVE, I WOULD NOT HAVE BROUGHT YOU ALL THIS WAY...
...FOR ANYTHING LESS THAN A *MULTITUDE!*
ALL THEY REQUIRE NOW IS THAT FRUSTRATINGLY ELUSIVE *SPARK* OF TRUE LIFE.
THE CARGO CAN BE FOUND IN THE PYRCU-PI NEBULA. TRANSMITTING COORDINATES TO YOUR ONBOARD NAVIGATION SYSTEMS--*NOW*.
SET COURSE! GLORIOUS, INTOXICATING REVENGE IS AT LAST WITHIN REACH!

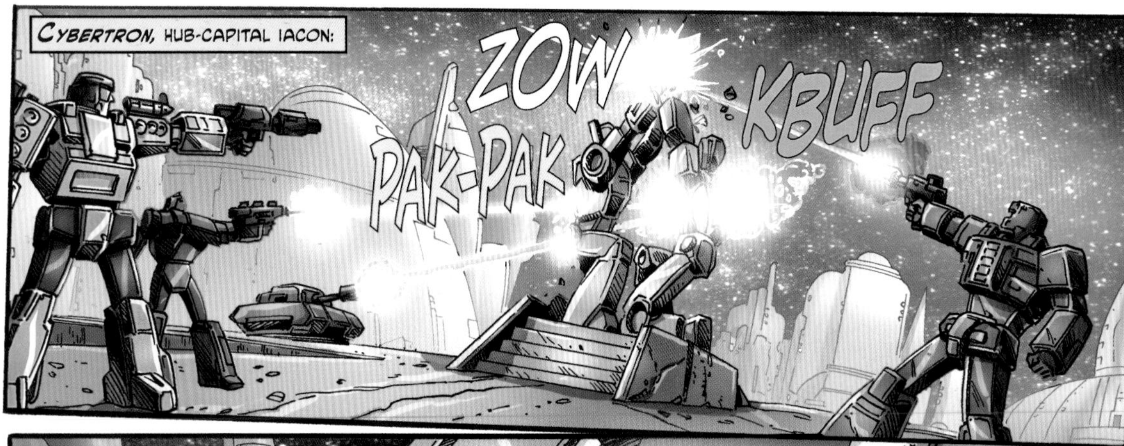
CYBERTRON, HUB-CAPITAL IACON:
ZOW
PAK-PAK
KBUFF
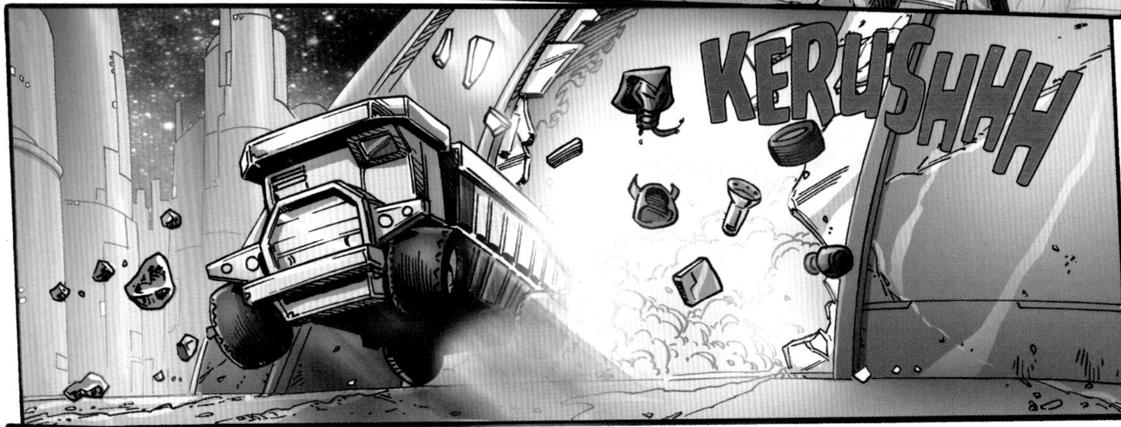
KERUSHHH
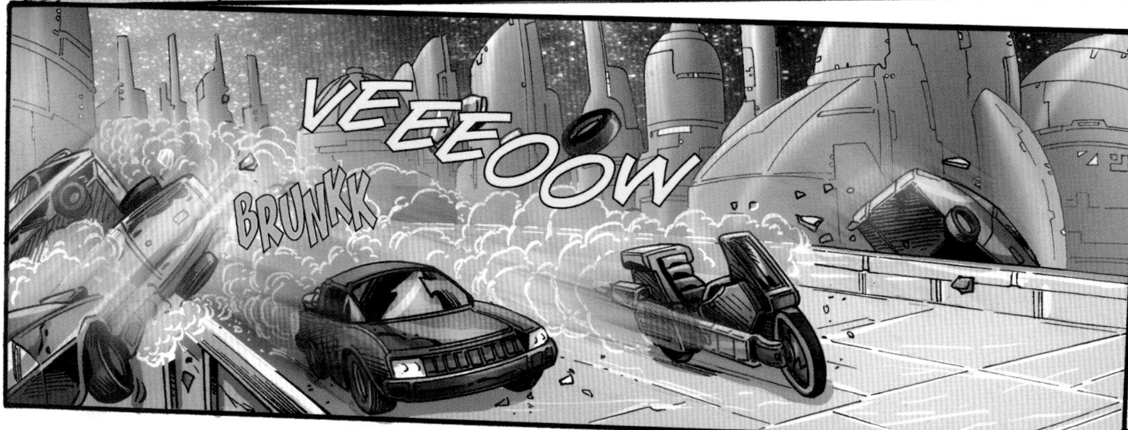
VEEEOOW
BRUNKK
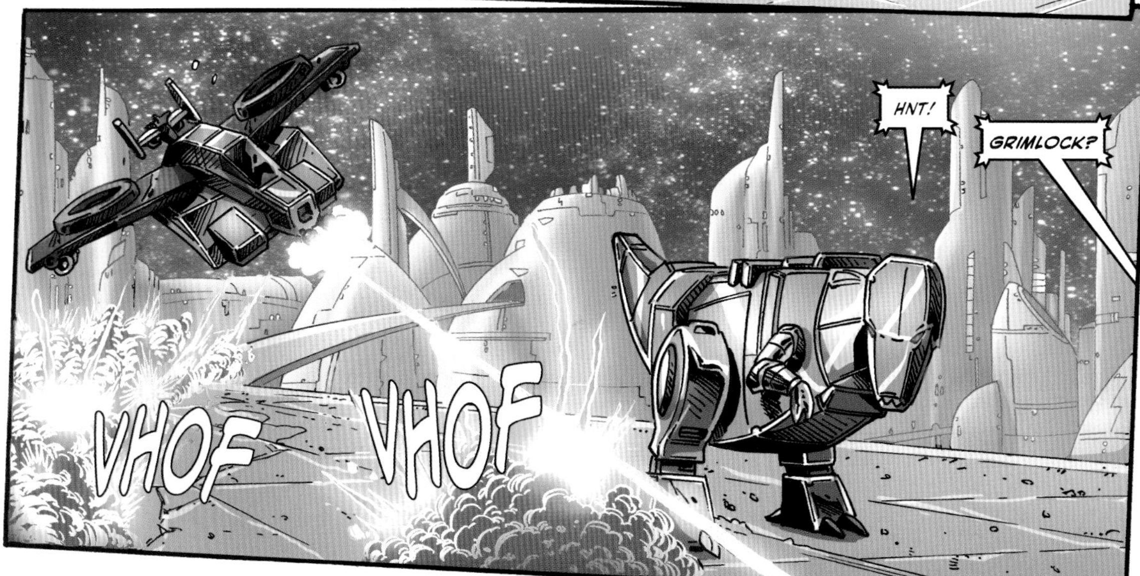
HNT!
GRIMLOCK?
VHOF
VHOF

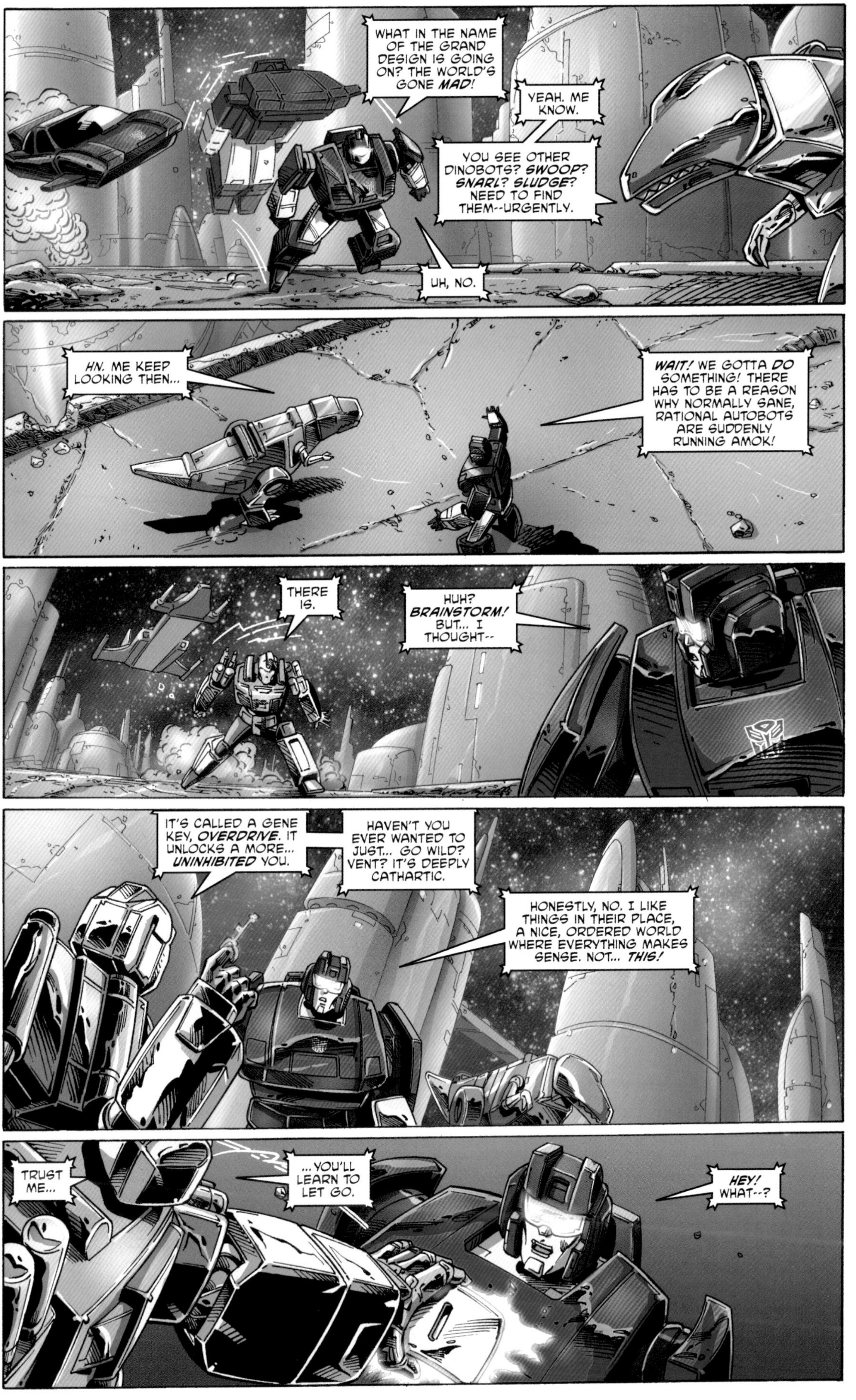
WHAT IN THE NAME OF THE GRAND DESIGN IS GOING ON? THE WORLD'S GONE *MAD!*
YEAH. ME KNOW.
YOU SEE OTHER DINOBOTS? *SWOOP? SNARL? SLUDGE?* NEED TO FIND THEM--URGENTLY.
UH, NO.
HN. ME KEEP LOOKING THEN...
WAIT! WE GOTTA *DO* SOMETHING! THERE HAS TO BE A REASON WHY NORMALLY SANE, RATIONAL AUTOBOTS ARE SUDDENLY RUNNING AMOK!
THERE IS.
HUH? *BRAINSTORM!* BUT... I THOUGHT--
IT'S CALLED A GENE KEY, *OVERDRIVE.* IT UNLOCKS A MORE... *UNINHIBITED* YOU.
HAVEN'T YOU EVER WANTED TO JUST... GO WILD? VENT? IT'S DEEPLY CATHARTIC.
HONESTLY, NO. I LIKE THINGS IN THEIR PLACE, A NICE, ORDERED WORLD WHERE EVERYTHING MAKES SENSE. NOT... *THIS!*
TRUST ME...
...YOU'LL LEARN TO LET GO.
HEY! WHAT--?

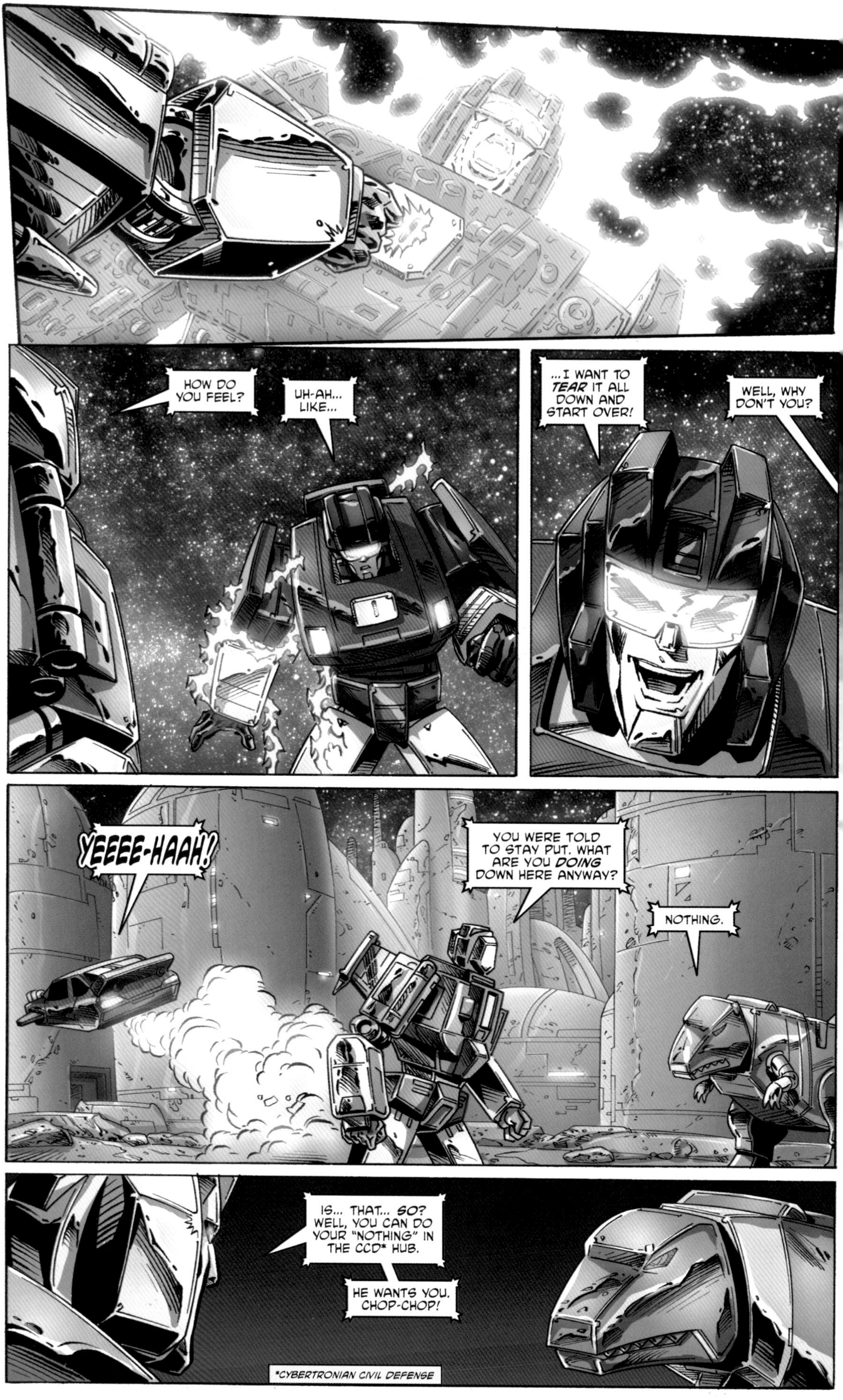
HOW DO YOU FEEL?
UH-AH... LIKE...
...I WANT TO TEAR IT ALL DOWN AND START OVER!
WELL, WHY DON'T YOU?
YEEEE-HAAH!
YOU WERE TOLD TO STAY PUT. WHAT ARE YOU DOING DOWN HERE ANYWAY?
NOTHING.
IS... THAT... SO? WELL, YOU CAN DO YOUR "NOTHING" IN THE CCD* HUB.
HE WANTS YOU. CHOP-CHOP!
*CYBERTRONIAN CIVIL DEFENSE

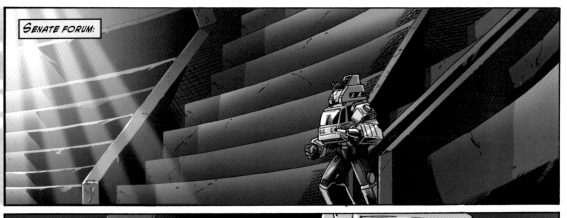

GRAPPLE...

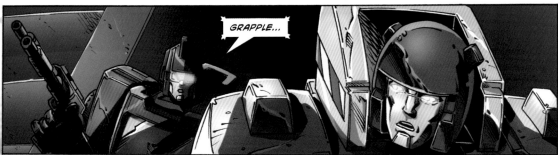

CROSSHAIRS! ARE YOU--?

STILL ME? UH-HUH. ONLY SHOOT WHEN I SEE THE WIRES IN THEIR EYES.

YOU?

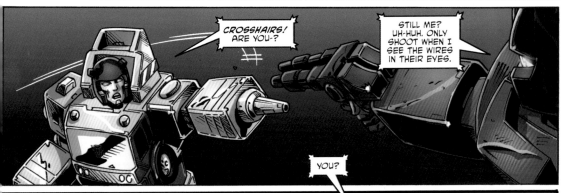

STILL RATHER BUILDING THAN DESTROYING.

PHEW. IT'S HARD TO KNOW WHO TO TRUST ANYMORE. YOU ALONE?

HOSEHEAD, BLURR... YOU CAN COME OUT NOW.

GOOD TO SEE YOU, GRAPPLE. BUT WE NEED TO GO--NOW. IT'S NOT SAFE HERE.

THOUGHTYOU*MIGHT* KNOWABACKDOOR-- SOMETHINGNOTONANY BLUEPRINTS?

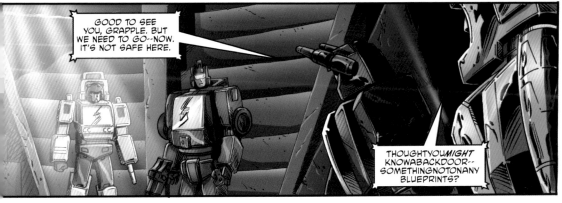

"FOLLOW ME..."

ALRIGHT...

PERCEPTOR? HOIST? SPLASHDOWN?

PERCEPTOR WE *KNOW* HAS BEEN TURNED. SPLASHDOWN... PRETTY SURE... DON'T KNOW ABOUT HOIST.

ANYONE HAVE A *CLUE* WHAT'S ACTUALLY GOING ON? OR WHO'S RESPONSIBLE?

FIRST I KNEW WAS WHEN LANDMINE TRIED TO THROW ME *OFF* A BALCONY!

WE'REJUSTASIN THEDARKBUT ISAWPERCEPTORUSE SOMETHINGAWEAPON ORDEVICEON OVER-RUN.

ALL WE KNOW FOR SURE IS, US AUTOBOTS ARE NOW AN ENDANGERED SPECIES!

HOT ROD?

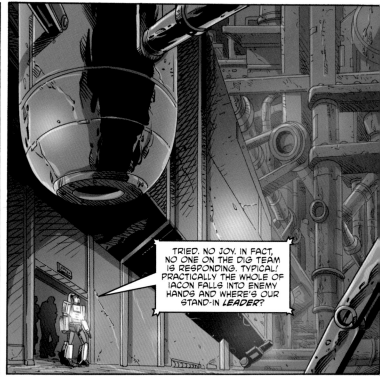

TRIED. NO JOY. IN FACT, NO ONE ON THE DIG TEAM IS RESPONDING. TYPICAL! PRACTICALLY THE WHOLE OF IACON FALLS INTO ENEMY HANDS AND WHERE'S OUR STAND-IN *LEADER*?

"HAPPILY GRUBBING AROUND FOR DUSTY ARTIFACTS IN THE DEPTHS OF CYBERTRON!"

HN-- HN-- HN--

HNNNH--

DID--?

KTKRR-KTKRR-KTKRR
NO!
SKAAAR!

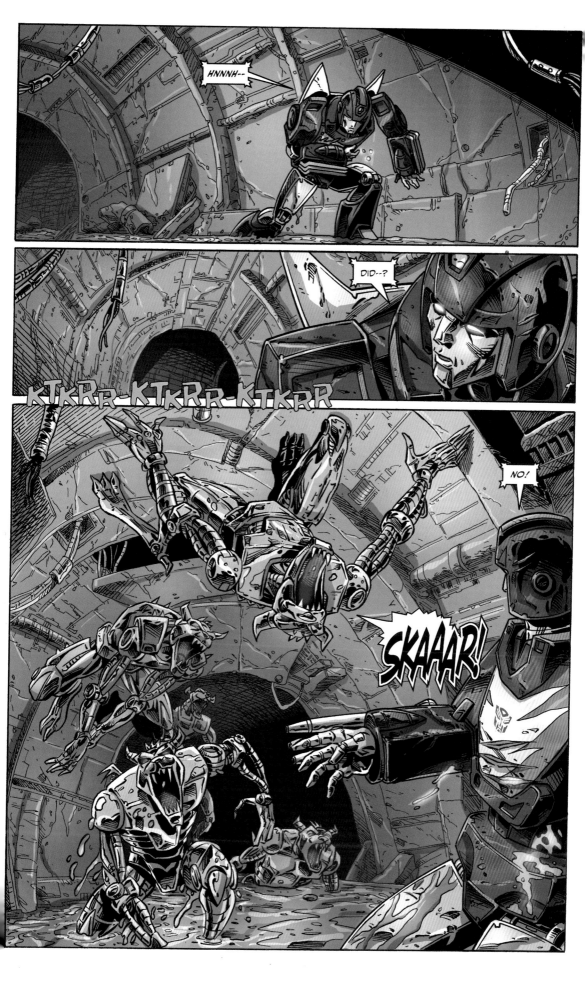

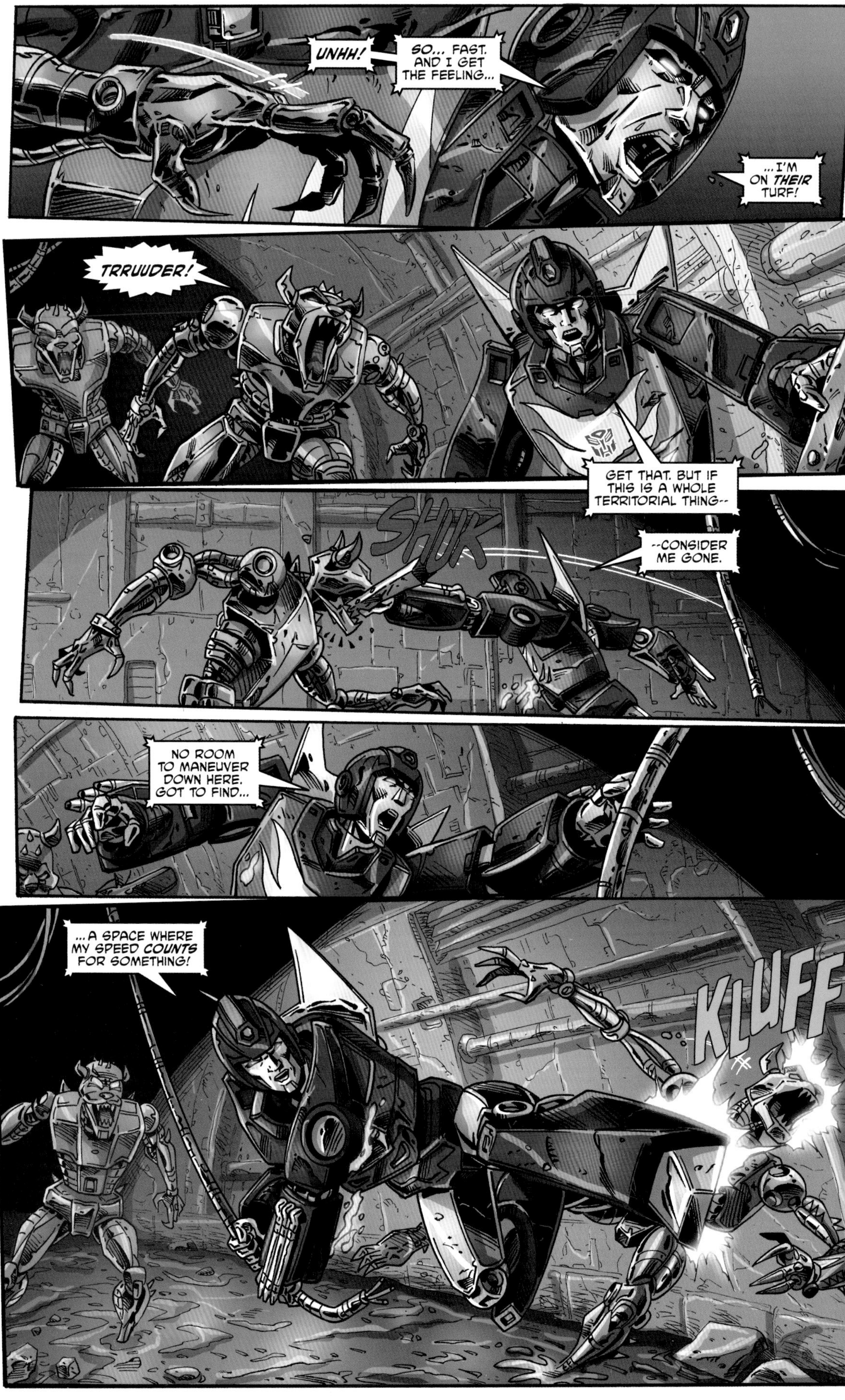

UNHH!
SO... FAST. AND I GET THE FEELING...
...I'M ON THEIR TURF!
TRRUUDER!
GET THAT. BUT IF THIS IS A WHOLE TERRITORIAL THING--
SHUK
--CONSIDER ME GONE.
NO ROOM TO MANEUVER DOWN HERE. GOT TO FIND...
...A SPACE WHERE MY SPEED COUNTS FOR SOMETHING!
KLUFF

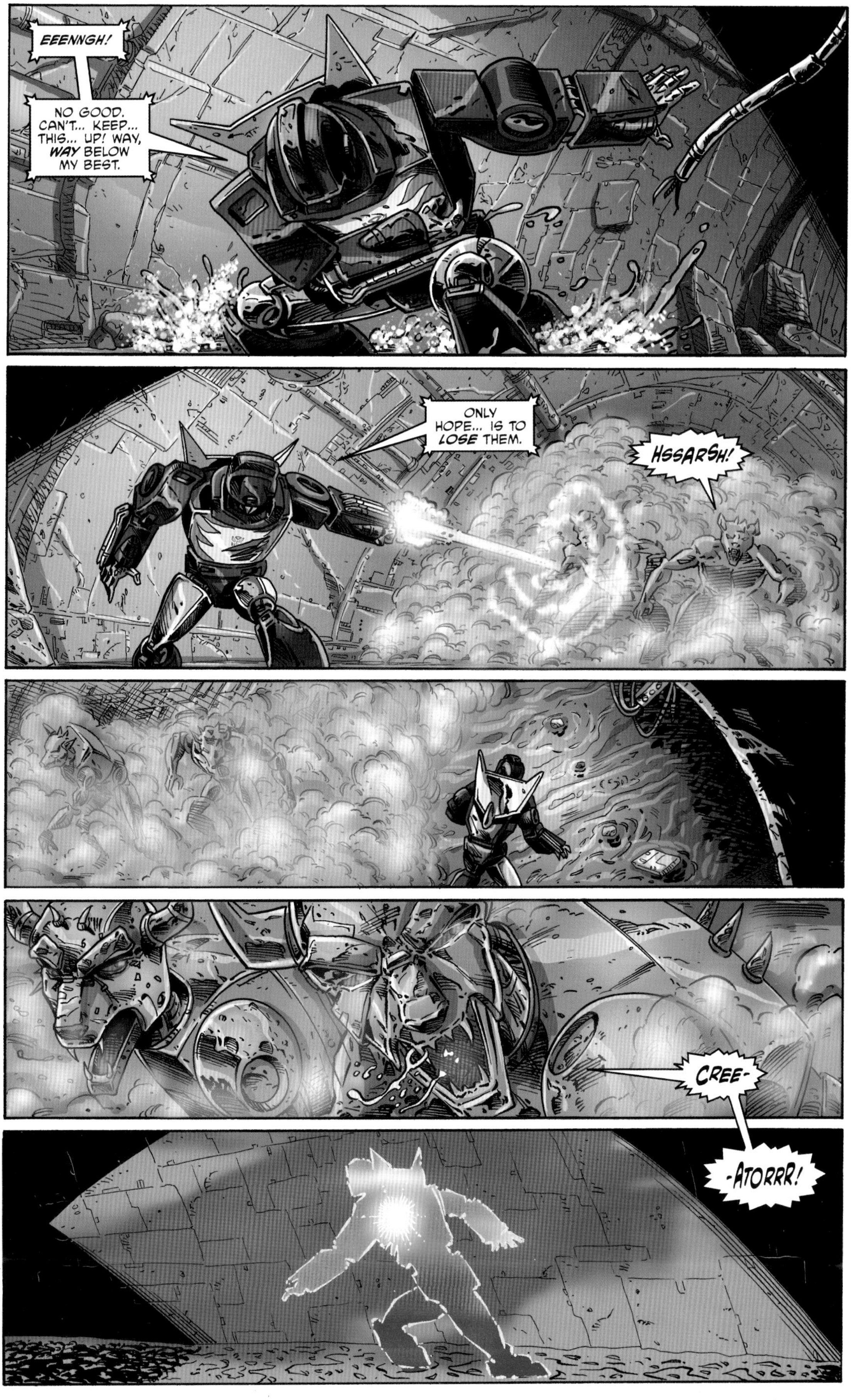

EEENNGH!
NO GOOD. CAN'T... KEEP... THIS... UP! WAY, WAY BELOW MY BEST.
ONLY HOPE... IS TO LOSE THEM.
HSSARSH!
CREE-
-ATORRR!

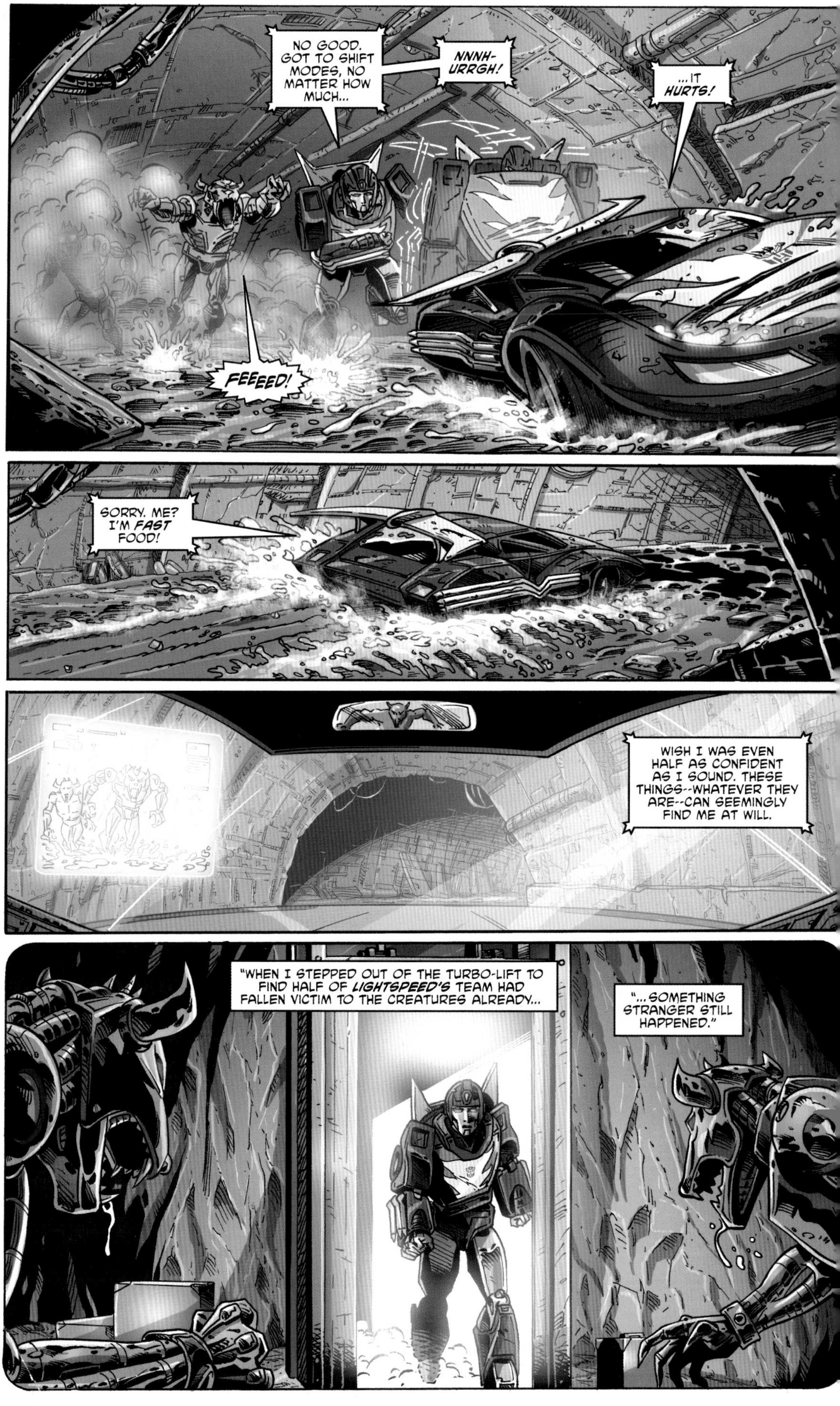
NO GOOD. GOT TO SHIFT MODES, NO MATTER HOW MUCH...
NNNH-URRGH!
...IT HURTS!
FEEEED!
SORRY. ME? I'M FAST FOOD!
WISH I WAS EVEN HALF AS CONFIDENT AS I SOUND. THESE THINGS--WHATEVER THEY ARE--CAN SEEMINGLY FIND ME AT WILL.
"WHEN I STEPPED OUT OF THE TURBO-LIFT TO FIND HALF OF LIGHTSPEED'S TEAM HAD FALLEN VICTIM TO THE CREATURES ALREADY...
"...SOMETHING STRANGER STILL HAPPENED."

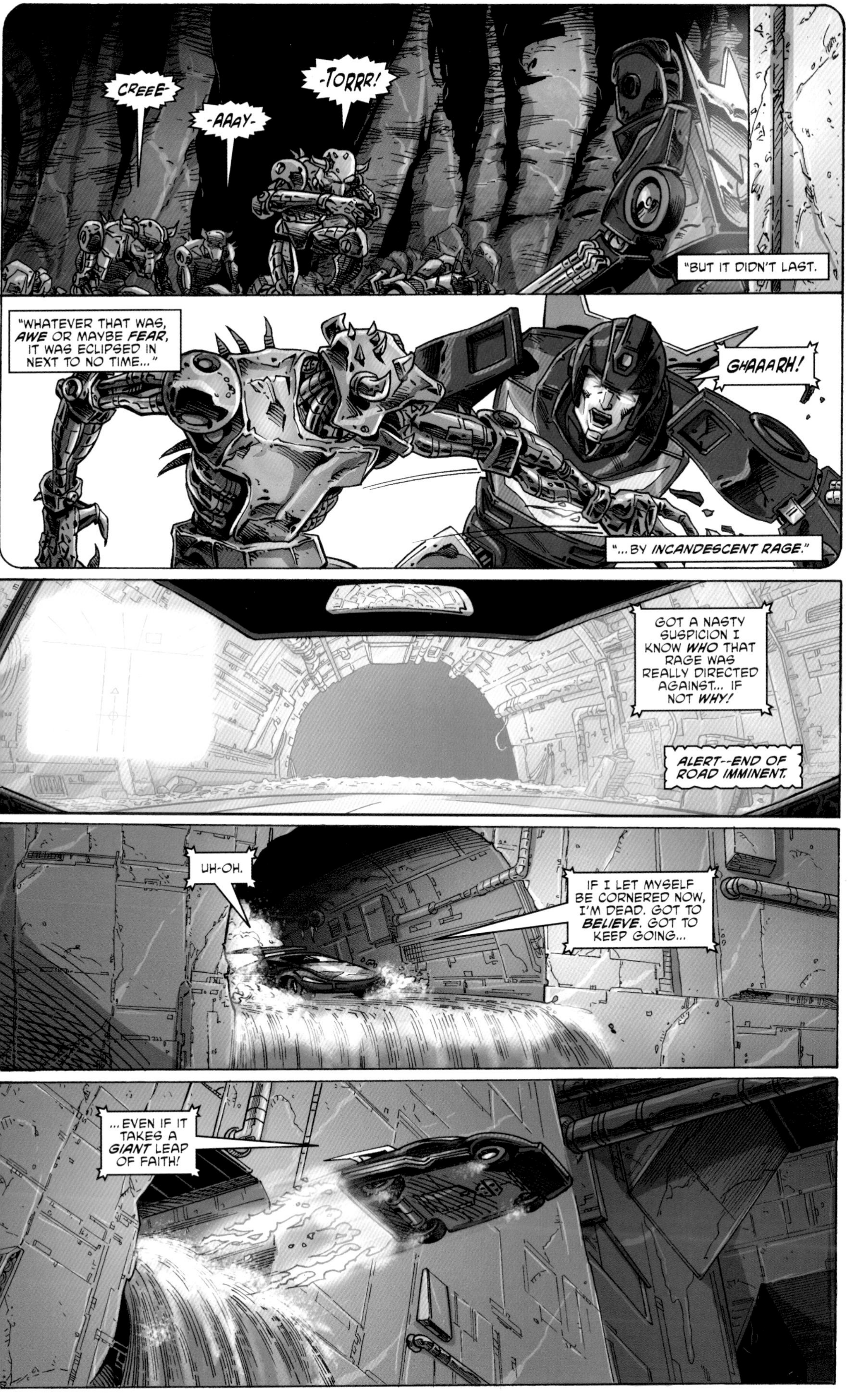
CREEE-
-AAAY-
-TORRR!
"BUT IT DIDN'T LAST.
"WHATEVER THAT WAS, AWE OR MAYBE FEAR, IT WAS ECLIPSED IN NEXT TO NO TIME..."
GHAAARH!
"...BY INCANDESCENT RAGE."
GOT A NASTY SUSPICION I KNOW WHO THAT RAGE WAS REALLY DIRECTED AGAINST... IF NOT WHY!
ALERT--END OF ROAD IMMINENT.
UH-OH.
IF I LET MYSELF BE CORNERED NOW, I'M DEAD. GOT TO BELIEVE. GOT TO KEEP GOING...
...EVEN IF IT TAKES A GIANT LEAP OF FAITH!

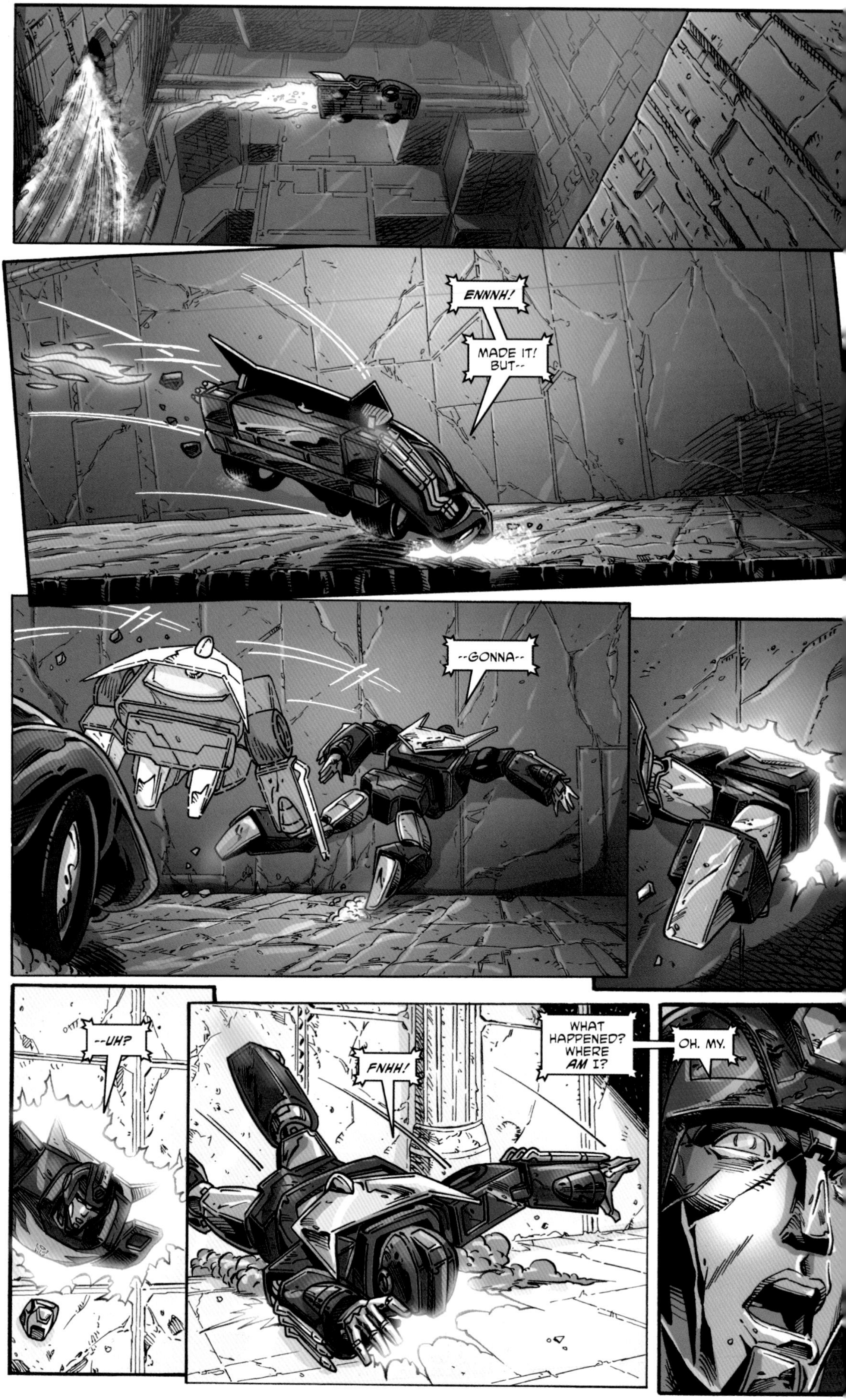
ENNNH!
MADE IT! BUT--
--GONNA--
--UH?
FNHH!
WHAT HAPPENED? WHERE AM I?
OH. MY.

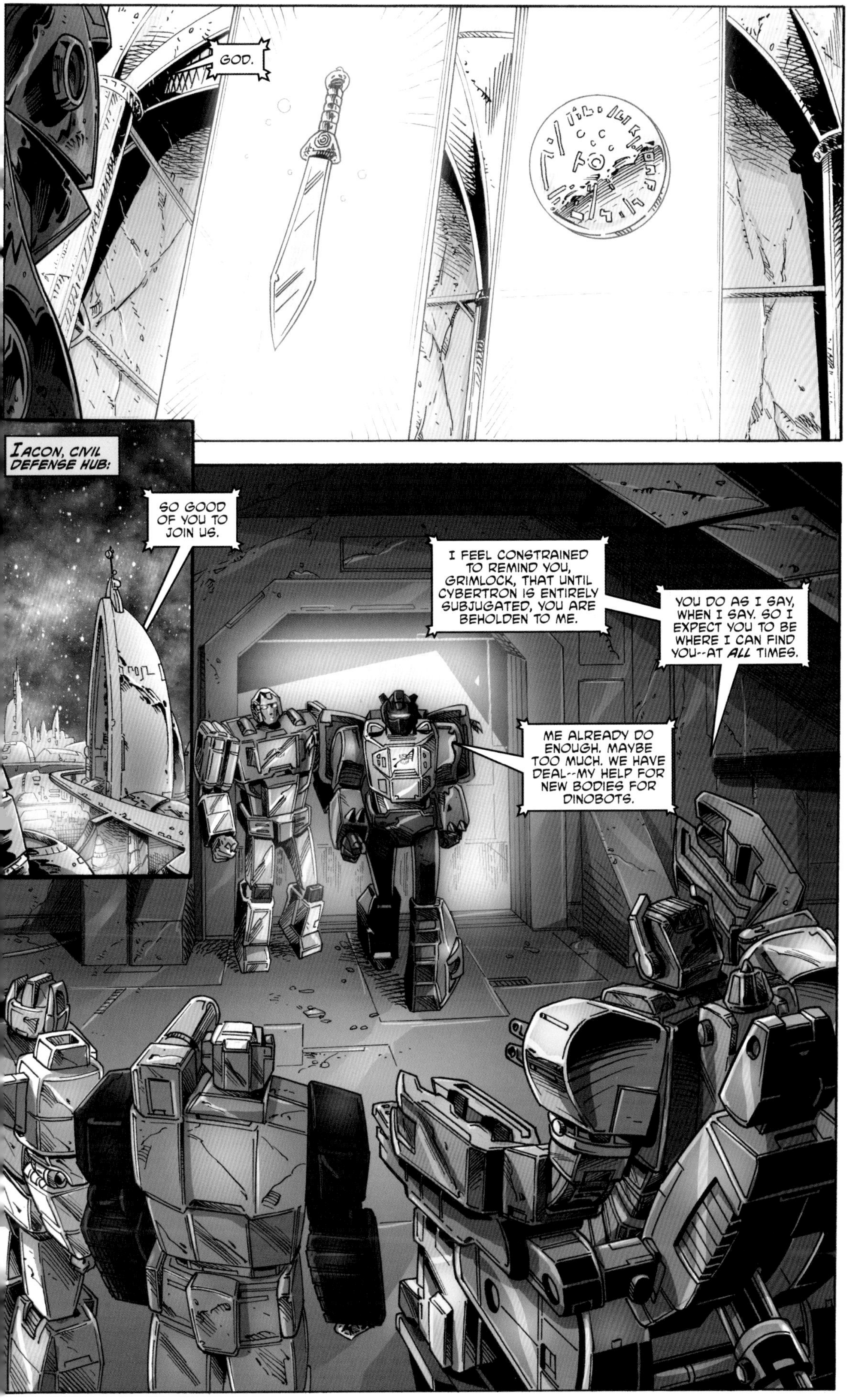
GOD.
IACON, CIVIL DEFENSE HUB:
SO GOOD OF YOU TO JOIN US.
I FEEL CONSTRAINED TO REMIND YOU, GRIMLOCK, THAT UNTIL CYBERTRON IS ENTIRELY SUBJUGATED, YOU ARE BEHOLDEN TO ME.
YOU DO AS I SAY, WHEN I SAY. SO I EXPECT YOU TO BE WHERE I CAN FIND YOU--AT ALL TIMES.
ME ALREADY DO ENOUGH. MAYBE TOO MUCH. WE HAVE DEAL--MY HELP FOR NEW BODIES FOR DINOBOTS.

GRIMLOCK, GRIMLOCK...

...YOU HAVE BARELY *BEGUN* TO FULFILL YOUR END OF THE BARGAIN. THAT FINE NEW BI-CONFIGURATIONAL FORM YOU NOW WEAR DOESN'T COME CHEAP.

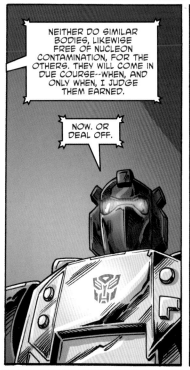

NEITHER DO SIMILAR BODIES, LIKEWISE FREE OF NUCLEON CONTAMINATION, FOR THE OTHERS. THEY WILL COME IN DUE COURSE--WHEN, AND ONLY WHEN, I JUDGE THEM EARNED.

NOW. OR DEAL OFF.

OH, DEAR, OH, DEAR. NO. THAT WON'T DO AT ALL. BUT I EXPECTED AS MUCH. I NEED PROOF, GRIMLOCK, OF WHERE YOUR REAL LOYALTIES LIE.

FOR REASONS I CANNOT FATHOM, *PUNCH* HERE SEEMS IMMUNE TO MY GENE KEY'S PERSONALITY MODIFICATIONS. WHICH RATHER MAKES HIM *SURPLUS* TO REQUIREMENTS.

EXECUTE HIM.

DO AS I COMMAND... OR *SLAG* WILL BE LEFT TO STEW IN HIS REGRESSIVE STATE AND THE REST OF THE DINOBOTS HUNTED DOWN AND *TERMINATED*.

THE CHOICE IS YOURS.

NO.

GRIMLOCK? WHAT ARE YOU *DOING*?

YOU'RE ONE OF US. THIS SCUM... THEY'RE BENEATH YOU.

AH, BUT *ARE* WE? I BELIEVE THERE IS NO UPPER LIMIT TO WHAT GRIMLOCK WILL DO. HIS ONLY REAL ALLEGIANCE IS TO HIMSELF AND HIS FELLOW DINOBOTS. HE WILL BEND WITH THE PREVAILING WIND, WHICH RIGHT NOW...

...IS BLOWING FULL FORCE IN THE DIRECTION OF BLANKET DECEPTICON RULE!

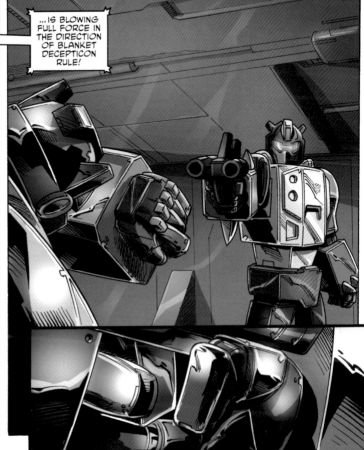

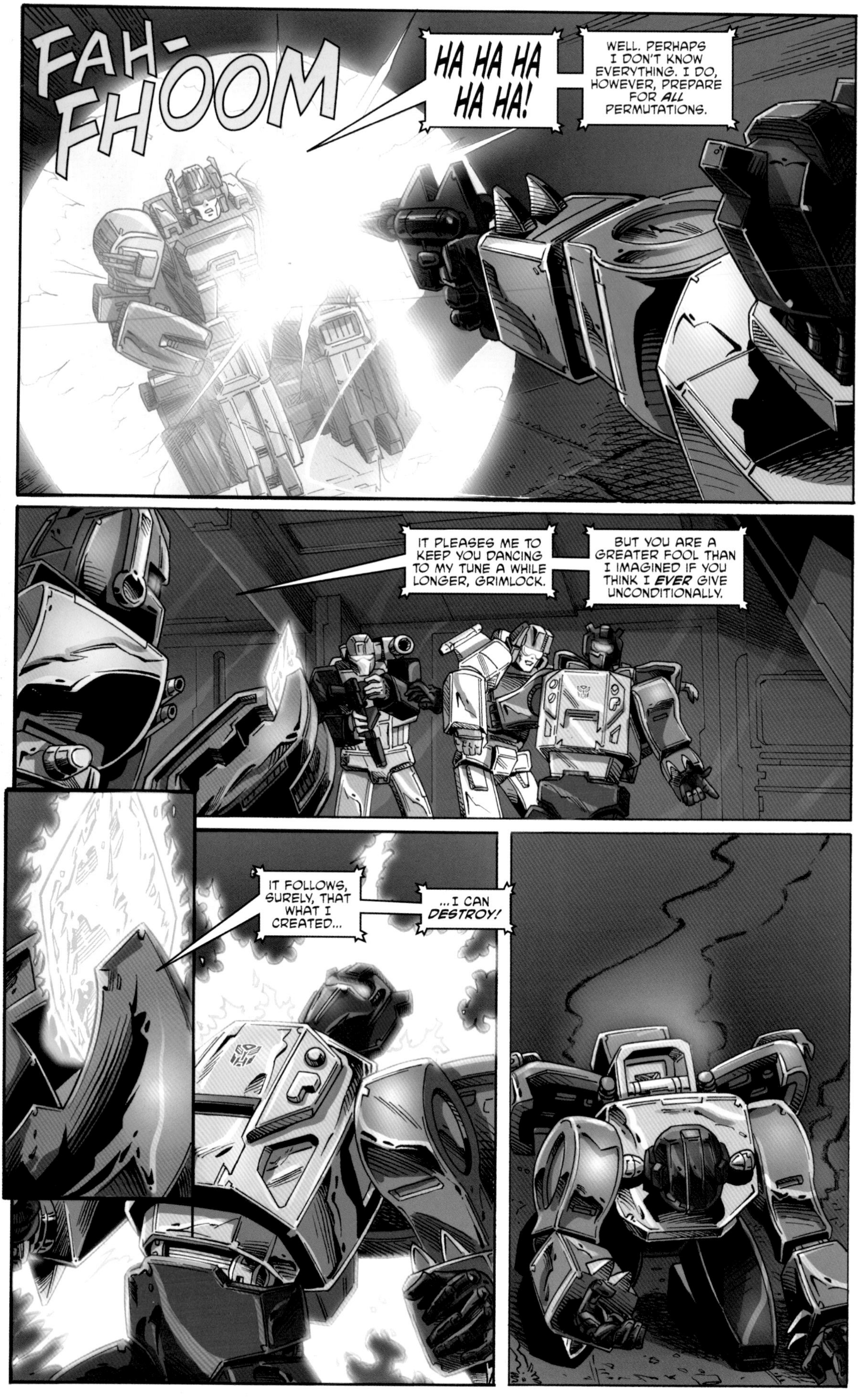
FAH-FHOOM
HA HA HA HA HA!
WELL. PERHAPS I DON'T KNOW EVERYTHING. I DO, HOWEVER, PREPARE FOR *ALL* PERMUTATIONS.
IT PLEASES ME TO KEEP YOU DANCING TO MY TUNE A WHILE LONGER, GRIMLOCK.
BUT YOU ARE A GREATER FOOL THAN I IMAGINED IF YOU THINK I *EVER* GIVE UNCONDITIONALLY.
IT FOLLOWS, SURELY, THAT WHAT I CREATED...
...I CAN *DESTROY!*

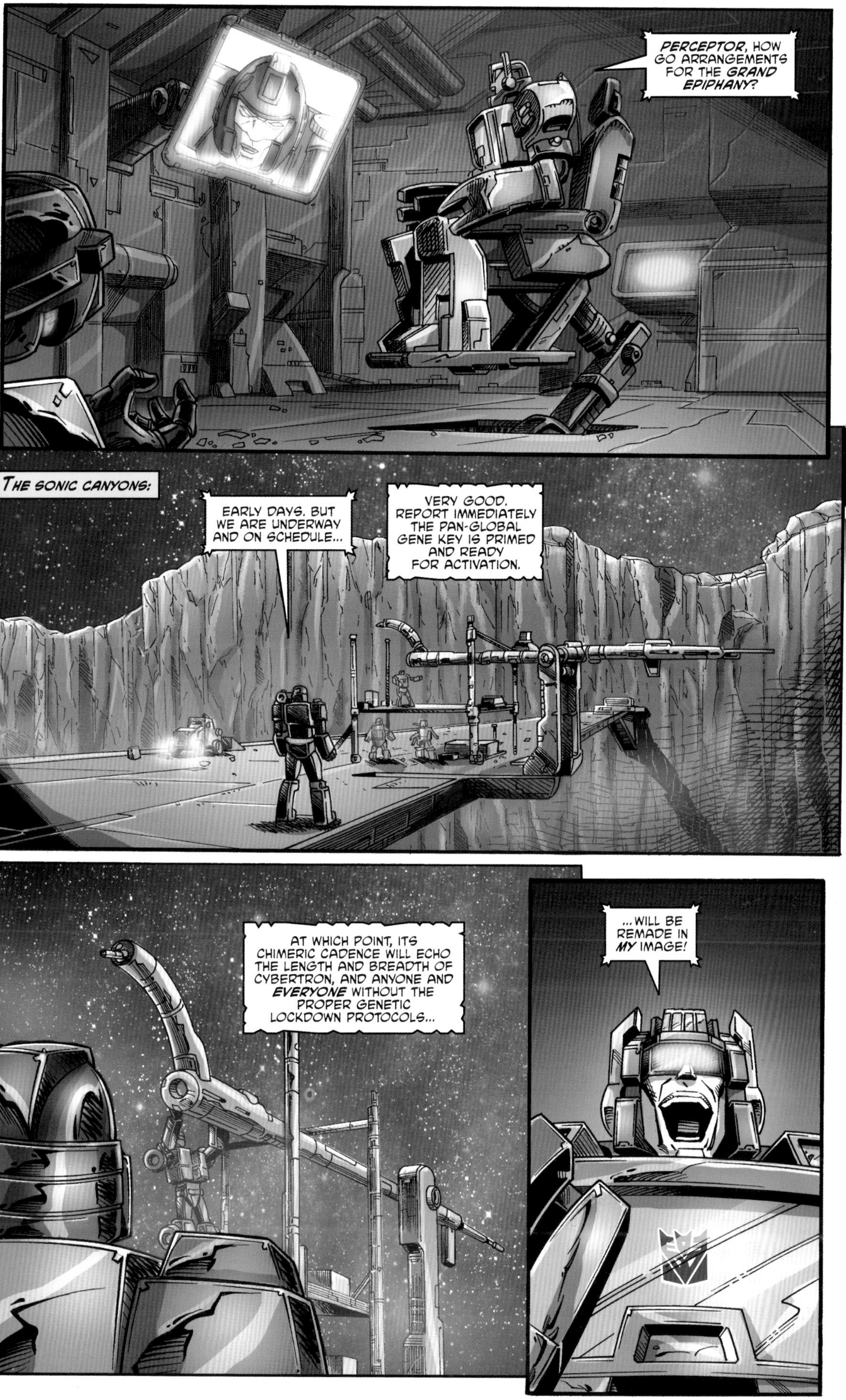
PERCEPTOR, HOW GO ARRANGEMENTS FOR THE GRAND EPIPHANY?
THE SONIC CANYONS:
EARLY DAYS. BUT WE ARE UNDERWAY AND ON SCHEDULE...
VERY GOOD. REPORT IMMEDIATELY THE PAN-GLOBAL GENE KEY IS PRIMED AND READY FOR ACTIVATION.
AT WHICH POINT, ITS CHIMERIC CADENCE WILL ECHO THE LENGTH AND BREADTH OF CYBERTRON, AND ANYONE AND EVERYONE WITHOUT THE PROPER GENETIC LOCKDOWN PROTOCOLS...
...WILL BE REMADE IN MY IMAGE!

MEGATRON, YOU DEVIOUS DEVIL...

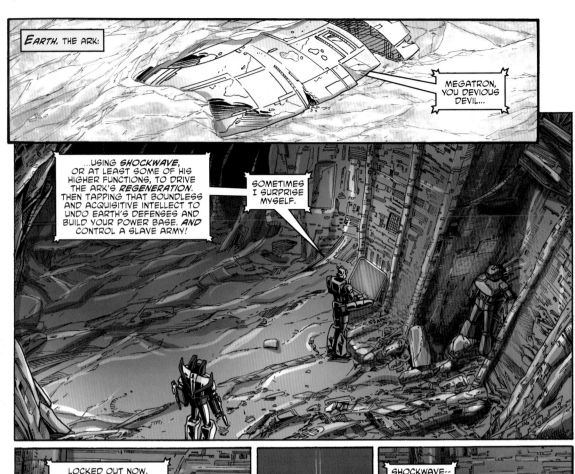

...USING *SHOCKWAVE,* OR AT LEAST SOME OF HIS HIGHER FUNCTIONS, TO DRIVE THE ARK'S *REGENERATION.* THEN TAPPING THAT BOUNDLESS AND ACQUISITIVE INTELLECT TO UNDO EARTH'S DEFENSES AND BUILD YOUR POWER BASE. *AND* CONTROL A SLAVE ARMY!

SOMETIMES I SURPRISE MYSELF.

LOCKED OUT NOW. A RESPONSE TO WHATEVER OR WHOEVER CRASHED AND BURNED THE "AUNTIE" FACADE... ACCESSIBLE *ONLY* BY MEGATRON...

...OR HIS FUTURE SELF.

SHOCKWAVE-- REPORT ARK STATUS.

ONBOARD PROPULSION SYSTEMS AT SIXTY-EIGHT PERCENT--HULL INTEGRITY NOW VIABLE THROUGH REDUNDANCY PROTOCOL--FULL FLIGHT CAPABILITY IN SIX SOLAR CYCLES--

YOU HEAR THAT, *STARSCREAM?*

WE'RE GOING HOME...

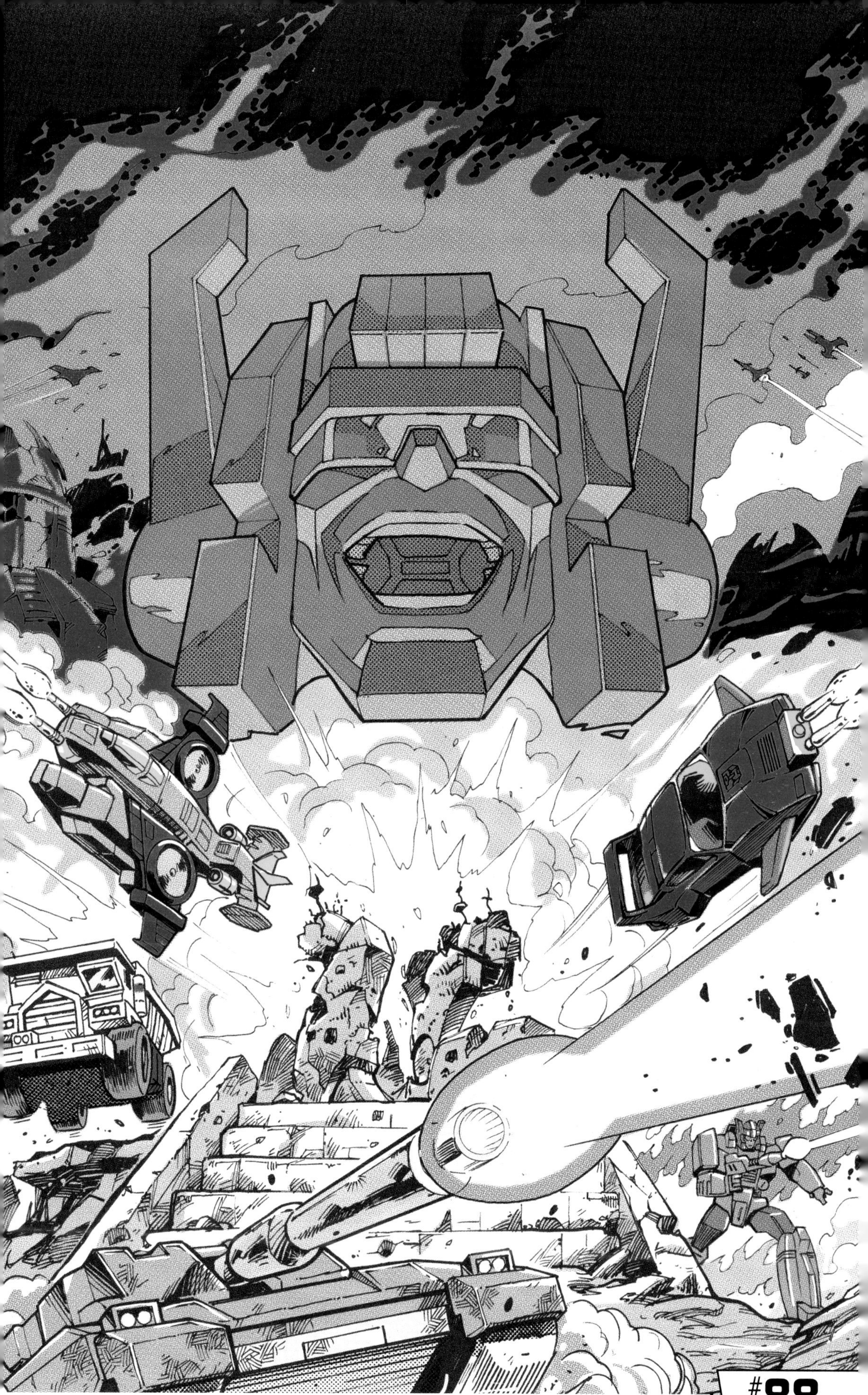
#88
COVER B: Art by GUIDO GUIDI

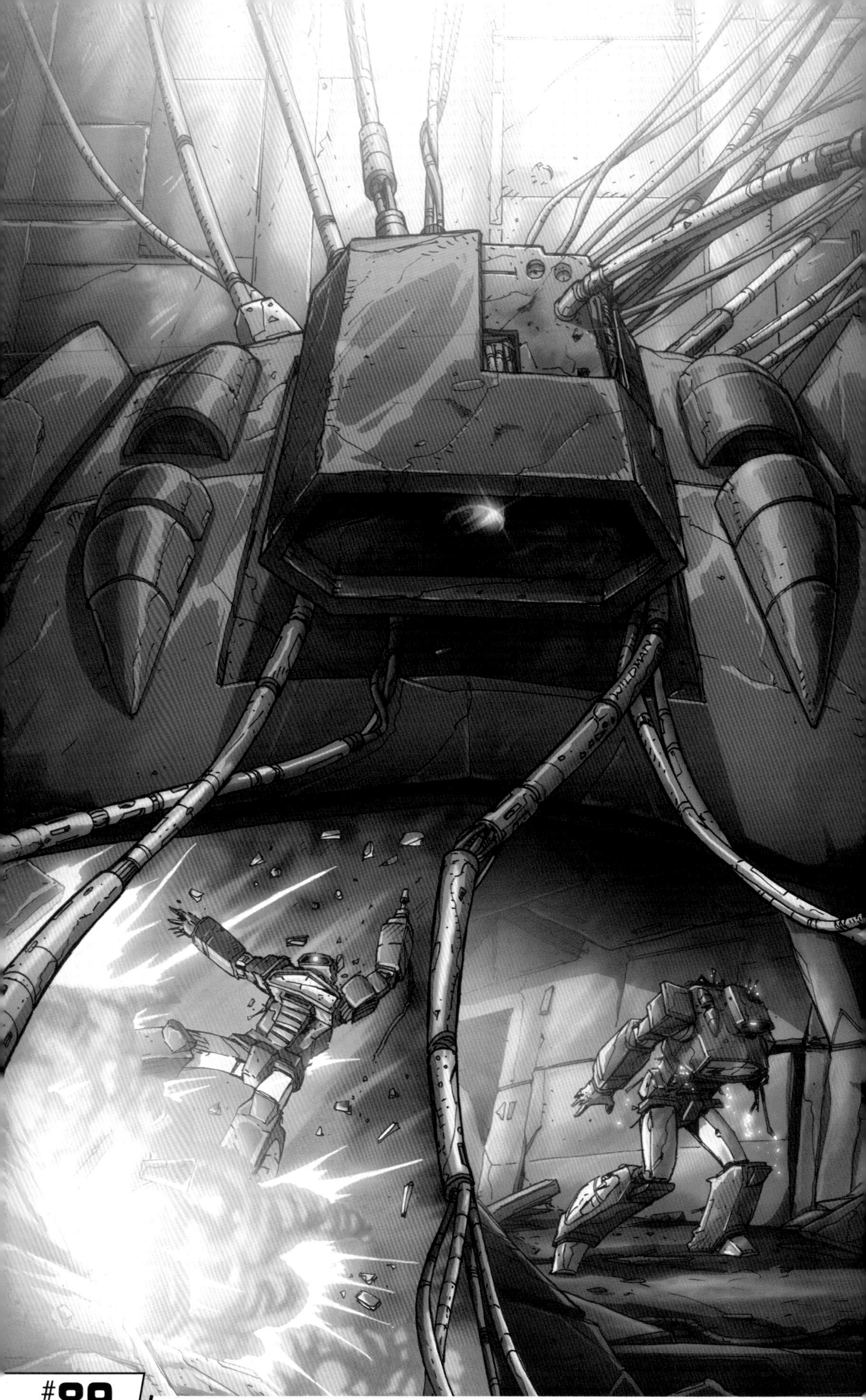

#89

COVER A: Art by ANDREW WILDMAN • Colors by JASON CARDY

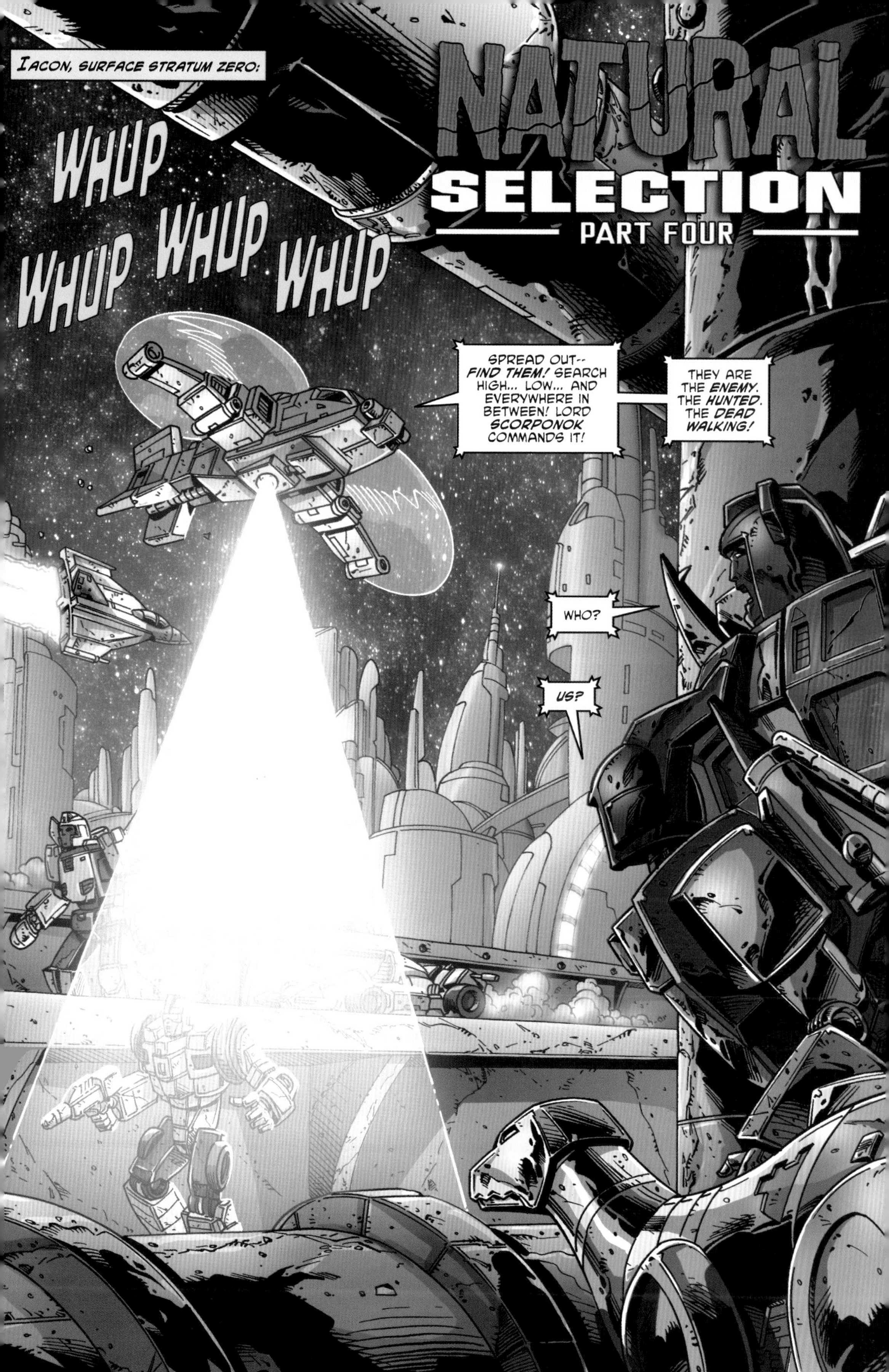
IACON, SURFACE STRATUM ZERO:
NATURAL SELECTION
PART FOUR
WHUP WHUP WHUP WHUP WHUP
SPREAD OUT-- FIND THEM! SEARCH HIGH... LOW... AND EVERYWHERE IN BETWEEN! LORD SCORPONOK COMMANDS IT!
THEY ARE THE ENEMY. THE HUNTED. THE DEAD WALKING!
WHO?
US?

WRITER IMON FURMAN
PENCILER ANDREW WILDMAN
INKER STEPHEN BASKERVILLE
COLORIST JOHN-PAUL BOVE
LETTERER CHRIS MOWRY
EDITOR JOHN BARBER
EDITOR-IN-CHIEF CHRIS RYALL

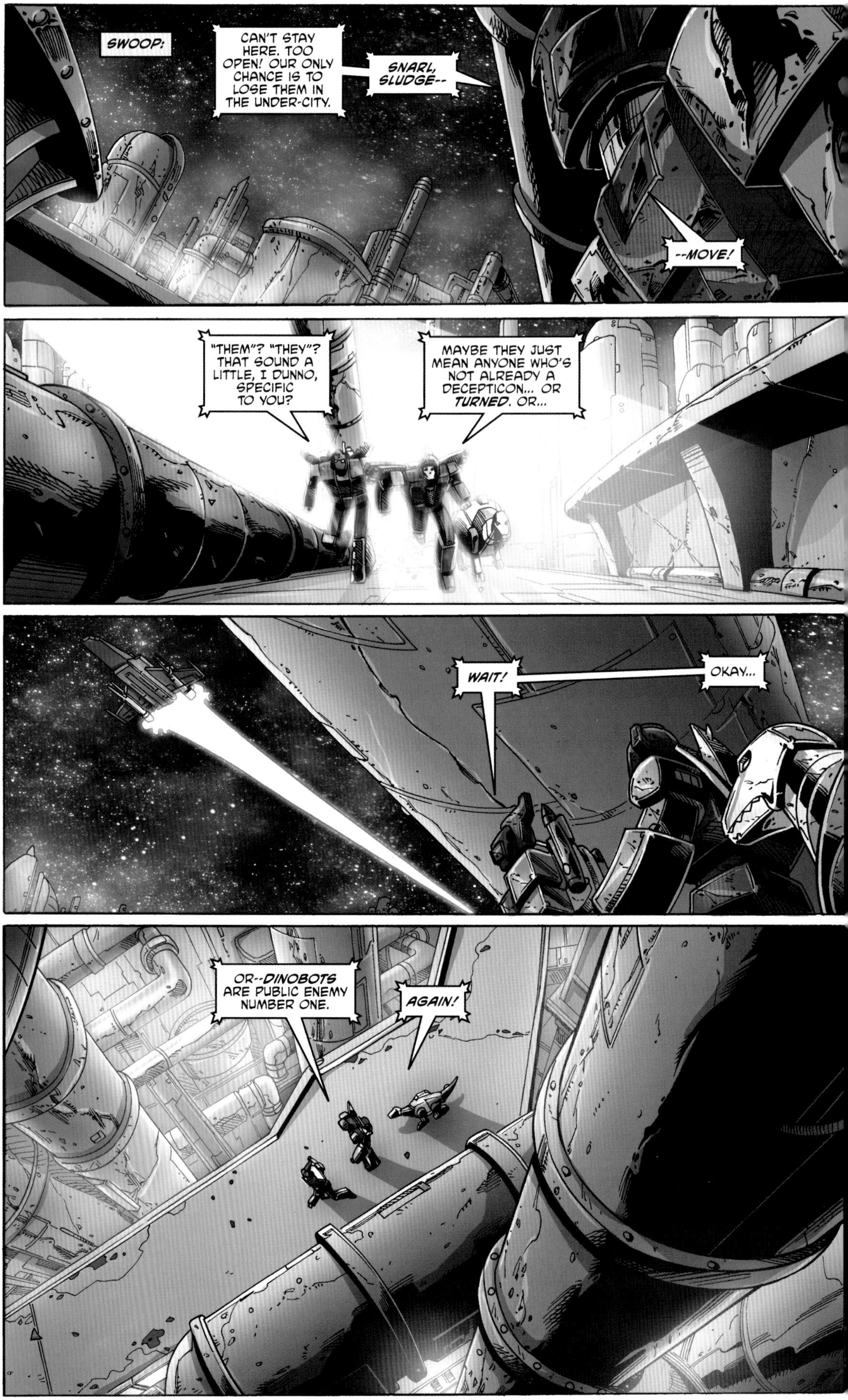
SWOOP:
CAN'T STAY HERE. TOO OPEN! OUR ONLY CHANCE IS TO LOSE THEM IN THE UNDER-CITY.
SNARL, SLUDGE--
--MOVE!
"THEM"? "THEY"? THAT SOUND A LITTLE, I DUNNO, SPECIFIC TO YOU?
MAYBE THEY JUST MEAN ANYONE WHO'S NOT ALREADY A DECEPTICON... OR TURNED. OR...
WAIT!
OKAY...
OR--DINOBOTS ARE PUBLIC ENEMY NUMBER ONE.
AGAIN!

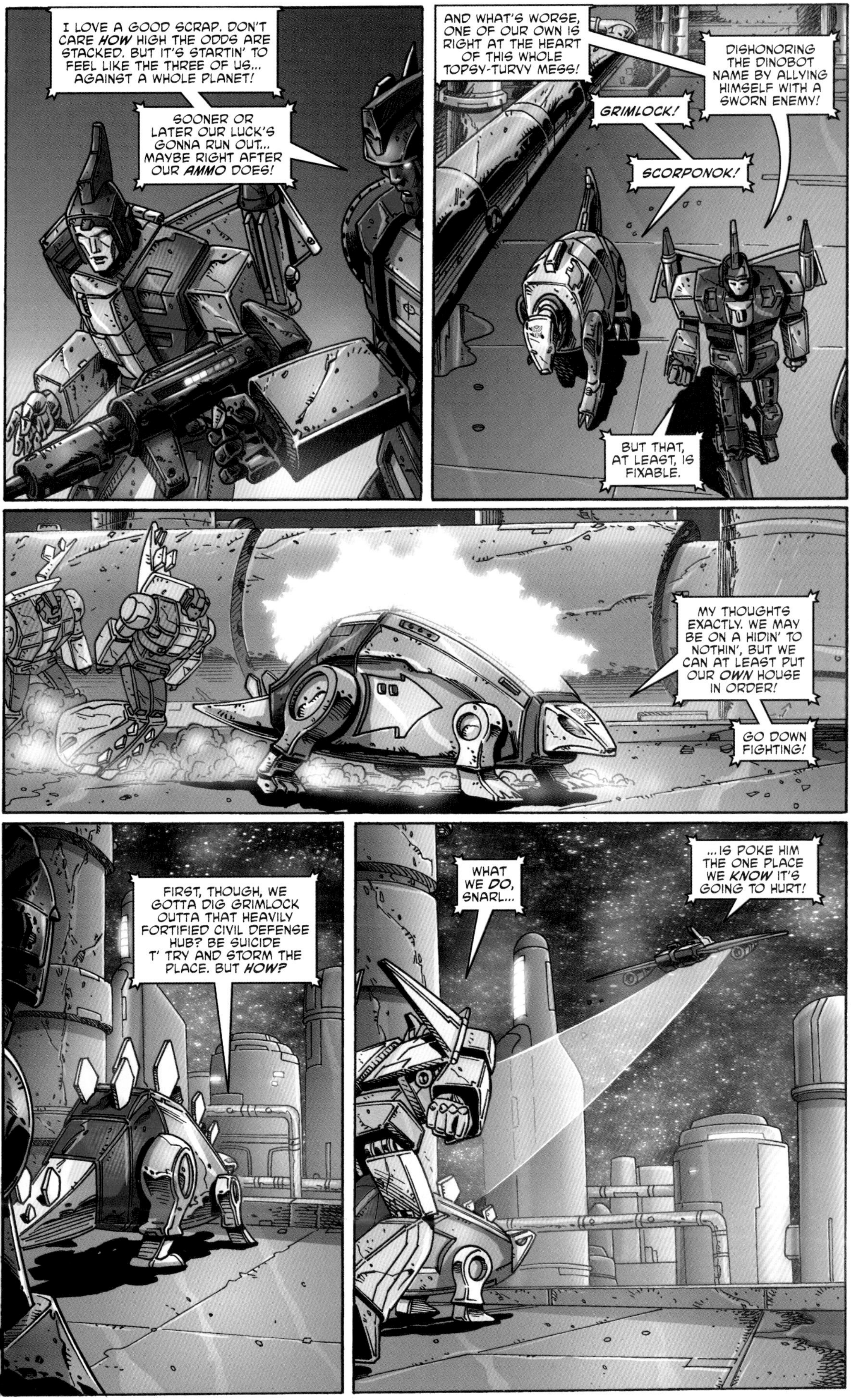
I LOVE A GOOD SCRAP. DON'T CARE *HOW* HIGH THE ODDS ARE STACKED. BUT IT'S STARTIN' TO FEEL LIKE THE THREE OF US... AGAINST A WHOLE PLANET!
SOONER OR LATER OUR LUCK'S GONNA RUN OUT... MAYBE RIGHT AFTER OUR *AMMO* DOES!
AND WHAT'S WORSE, ONE OF OUR OWN IS RIGHT AT THE HEART OF THIS WHOLE TOPSY-TURVY MESS!
DISHONORING THE DINOBOT NAME BY ALLYING HIMSELF WITH A SWORN ENEMY!
GRIMLOCK!
SCORPONOK!
BUT THAT, AT LEAST, IS FIXABLE.
MY THOUGHTS EXACTLY. WE MAY BE ON A HIDIN' TO NOTHIN', BUT WE CAN AT LEAST PUT OUR *OWN* HOUSE IN ORDER!
GO DOWN FIGHTING!
FIRST, THOUGH, WE GOTTA DIG GRIMLOCK OUTTA THAT HEAVILY FORTIFIED CIVIL DEFENSE HUB? BE SUICIDE T' TRY AND STORM THE PLACE. BUT *HOW?*
WHAT WE *DO*, SNARL...
...IS POKE HIM THE ONE PLACE WE *KNOW* IT'S GOING TO HURT!

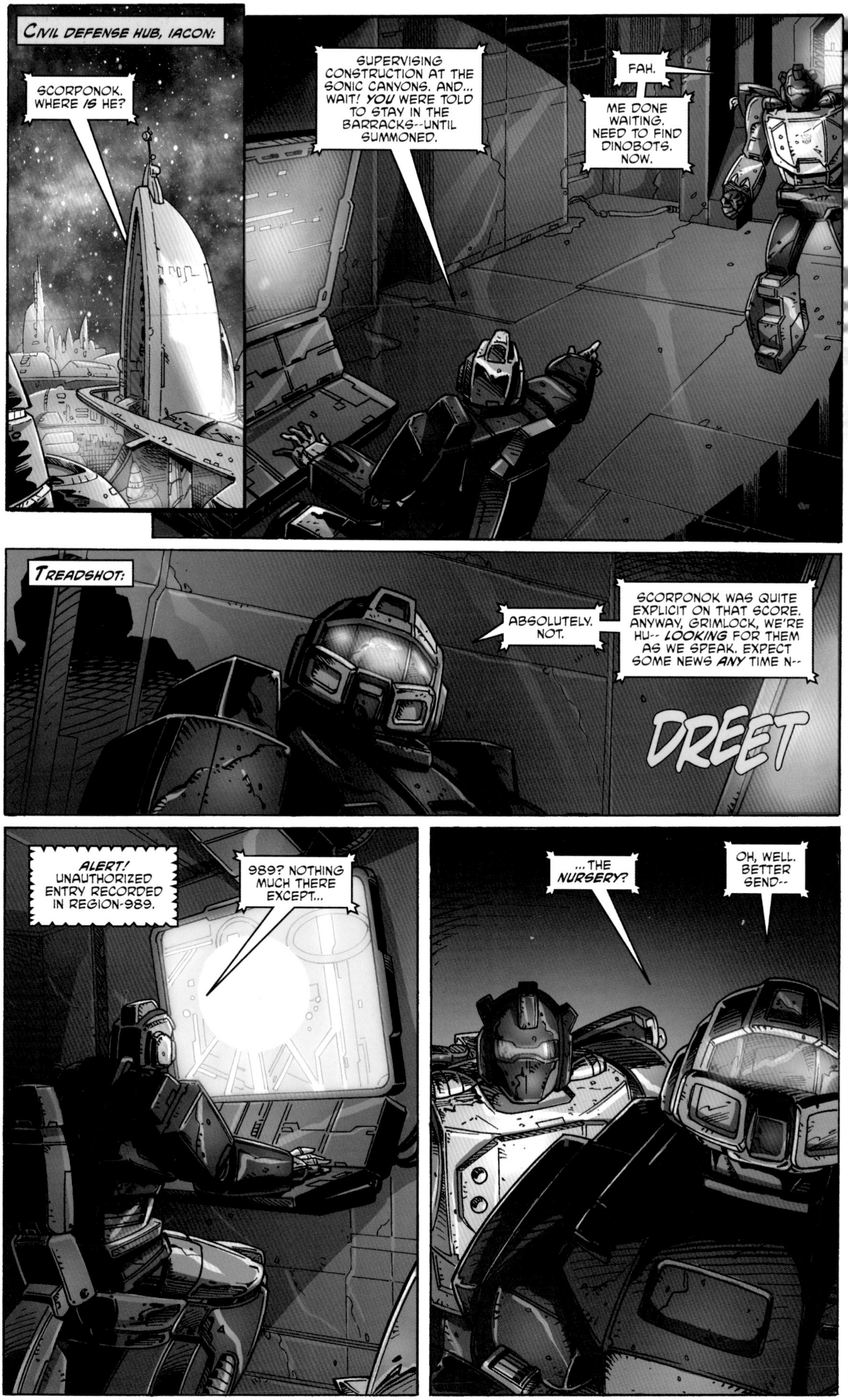
CIVIL DEFENSE HUB, IACON:
SCORPONOK. WHERE *IS* HE?
SUPERVISING CONSTRUCTION AT THE SONIC CANYONS. AND... WAIT! *YOU* WERE TOLD TO STAY IN THE BARRACKS--UNTIL SUMMONED.
FAH.
ME DONE WAITING. NEED TO FIND DINOBOTS. NOW.
TREADSHOT:
ABSOLUTELY. NOT.
SCORPONOK WAS QUITE EXPLICIT ON THAT SCORE. ANYWAY, GRIMLOCK, WE'RE HU-- *LOOKING* FOR THEM AS WE SPEAK. EXPECT SOME NEWS *ANY* TIME N--
DREET
ALERT! UNAUTHORIZED ENTRY RECORDED IN REGION-989.
989? NOTHING MUCH THERE EXCEPT...
...THE *NURSERY?*
OH, WELL. BETTER SEND--

SPZAKT

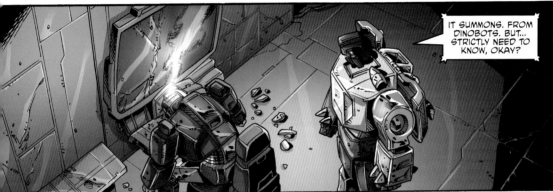

IT SUMMONS. FROM DINOBOTS. BUT... STRICTLY NEED TO KNOW, OKAY?

HE SONIC CANYONS:

FITTING, IS IT NOT, *PERCEPTOR*, THAT HERE WE STAND, IN ONE OF THE RAW, GAPING WOUNDS THAT SCAR CYBERTRON'S CELESTIAL PERFECTION...

...ON THE BRINK OF A TRUE AND LASTING *REUNIFICATION*: A HEALING OF THE CATASTROPHIC RIFT IN PRIMUS'S GRAND PLAN.

IF YOU SAY SO.

SCORPONOK:

THE SCHISM THAT DIVIDED PRIMUS'S CREATIONS IS ABOUT TO BE MENDED. HEALED. AND WHOEVER CAME FIRST-- AUTOBOT OR DECEPTICON-- WE WILL SOON *ALL* BE ONE!

AT A STROKE, I WILL HAVE ACCOMPLISHED WHAT THE PIOUS, THE PITILESS, AND THE PRINCIPLED COULD NOT. MY NAME, SO LONG SYNONYMOUS WITH WAR, WILL LIVE *FOREVER*... AS THE ARCHITECT OF *PEACE!*

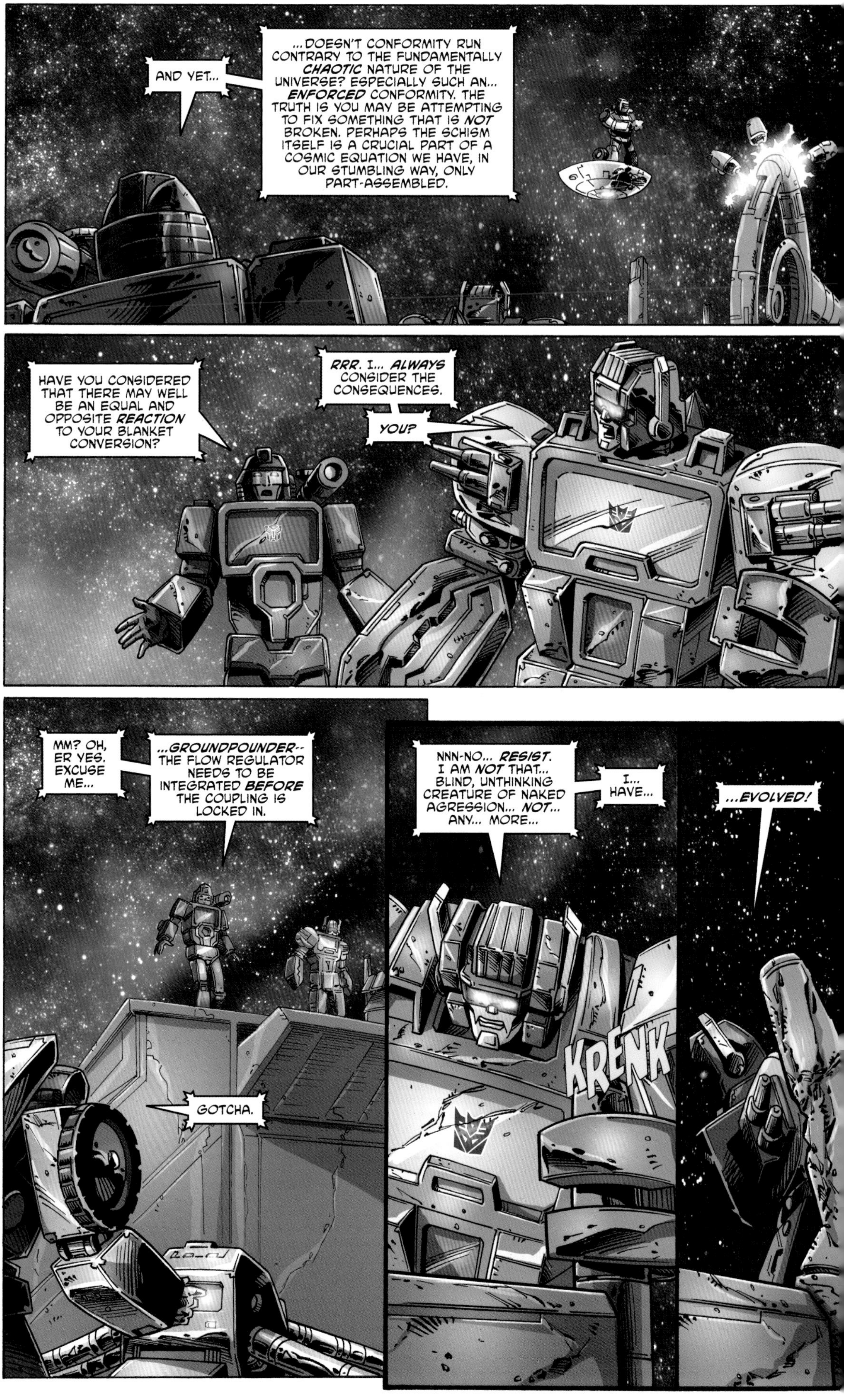
AND YET...
...DOESN'T CONFORMITY RUN CONTRARY TO THE FUNDAMENTALLY *CHAOTIC* NATURE OF THE UNIVERSE? ESPECIALLY SUCH AN... *ENFORCED* CONFORMITY. THE TRUTH IS YOU MAY BE ATTEMPTING TO FIX SOMETHING THAT IS *NOT* BROKEN. PERHAPS THE SCHISM ITSELF IS A CRUCIAL PART OF A COSMIC EQUATION WE HAVE, IN OUR STUMBLING WAY, ONLY PART-ASSEMBLED.
HAVE YOU CONSIDERED THAT THERE MAY WELL BE AN EQUAL AND OPPOSITE *REACTION* TO YOUR BLANKET CONVERSION?
RRR. I... *ALWAYS* CONSIDER THE CONSEQUENCES.
YOU?
MM? OH, ER YES. EXCUSE ME...
...GROUNDPOUNDER-- THE FLOW REGULATOR NEEDS TO BE INTEGRATED *BEFORE* THE COUPLING IS LOCKED IN.
GOTCHA.
NNN-NO... *RESIST*. I AM *NOT* THAT... BLIND, UNTHINKING CREATURE OF NAKED AGRESSION... *NOT*... ANY... MORE...
KRENK
I... HAVE...
...EVOLVED!

BELOW:

THIS... *CAN'T* BE JUST SOME RANDOM TWIST OF FATE...

...YOU *LED* ME HERE. DIDN'T YOU...

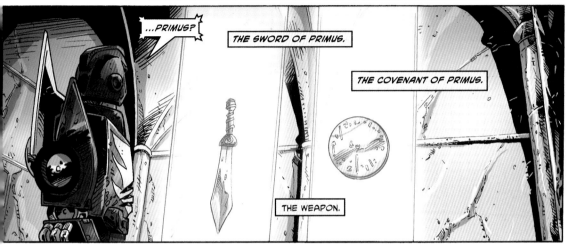

...PRIMUS?

THE SWORD OF PRIMUS.

THE COVENANT OF PRIMUS.

THE WEAPON.

OR THE KNOWLEDGE.

GETTING THE DISTINCT FEELING HERE...

...I'M SUPPOSED TO *CHOOSE*.

SKREEEGT

CAN *HEAR* THEM. CLOSER NOW. *MUCH* CLOSER.

HOMING IN WITH UNERRING, UNWAVERING PRECISION. DRIVEN BY FORCES AND GUIDED BY SENSES I CAN'T EVEN BEGIN TO UNDERSTAND.

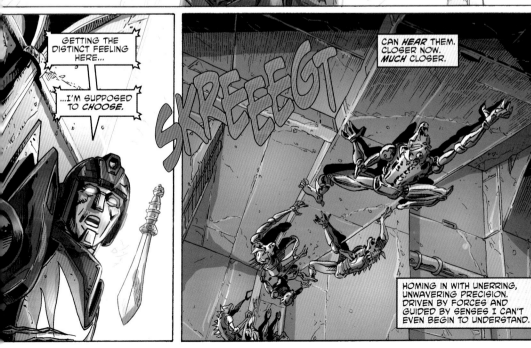

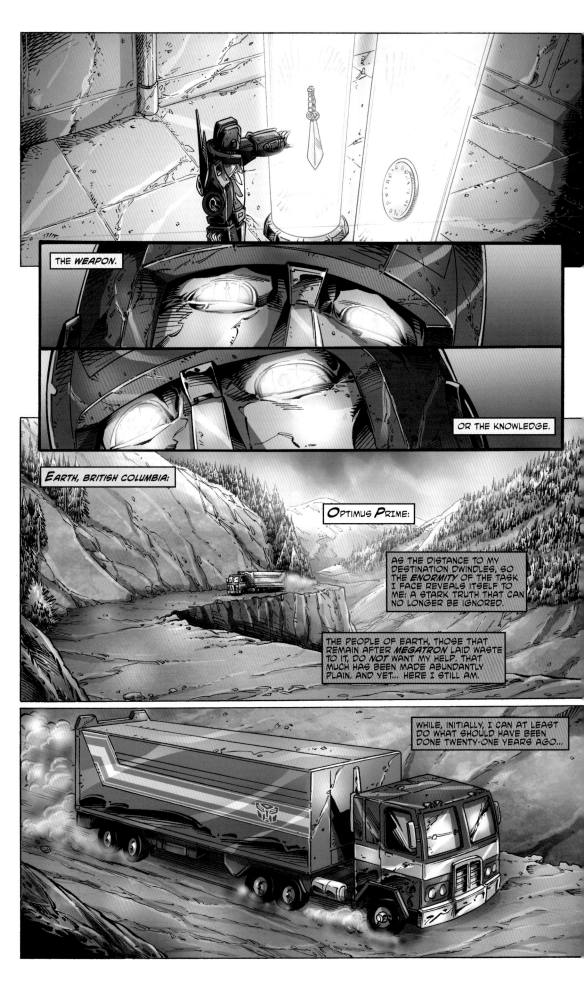

THE *WEAPON.*

OR THE KNOWLEDGE.

EARTH, BRITISH COLUMBIA:

OPTIMUS PRIME:

AS THE DISTANCE TO MY DESTINATION DWINDLES, SO THE *ENORMITY* OF THE TASK I FACE REVEALS ITSELF TO ME: A STARK TRUTH THAT CAN NO LONGER BE IGNORED.

THE PEOPLE OF EARTH, THOSE THAT REMAIN AFTER *MEGATRON* LAID WASTE TO IT, DO *NOT* WANT MY HELP. THAT MUCH HAS BEEN MADE ABUNDANTLY PLAIN. AND YET... HERE I STILL AM.

WHILE, INITIALLY, I CAN AT LEAST DO WHAT SHOULD HAVE BEEN DONE TWENTY-ONE YEARS AGO...

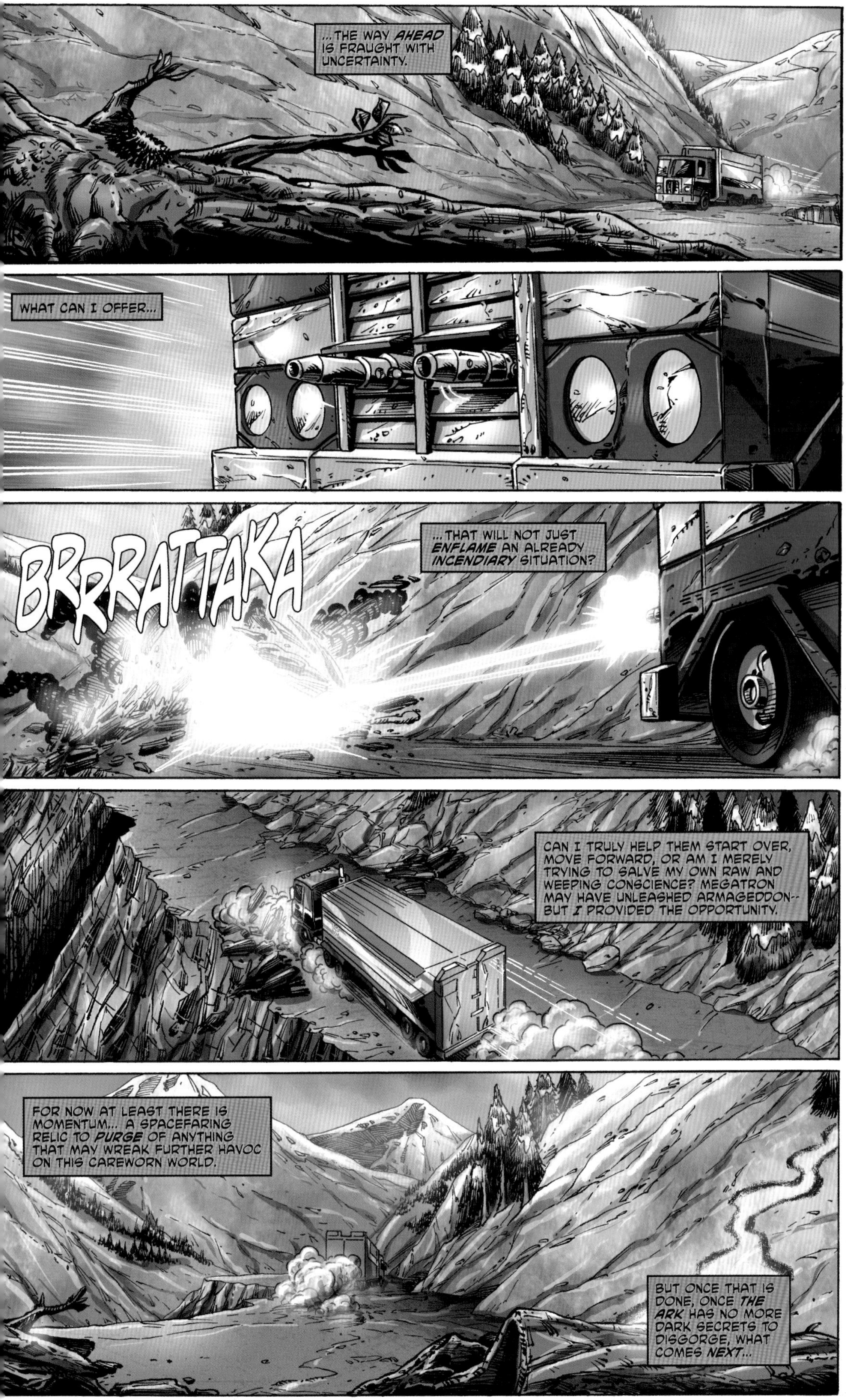
...THE WAY *AHEAD* IS FRAUGHT WITH UNCERTAINTY.
WHAT CAN I OFFER...
BRRRATTAKA
...THAT WILL NOT JUST *ENFLAME* AN ALREADY *INCENDIARY* SITUATION?
CAN I TRULY HELP THEM START OVER, MOVE FORWARD, OR AM I MERELY TRYING TO SALVE MY OWN RAW AND WEEPING CONSCIENCE? MEGATRON MAY HAVE UNLEASHED ARMAGEDDON-- BUT *I* PROVIDED THE OPPORTUNITY.
FOR NOW AT LEAST THERE IS MOMENTUM... A SPACEFARING RELIC TO *PURGE* OF ANYTHING THAT MAY WREAK FURTHER HAVOC ON THIS CAREWORN WORLD.
BUT ONCE THAT IS DONE, ONCE *THE ARK* HAS NO MORE DARK SECRETS TO DISGORGE, WHAT COMES *NEXT*...

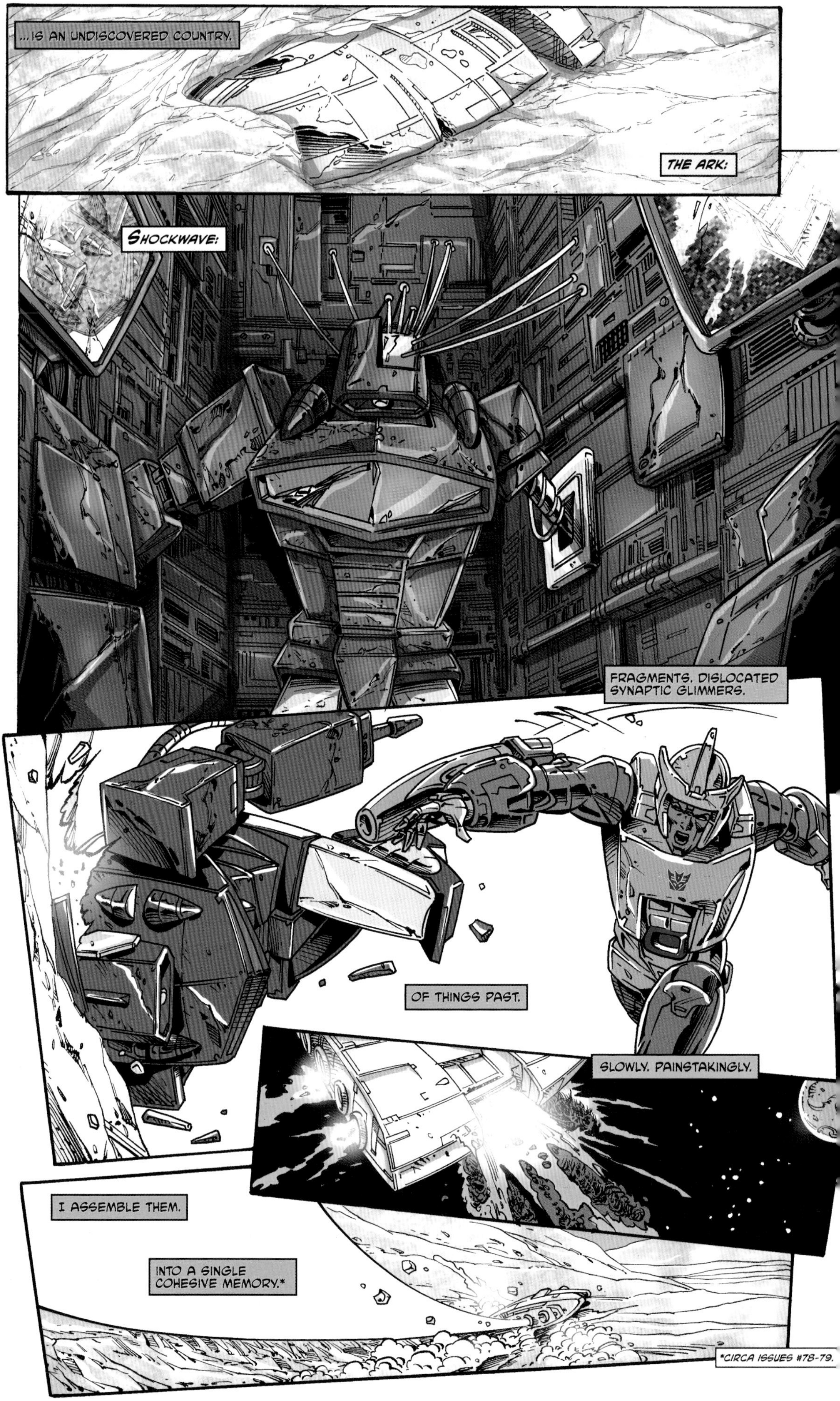

...IS AN UNDISCOVERED COUNTRY.
THE ARK:
SHOCKWAVE:
FRAGMENTS. DISLOCATED SYNAPTIC GLIMMERS.
OF THINGS PAST.
SLOWLY. PAINSTAKINGLY.
I ASSEMBLE THEM.
INTO A SINGLE COHESIVE MEMORY.*
*CIRCA ISSUES #78-79.

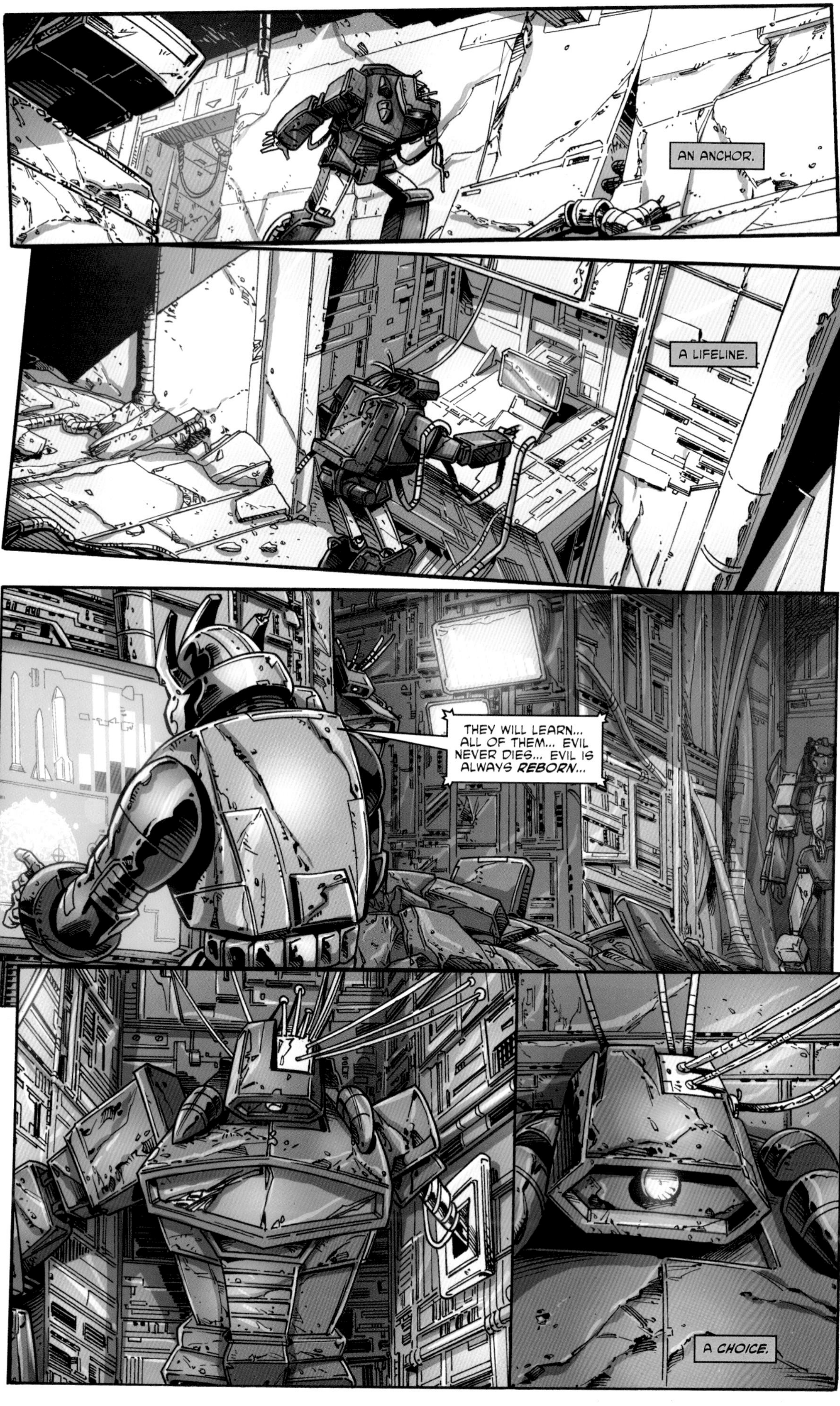
AN ANCHOR.
A LIFELINE.
THEY WILL LEARN... ALL OF THEM... EVIL NEVER DIES... EVIL IS ALWAYS *REBORN*...
A *CHOICE.*

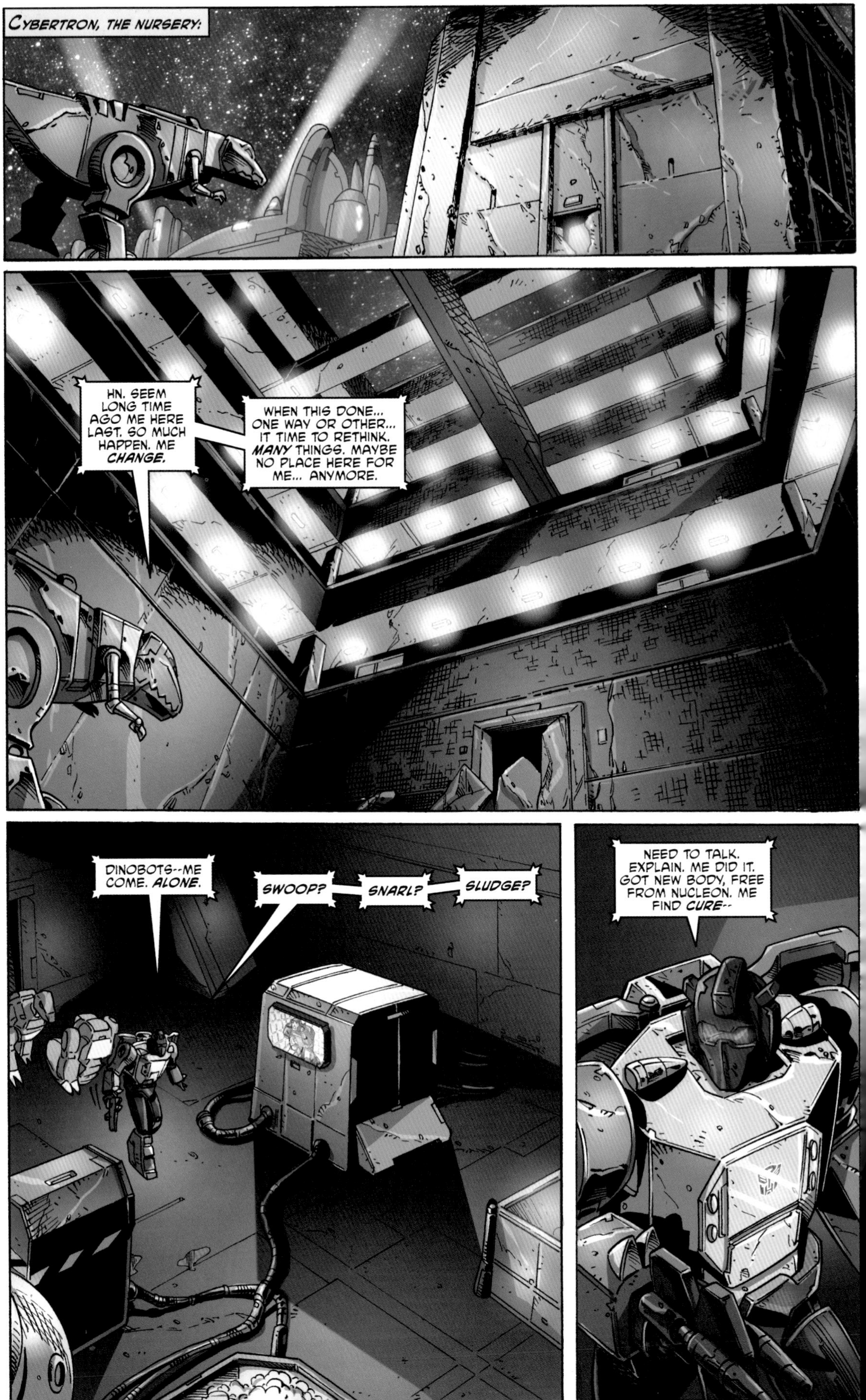
CYBERTRON, THE NURSERY:
HN. SEEM LONG TIME AGO ME HERE LAST. SO MUCH HAPPEN. ME CHANGE.
WHEN THIS DONE... ONE WAY OR OTHER... IT TIME TO RETHINK. MANY THINGS. MAYBE NO PLACE HERE FOR ME... ANYMORE.
DINOBOTS--ME COME. ALONE.
SWOOP?
SNARL?
SLUDGE?
NEED TO TALK. EXPLAIN. ME DID IT. GOT NEW BODY, FREE FROM NUCLEON. ME FIND CURE--

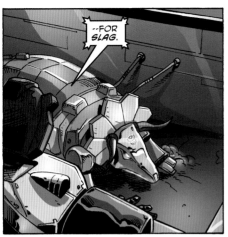

--FOR SLAG.

AT WHAT PRICE?

THE COMPLETE SUBJUGATION OF CYBERTRON? THE BETRAYAL OF EVERYONE AND EVERYTHING YOU ONCE HELD DEAR?

YOU WENT TOO FAR, GRIMLOCK. LOST PERSPECTIVE.

LIKE ALWAYS.

NO. ME HAVE PLAN. STRING SCORPONOK ALONG 'TIL WE GET WHAT WE NEED. THEN WE--

YOU CROSSED A LINE.

AN' THERE IS NO "WE"!

WAIT! JUST-- FNUH!

SHAAAK

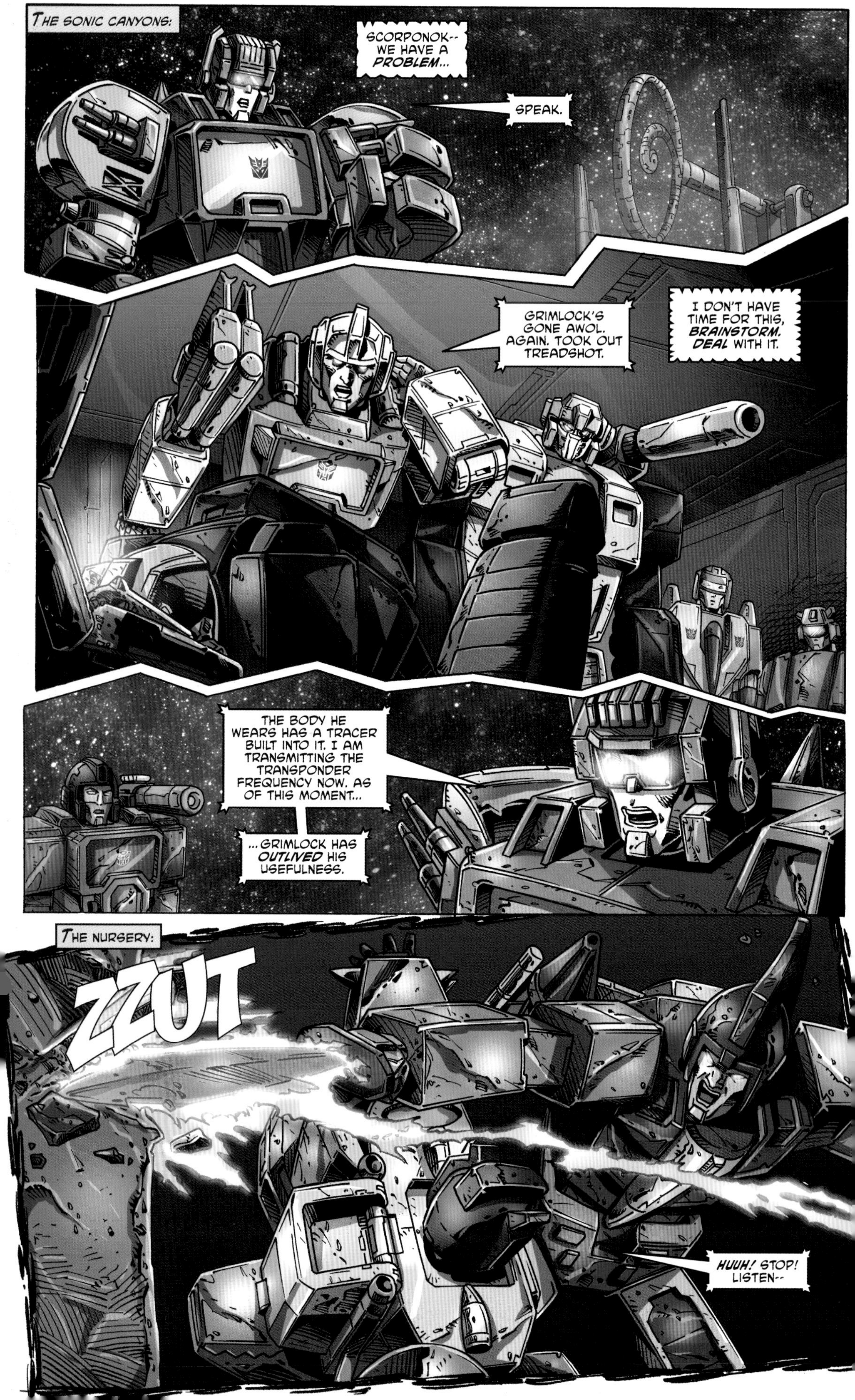
THE SONIC CANYONS:
SCORPONOK-- WE HAVE A *PROBLEM*...
SPEAK.
GRIMLOCK'S GONE AWOL. AGAIN. TOOK OUT TREADSHOT.
I DON'T HAVE TIME FOR THIS, *BRAINSTORM. DEAL* WITH IT.
THE BODY HE WEARS HAS A TRACER BUILT INTO IT. I AM TRANSMITTING THE TRANSPONDER FREQUENCY NOW. AS OF THIS MOMENT...
...GRIMLOCK HAS *OUTLIVED* HIS USEFULNESS.
THE NURSERY:
ZZUT
HUUH! STOP! LISTEN--

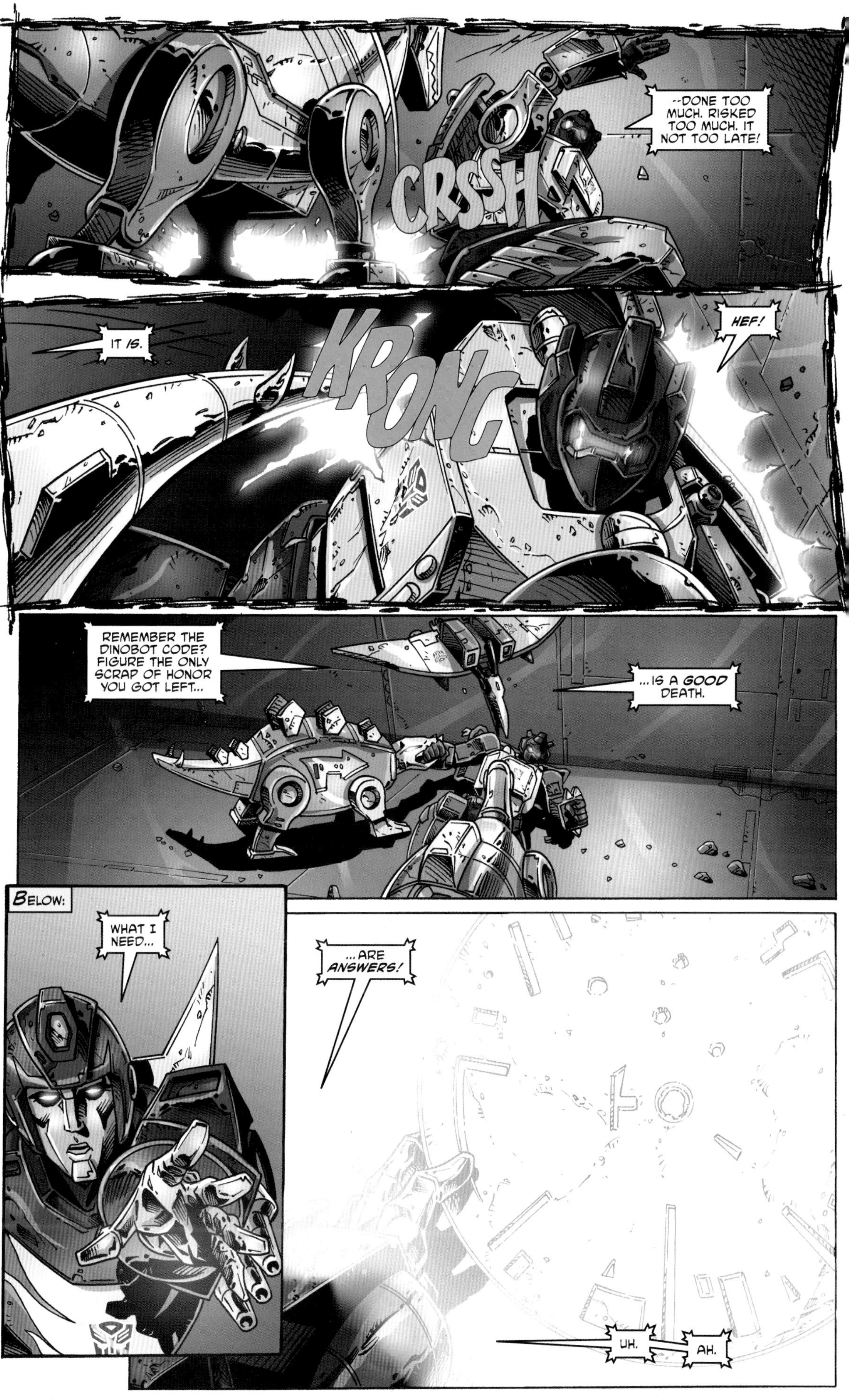

--DONE TOO MUCH. RISKED TOO MUCH. IT NOT TOO LATE!
CRSH
IT *IS*.
KRONG
HEF!
REMEMBER THE DINOBOT CODE? FIGURE THE ONLY SCRAP OF HONOR YOU GOT LEFT...
...IS A *GOOD* DEATH.
BELOW:
WHAT I NEED...
...ARE *ANSWERS!*
UH.
AH.

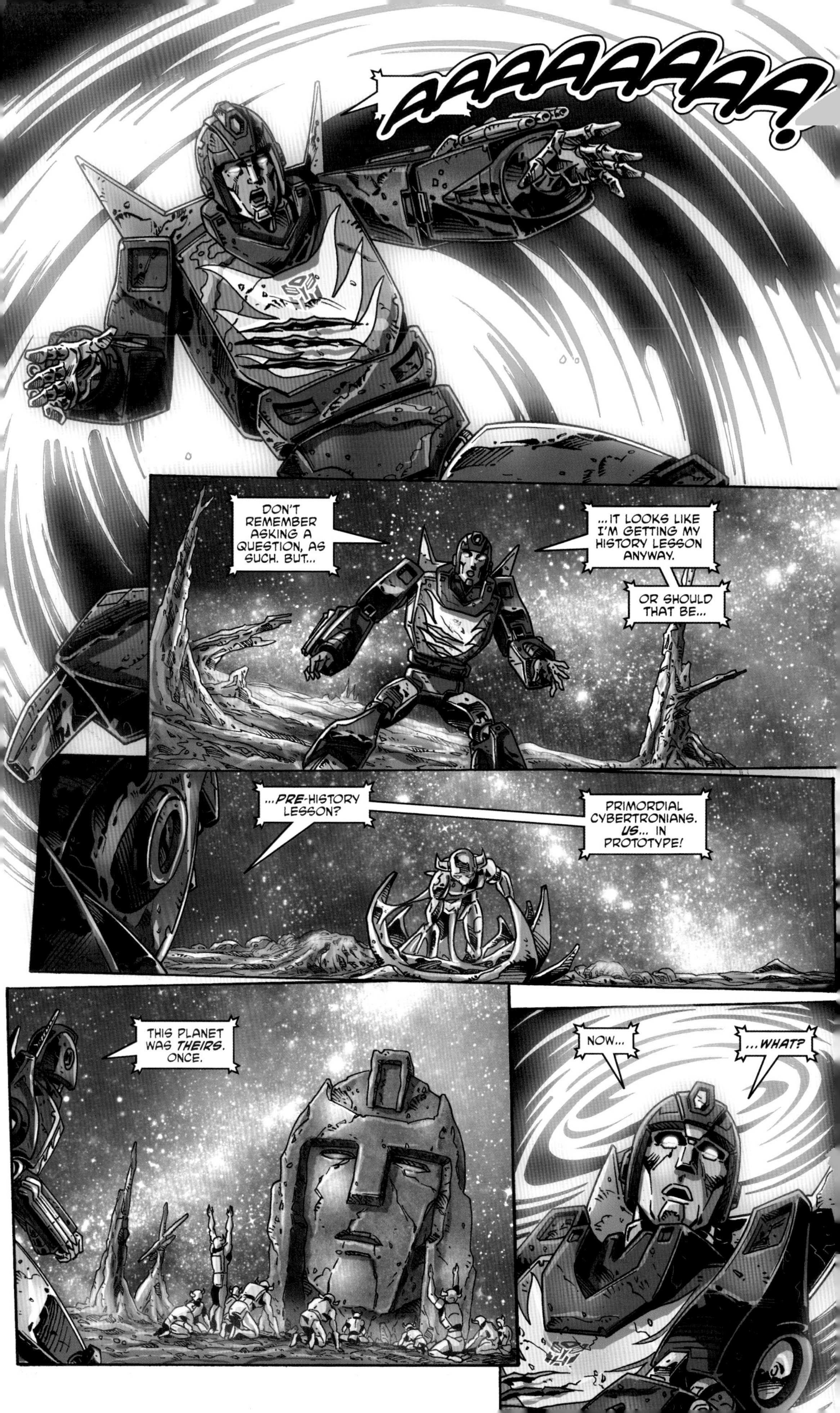
AAAAAAAA!
DON'T REMEMBER ASKING A QUESTION, AS SUCH. BUT...
...IT LOOKS LIKE I'M GETTING MY HISTORY LESSON ANYWAY.
OR SHOULD THAT BE...
...*PRE*-HISTORY LESSON?
PRIMORDIAL CYBERTRONIANS. *US*... IN PROTOTYPE!
THIS PLANET WAS *THEIRS*. ONCE.
NOW...
...*WHAT?*

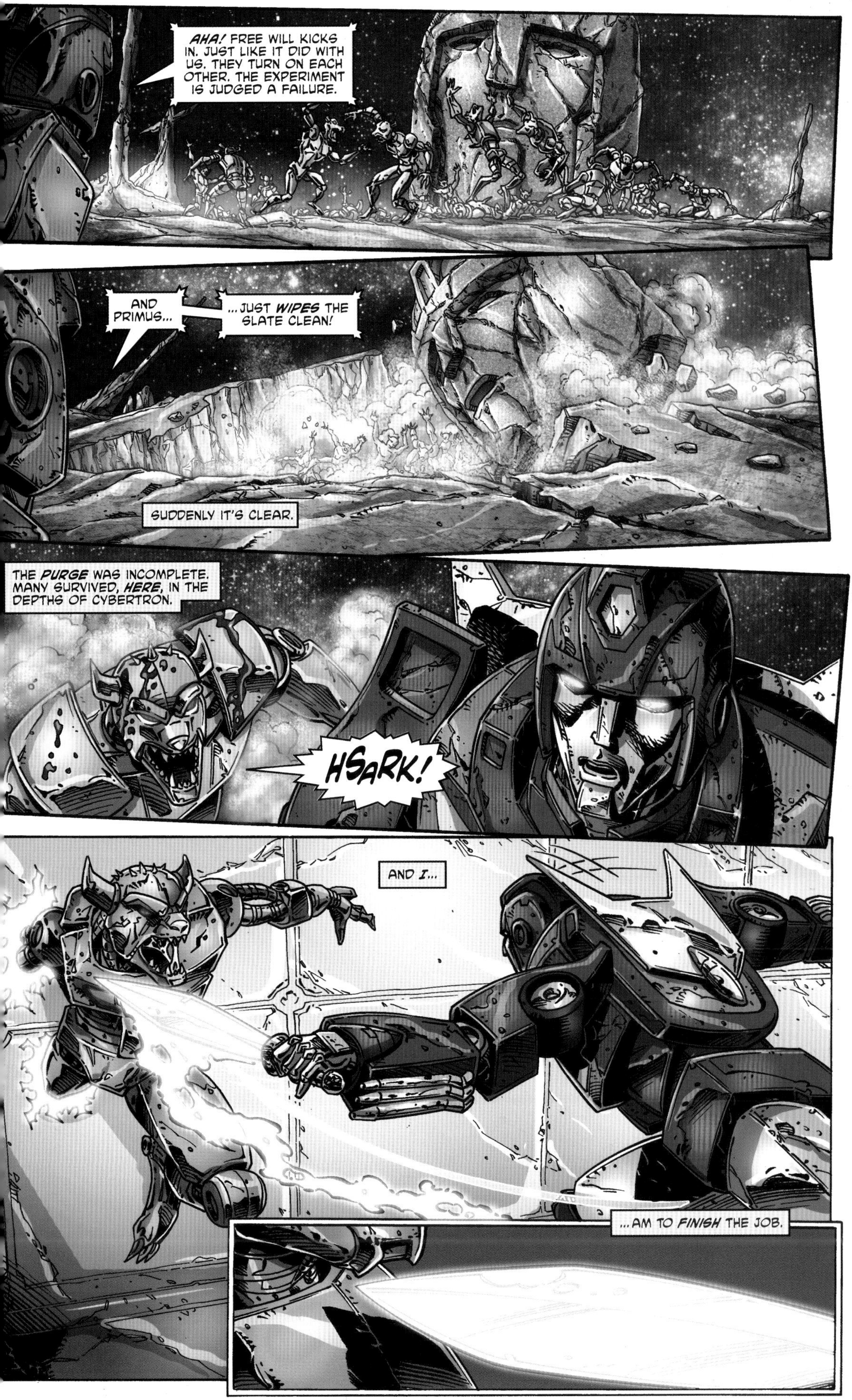
AHA! FREE WILL KICKS IN. JUST LIKE IT DID WITH US. THEY TURN ON EACH OTHER. THE EXPERIMENT IS JUDGED A FAILURE.
AND PRIMUS...
...JUST WIPES THE SLATE CLEAN!
SUDDENLY IT'S CLEAR.
THE PURGE WAS INCOMPLETE. MANY SURVIVED, HERE, IN THE DEPTHS OF CYBERTRON.
HSARK!
AND I...
...AM TO FINISH THE JOB.

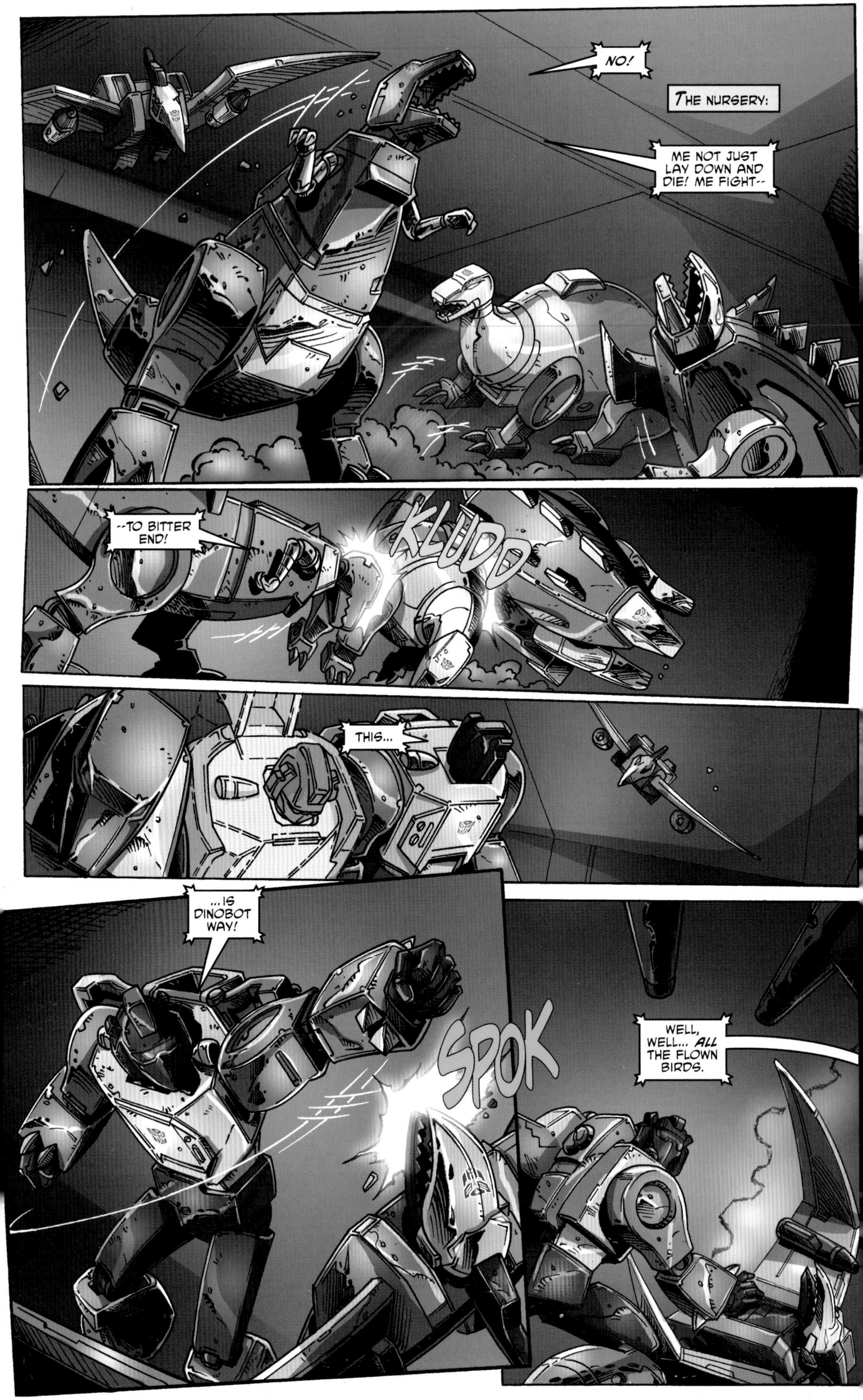
NO!
THE NURSERY:
ME NOT JUST LAY DOWN AND DIE! ME FIGHT--
--TO BITTER END!
KLUDD
THIS...
...IS DINOBOT WAY!
SPOK
WELL, WELL... ALL THE FLOWN BIRDS.

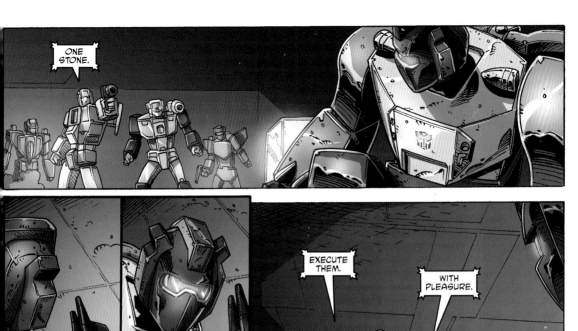

ONE STONE.

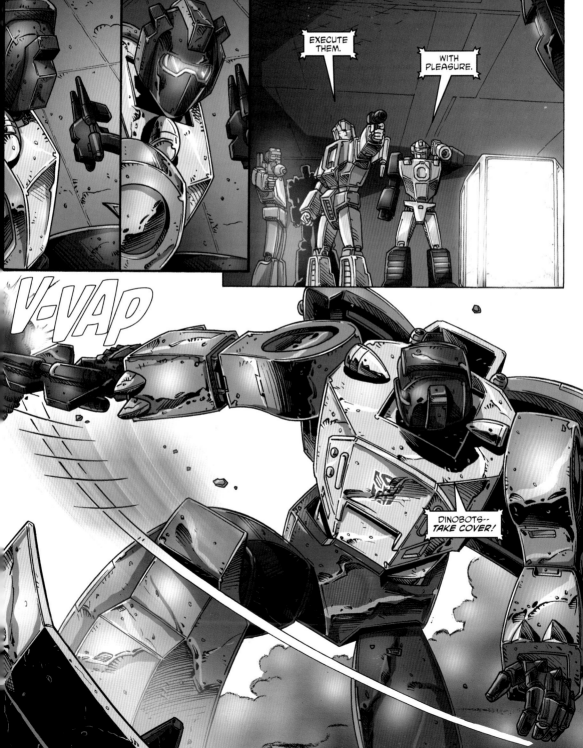

V-VAP

EXECUTE THEM.

WITH PLEASURE.

DINOBOTS—TAKE COVER!

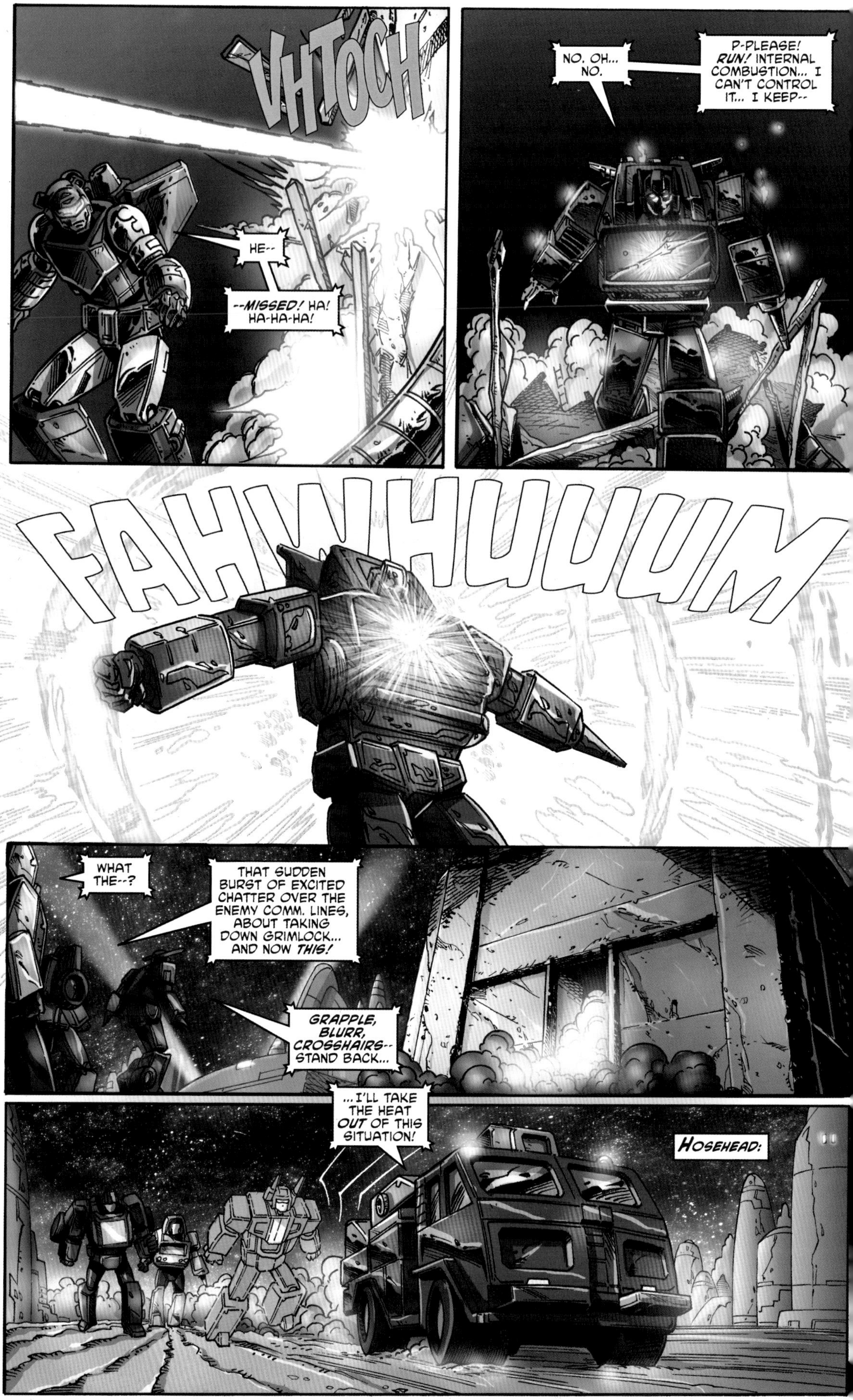
VHTOOM
HE--
--MISSED! HA! HA-HA-HA!
NO. OH... NO.
P-PLEASE! RUN! INTERNAL COMBUSTION... I CAN'T CONTROL IT... I KEEP--
FAHWHUUUM
WHAT THE--?
THAT SUDDEN BURST OF EXCITED CHATTER OVER THE ENEMY COMM. LINES, ABOUT TAKING DOWN GRIMLOCK... AND NOW THIS!
GRAPPLE, BLURR, CROSSHAIRS-- STAND BACK...
...I'LL TAKE THE HEAT OUT OF THIS SITUATION!
HOSEHEAD:

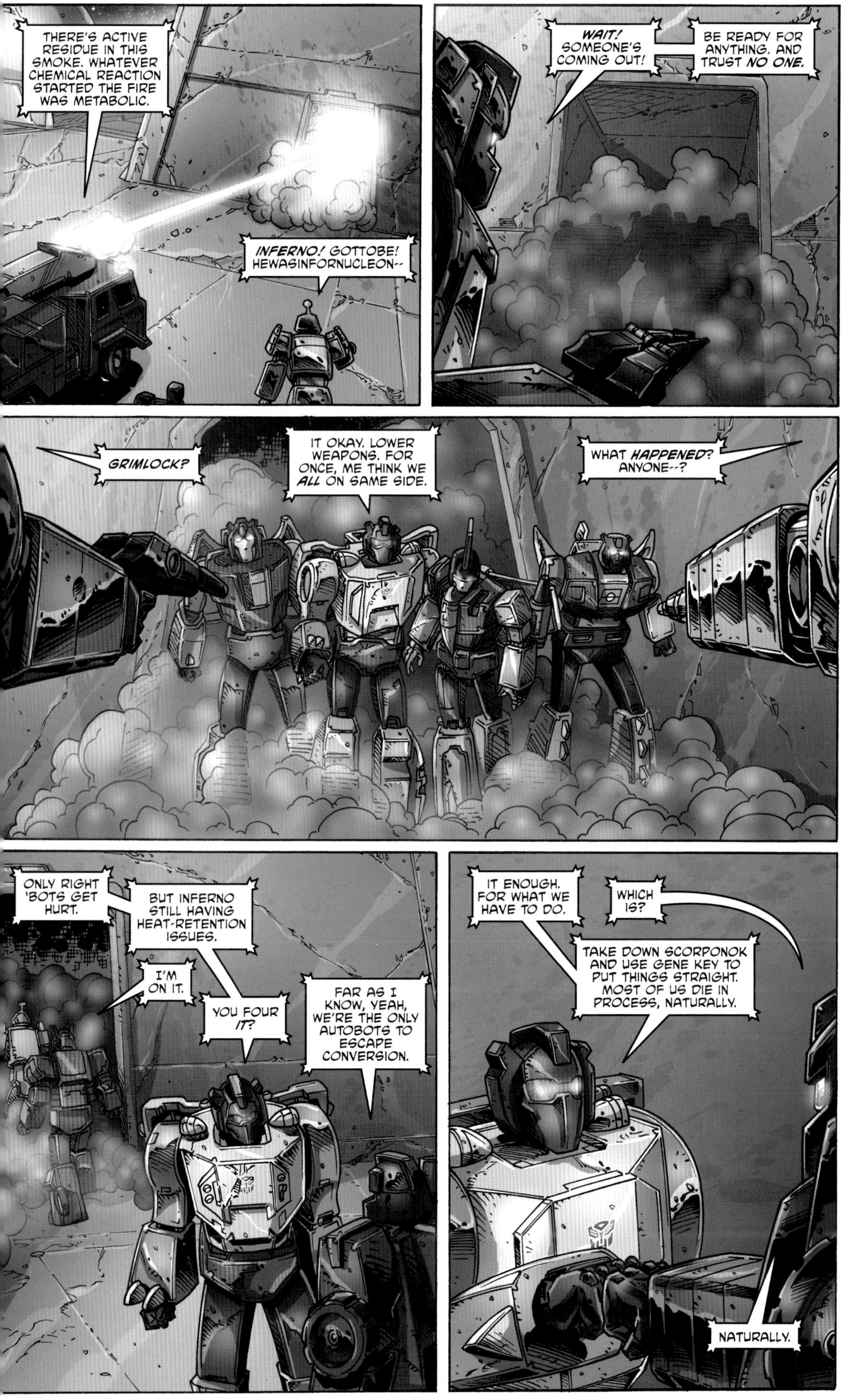
THERE'S ACTIVE RESIDUE IN THIS SMOKE. WHATEVER CHEMICAL REACTION STARTED THE FIRE WAS METABOLIC.
INFERNO! GOTTOBE! HEWASINFORNUCLEON--
WAIT! SOMEONE'S COMING OUT!
BE READY FOR ANYTHING. AND TRUST NO ONE.
GRIMLOCK?
IT OKAY. LOWER WEAPONS. FOR ONCE, ME THINK WE ALL ON SAME SIDE.
WHAT HAPPENED? ANYONE--?
ONLY RIGHT 'BOTS GET HURT.
BUT INFERNO STILL HAVING HEAT-RETENTION ISSUES.
I'M ON IT.
YOU FOUR IT?
FAR AS I KNOW, YEAH, WE'RE THE ONLY AUTOBOTS TO ESCAPE CONVERSION.
IT ENOUGH. FOR WHAT WE HAVE TO DO.
WHICH IS?
TAKE DOWN SCORPONOK AND USE GENE KEY TO PUT THINGS STRAIGHT. MOST OF US DIE IN PROCESS, NATURALLY.
NATURALLY.

CYBERTRONIAN SPACE:

IACON WATCHTOWER-- THIS IS HYPER-CRUISER *VALIANT*, REQUESTING PLANETARY APPROACH FUNNEL.

PLEASE BE AWARE WE ARE CARRYING CASUALTIES, SOME IN CRITICAL CONDITION. WE NEED MEDI-SUPPORT STANDING BY ON THE PAD.

WATCHTOWER, ARE YOU RECEIVING? PLEASE ACKNOWLEDGE.

IT'S THE AUTOBOTS WHO TRAVELLED TO EARTH WITH PRIME. *ULTRA MAGNUS*... AND THE OTHERS... WHAT DO I SAY? DO?

WAIT!

OKAY. UH-HUH. OKAY.

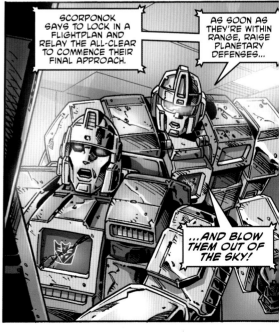

SCORPONOK SAYS TO LOCK IN A FLIGHTPLAN AND RELAY THE ALL-CLEAR TO COMMENCE THEIR FINAL APPROACH.

AS SOON AS THEY'RE WITHIN RANGE, RAISE PLANETARY DEFENSES...

...AND BLOW THEM OUT OF THE SKY!

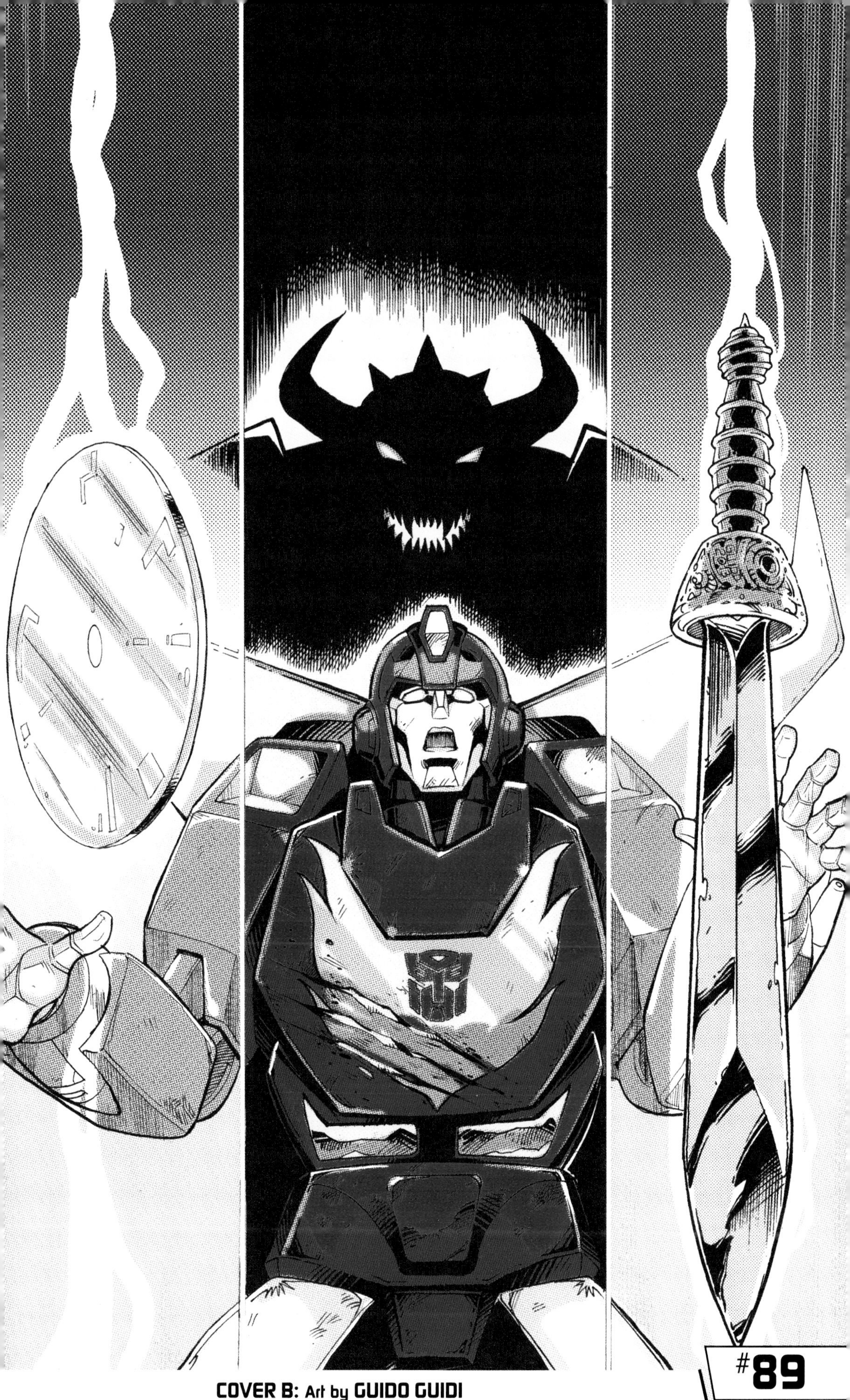

#89

COVER B: Art by GUIDO GUIDI

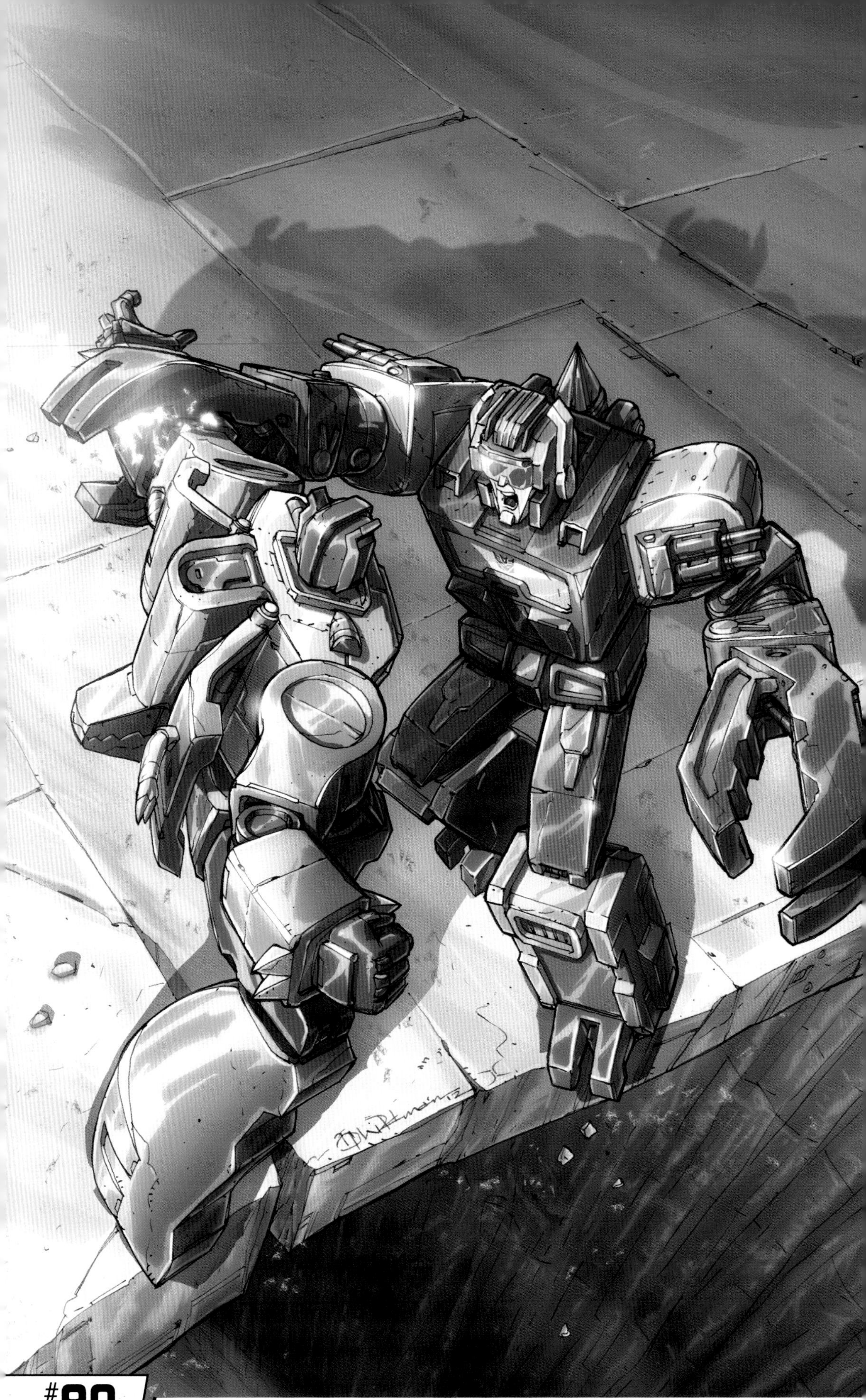

#90

COVER A: Art by ANDREW WILDMAN • Colors by JASON CARDY

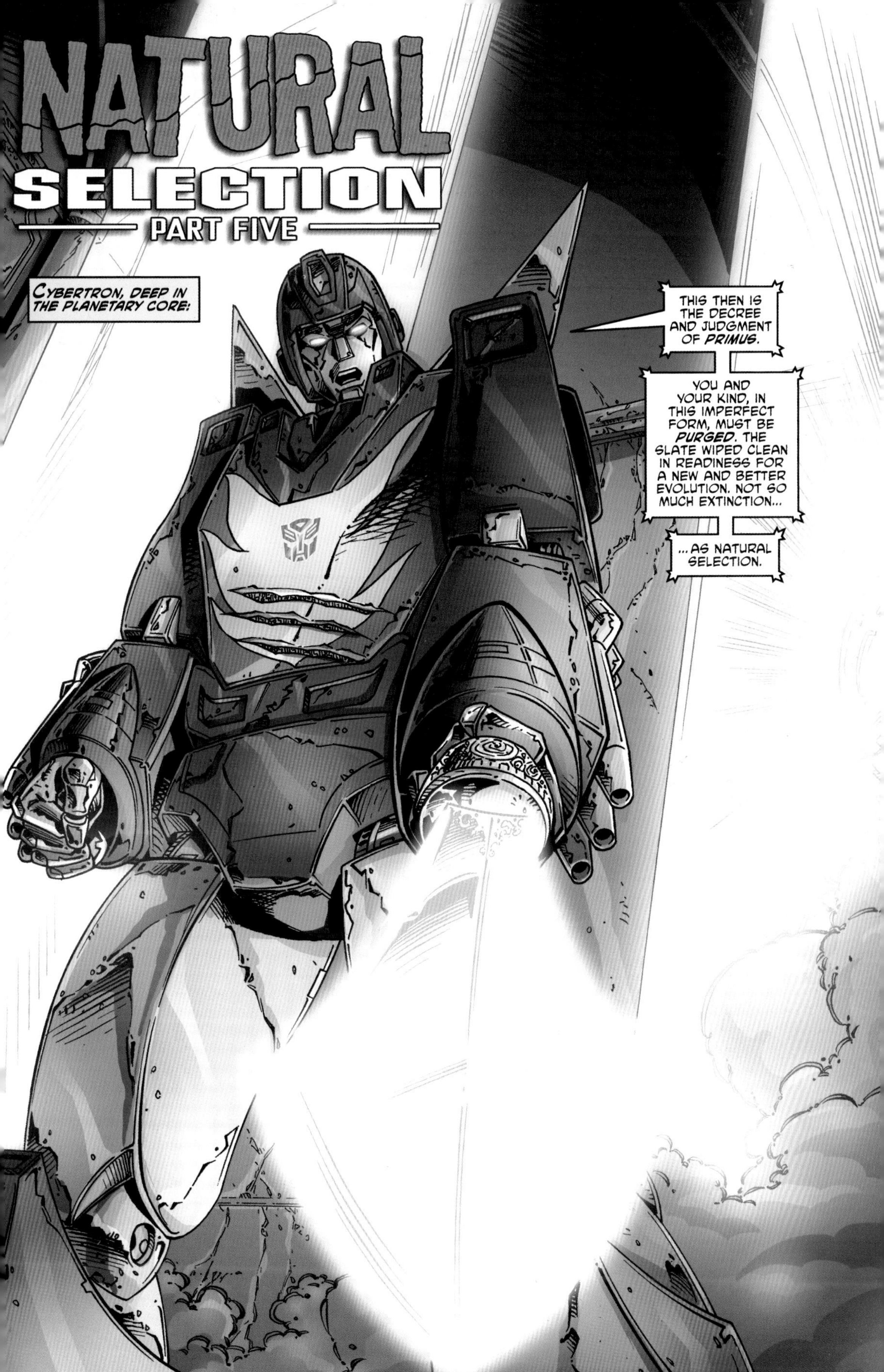
NATURAL SELECTION
PART FIVE
CYBERTRON, DEEP IN THE PLANETARY CORE:
THIS THEN IS THE DECREE AND JUDGMENT OF *PRIMUS*.
YOU AND YOUR KIND, IN THIS IMPERFECT FORM, MUST BE *PURGED*. THE SLATE WIPED CLEAN IN READINESS FOR A NEW AND BETTER EVOLUTION. NOT SO MUCH EXTINCTION...
...AS NATURAL SELECTION.

WRITER	PENCILER	INKER	COLORIST	COLORING ASSIST	LETTERER	EDITOR	EDITOR-IN-CHIEF
MON FURMAN	ANDREW WILDMAN	STEPHEN BASKERVILLE	JOHN-PAUL BOVE	JAMES STAYTE	CHRIS MOWRY	JOHN BARBER	CHRIS RYALL

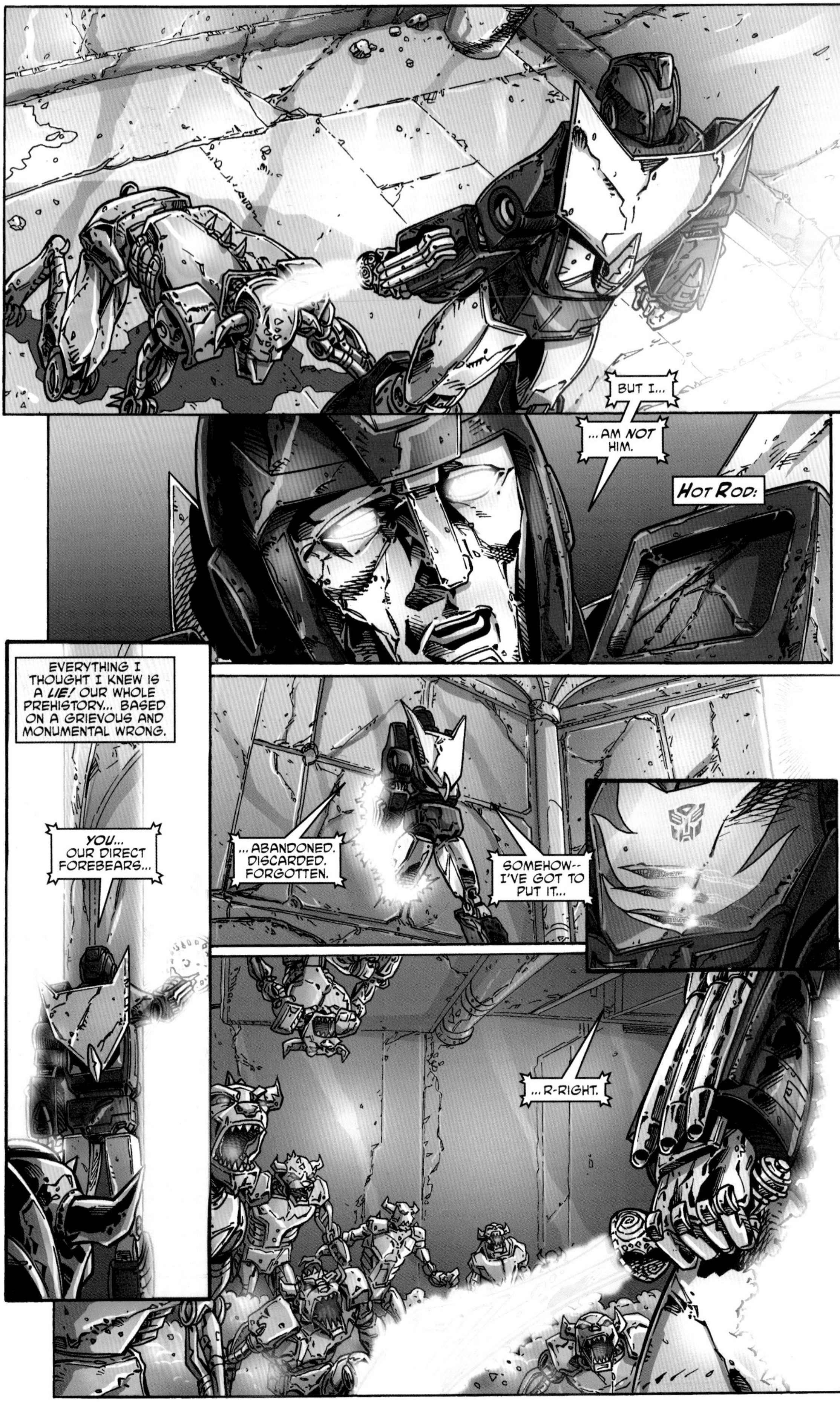
BUT I...
...AM NOT HIM.
HOT ROD:
EVERYTHING I THOUGHT I KNEW IS A LIE! OUR WHOLE PREHISTORY... BASED ON A GRIEVOUS AND MONUMENTAL WRONG.
YOU... OUR DIRECT FOREBEARS...
...ABANDONED. DISCARDED. FORGOTTEN.
SOMEHOW-- I'VE GOT TO PUT IT...
...R-RIGHT.

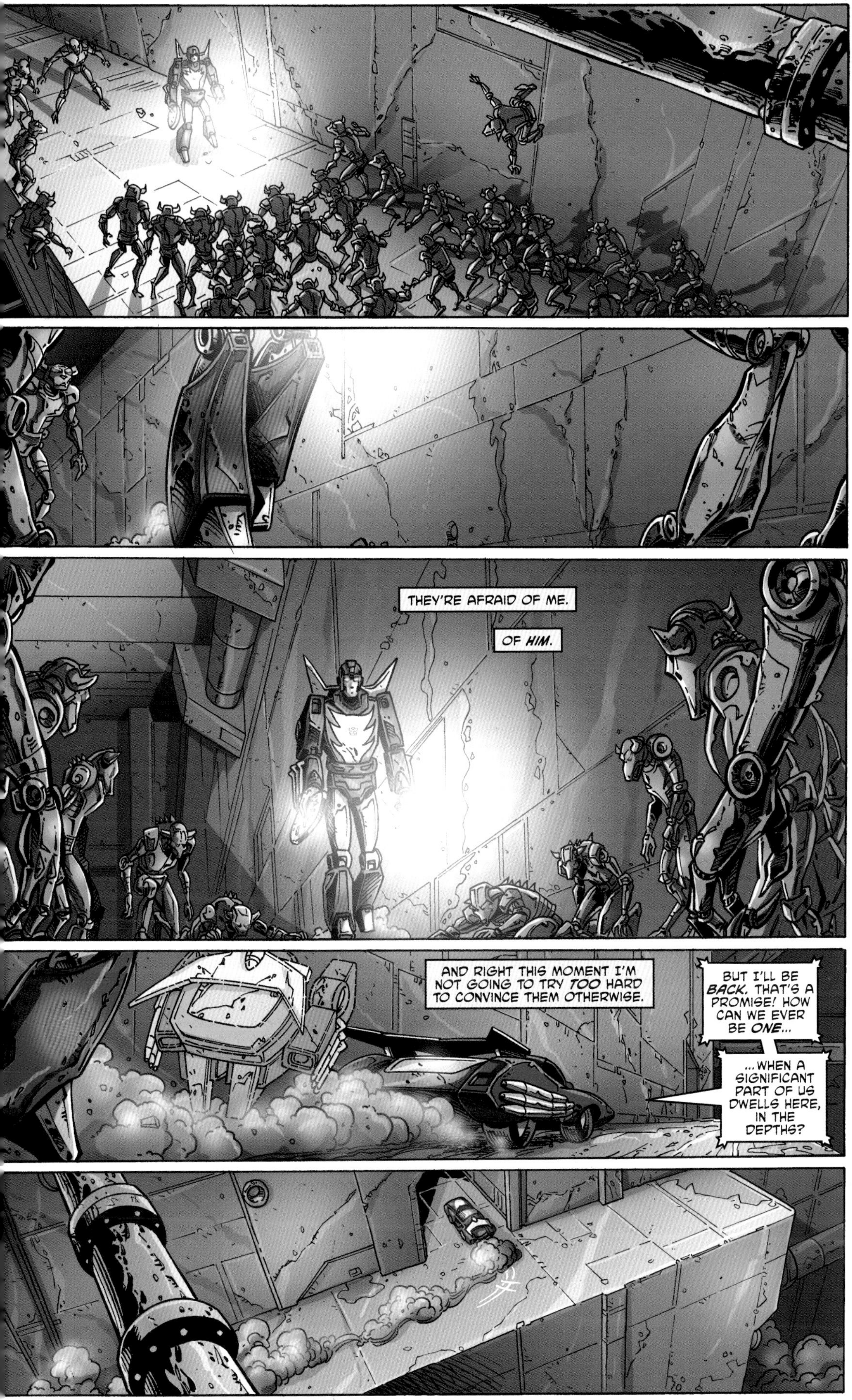
THEY'RE AFRAID OF ME.
OF *HIM*.
AND RIGHT THIS MOMENT I'M NOT GOING TO TRY *TOO* HARD TO CONVINCE THEM OTHERWISE.
BUT I'LL BE *BACK*. THAT'S A PROMISE! HOW CAN WE EVER BE *ONE*...
...WHEN A SIGNIFICANT PART OF US DWELLS HERE, IN THE DEPTHS?

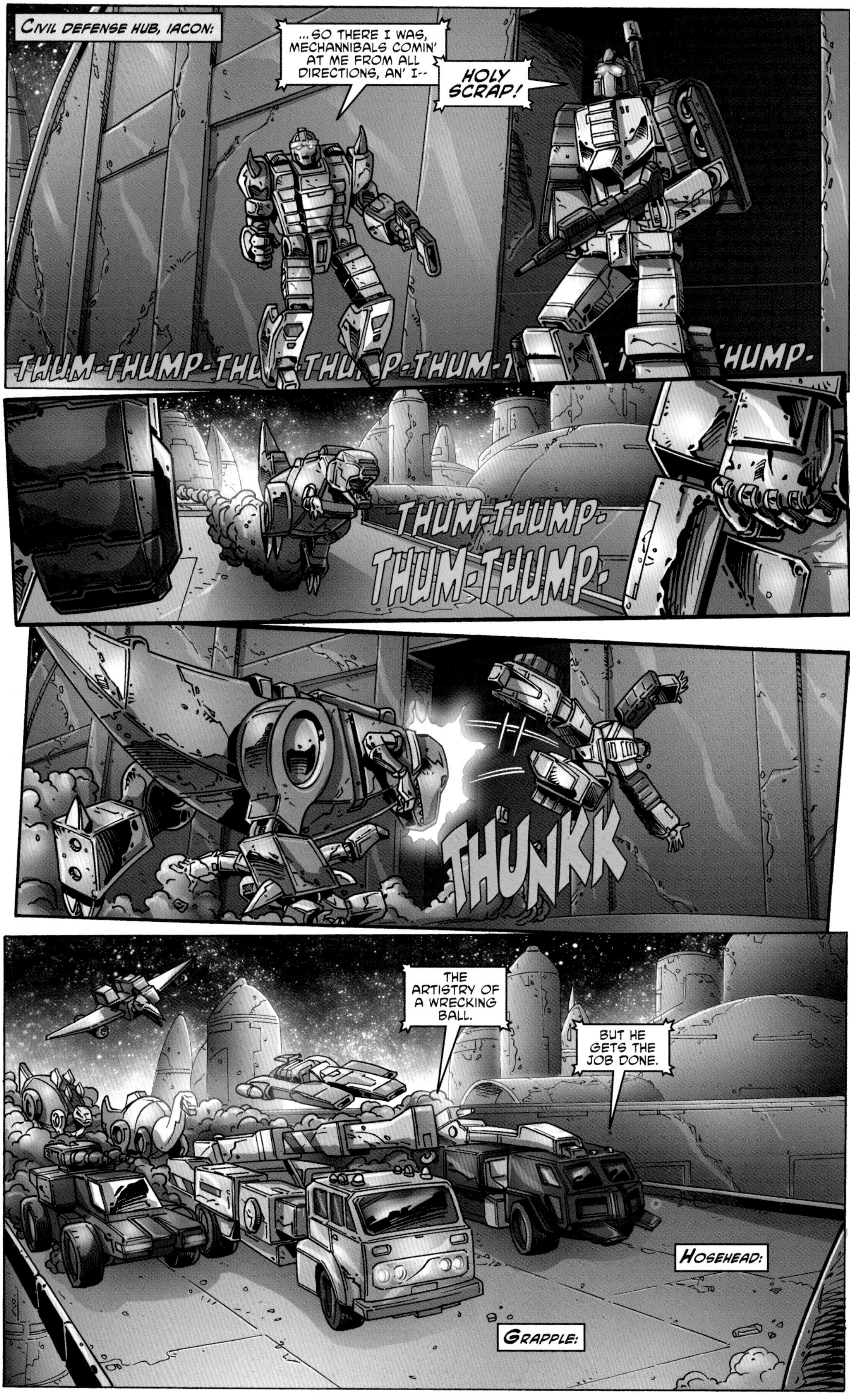

Civil defense hub, Iacon:
...So there I was, Mechannibals comin' at me from all directions, an' I--
HOLY SCRAP!
THUM-THUMP-THUM-THUMP-THUM-THUMP-
THUM-THUMP-
THUM-THUMP-
THUNKK
THE ARTISTRY OF A WRECKING BALL.
BUT HE GETS THE JOB DONE.
Hosehead:
Grapple:

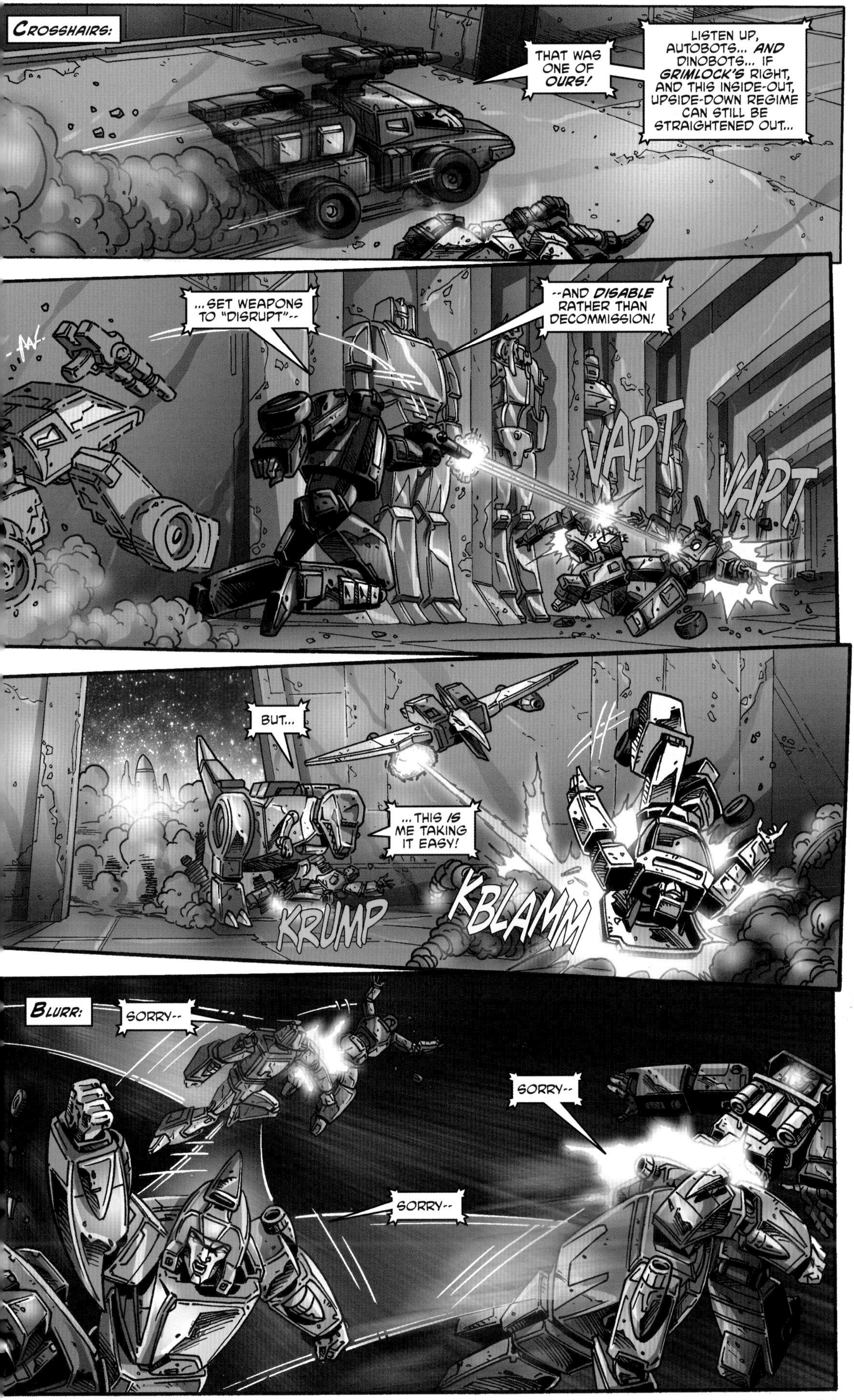

CROSSHAIRS:
THAT WAS ONE OF OURS!
LISTEN UP, AUTOBOTS... AND DINOBOTS... IF GRIMLOCK'S RIGHT, AND THIS INSIDE-OUT, UPSIDE-DOWN REGIME CAN STILL BE STRAIGHTENED OUT...
...SET WEAPONS TO "DISRUPT"--
--AND DISABLE RATHER THAN DECOMMISSION!
VAPT
VAPT
BUT...
...THIS IS ME TAKING IT EASY!
KRUMP
KBLAMM
BLURR:
SORRY--
SORRY--
SORRY--

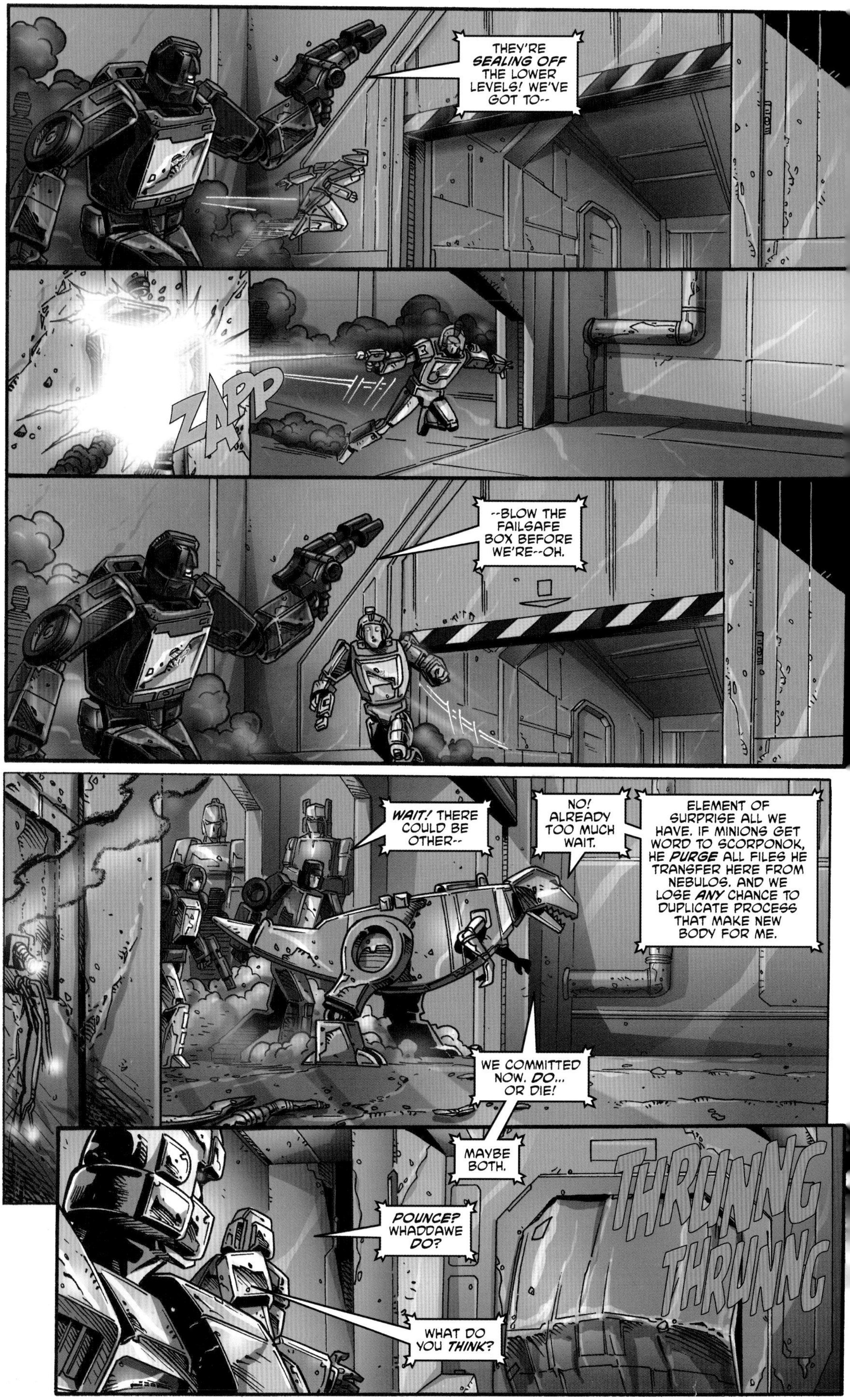
THEY'RE *SEALING OFF* THE LOWER LEVELS! WE'VE GOT TO--
ZAPP
--BLOW THE FAILSAFE BOX BEFORE WE'RE--OH.
WAIT! THERE COULD BE OTHER--
NO! ALREADY TOO MUCH WAIT.
ELEMENT OF SURPRISE ALL WE HAVE. IF MINIONS GET WORD TO SCORPONOK, HE *PURGE* ALL FILES HE TRANSFER HERE FROM NEBULOS. AND WE LOSE *ANY* CHANCE TO DUPLICATE PROCESS THAT MAKE NEW BODY FOR ME.
WE COMMITTED NOW. *DO*... OR DIE!
MAYBE BOTH.
POUNCE? WHADDAWE *DO?*
THRUNNG THRUNNG
WHAT DO YOU *THINK?*

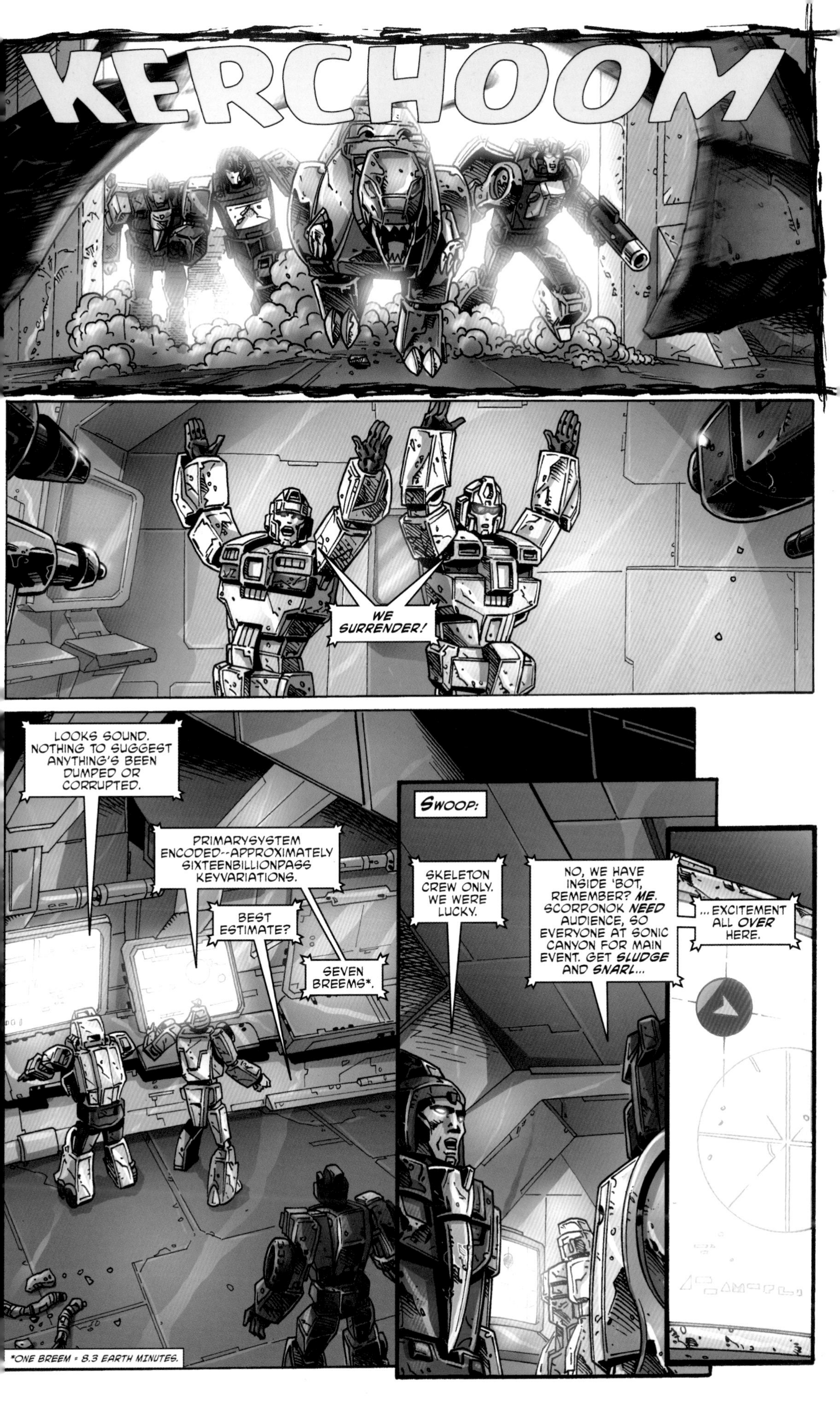
KERCHOOM
WE SURRENDER!
LOOKS SOUND. NOTHING TO SUGGEST ANYTHING'S BEEN DUMPED OR CORRUPTED.
PRIMARYSYSTEM ENCODED--APPROXIMATELY SIXTEENBILLIONPASS KEYVARIATIONS.
BEST ESTIMATE?
SEVEN BREEMS*.
*ONE BREEM = 8.3 EARTH MINUTES.
SWOOP:
SKELETON CREW ONLY. WE WERE LUCKY.
NO, WE HAVE INSIDE 'BOT, REMEMBER? ME. SCORPONOK NEED AUDIENCE, SO EVERYONE AT SONIC CANYON FOR MAIN EVENT. GET SLUDGE AND SNARL...
...EXCITEMENT ALL OVER HERE.

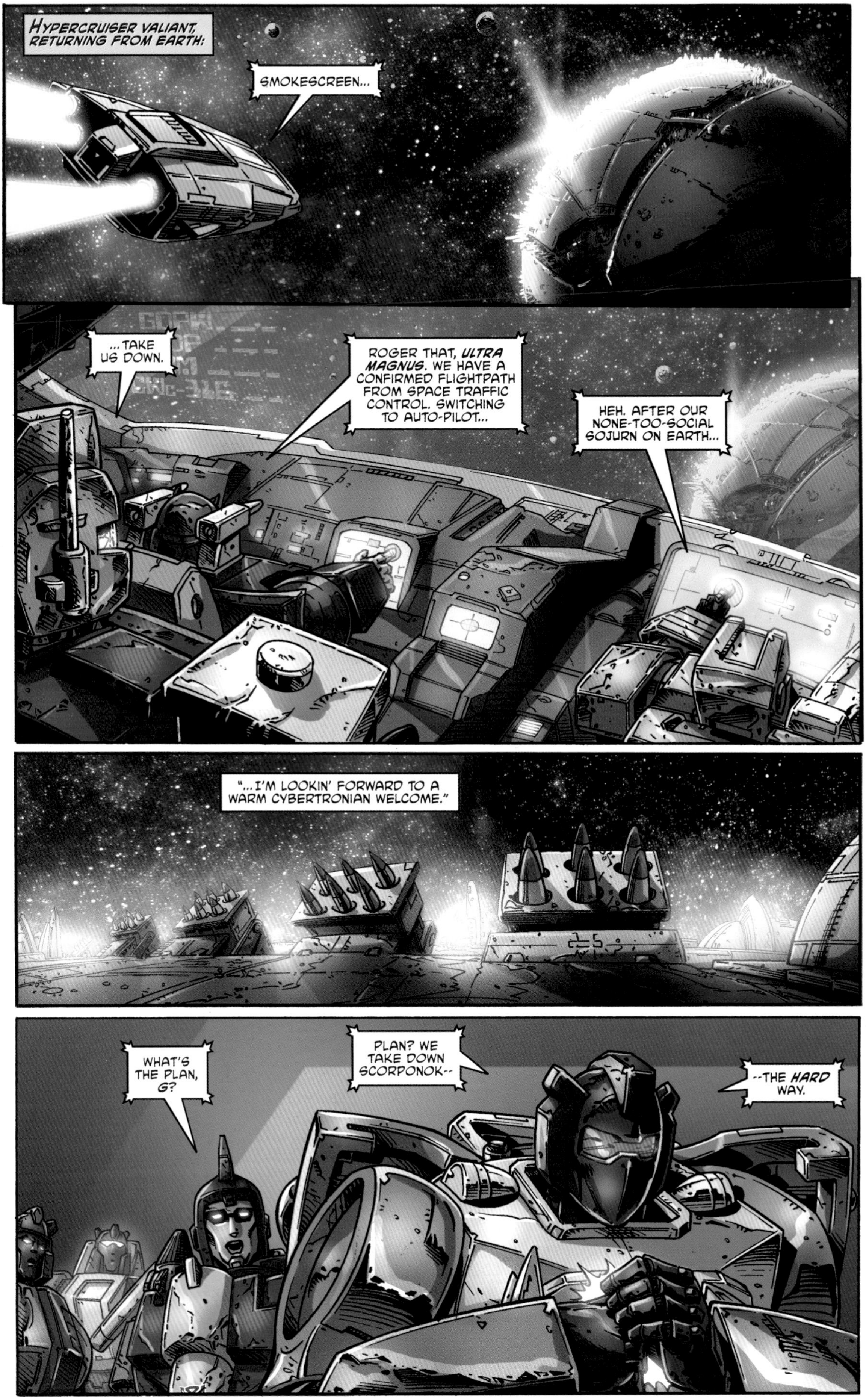
HYPERCRUISER VALIANT, RETURNING FROM EARTH:
SMOKESCREEN...
...TAKE US DOWN.
ROGER THAT, *ULTRA MAGNUS*. WE HAVE A CONFIRMED FLIGHTPATH FROM SPACE TRAFFIC CONTROL. SWITCHING TO AUTO-PILOT...
HEH. AFTER OUR NONE-TOO-SOCIAL SOJURN ON EARTH...
"...I'M LOOKIN' FORWARD TO A WARM CYBERTRONIAN WELCOME."
WHAT'S THE PLAN, G?
PLAN? WE TAKE DOWN SCORPONOK--
--THE *HARD* WAY.

YUKON TERRITORY, EARTH.

THE ARK:

SOON...

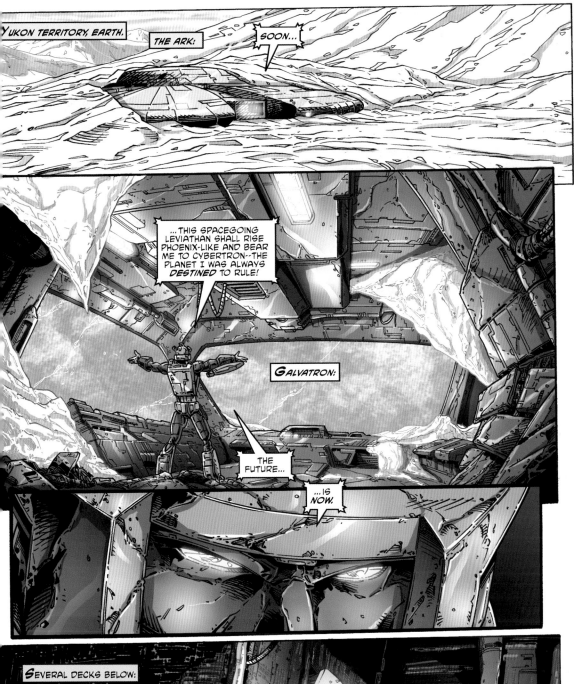

...THIS SPACEGOING LEVIATHAN SHALL RISE PHOENIX-LIKE AND BEAR ME TO CYBERTRON--THE PLANET I WAS ALWAYS *DESTINED* TO RULE!

GALVATRON:

THE FUTURE...

...IS NOW.

SEVERAL DECKS BELOW:

STARSCREAM__

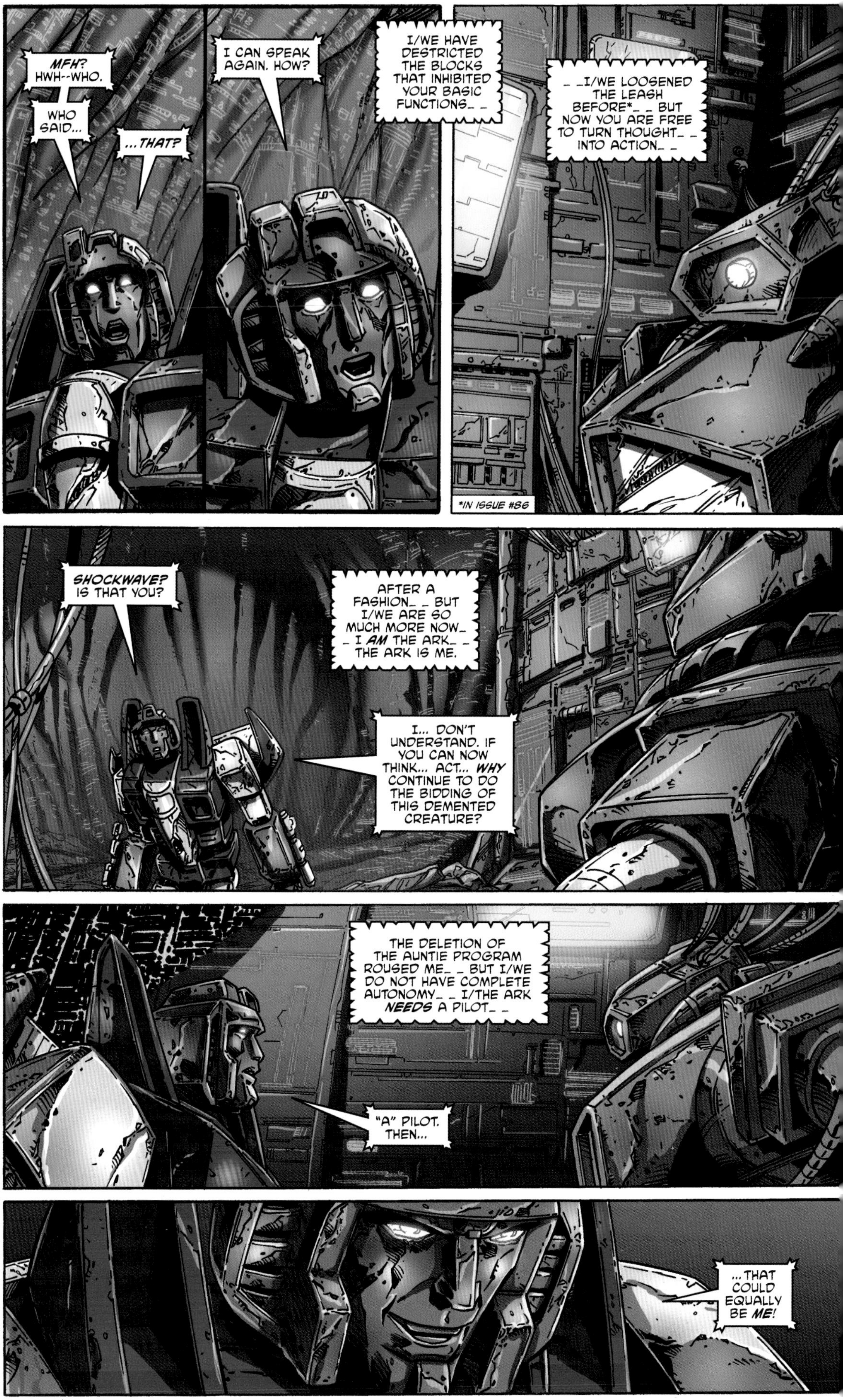
MFH? HWH--WHO.
WHO SAID...
...THAT?
I CAN SPEAK AGAIN. HOW?
I/WE HAVE DESTRICTED THE BLOCKS THAT INHIBITED YOUR BASIC FUNCTIONS_ _
_ _I/WE LOOSENED THE LEASH BEFORE*_ _ BUT NOW YOU ARE FREE TO TURN THOUGHT_ _ INTO ACTION_ _
*IN ISSUE #86
SHOCKWAVE? IS THAT YOU?
AFTER A FASHION_ _ BUT I/WE ARE SO MUCH MORE NOW_ _ I AM THE ARK_ _ THE ARK IS ME.
I... DON'T UNDERSTAND. IF YOU CAN NOW THINK... ACT... WHY CONTINUE TO DO THE BIDDING OF THIS DEMENTED CREATURE?
THE DELETION OF THE AUNTIE PROGRAM ROUSED ME_ _ BUT I/WE DO NOT HAVE COMPLETE AUTONOMY_ _ I/THE ARK NEEDS A PILOT_ _
"A" PILOT. THEN...
...THAT COULD EQUALLY BE ME!

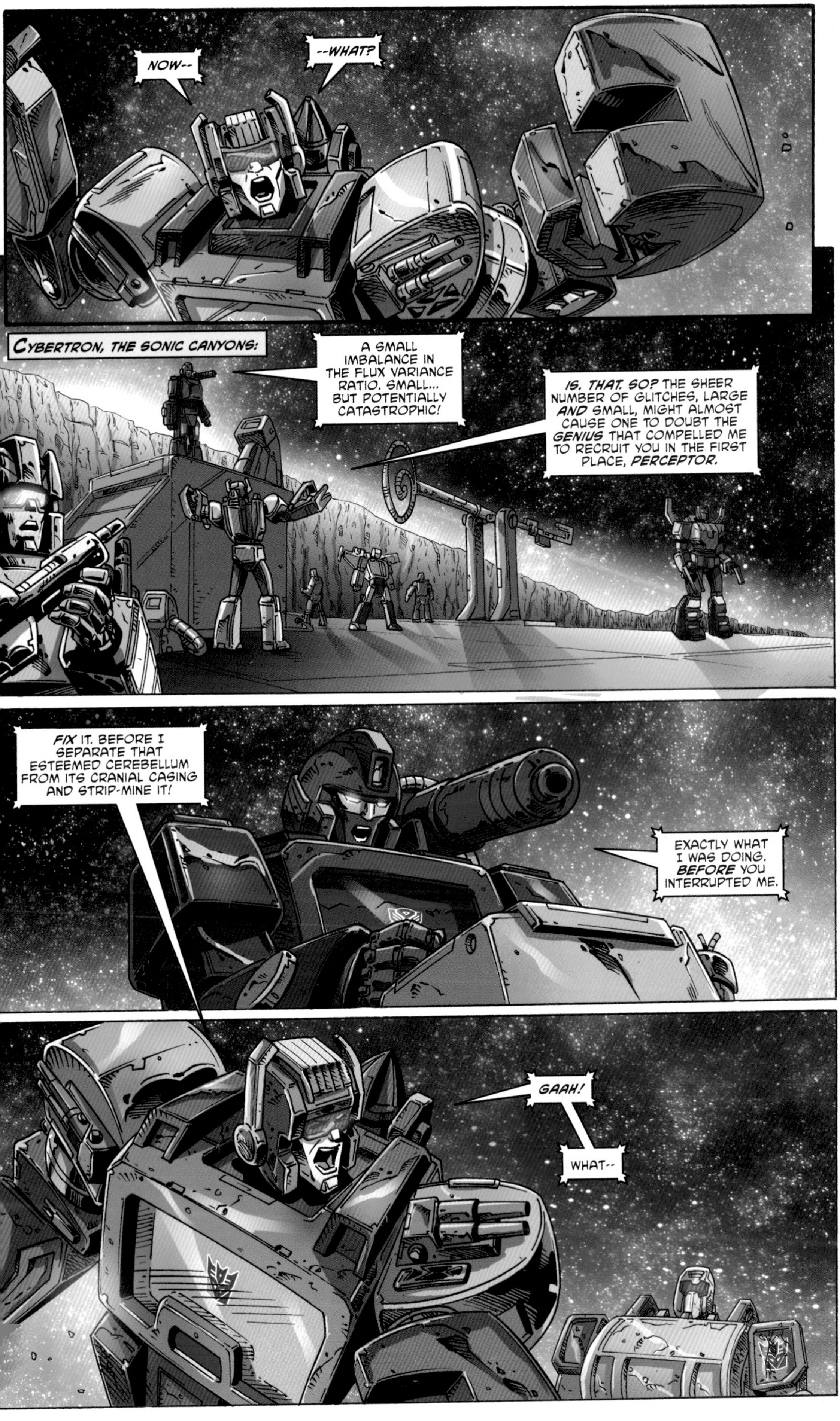
NOW--
--WHAT?
CYBERTRON, THE SONIC CANYONS:
A SMALL IMBALANCE IN THE FLUX VARIANCE RATIO. SMALL... BUT POTENTIALLY CATASTROPHIC!
IS. THAT. SO? THE SHEER NUMBER OF GLITCHES, LARGE AND SMALL, MIGHT ALMOST CAUSE ONE TO DOUBT THE GENIUS THAT COMPELLED ME TO RECRUIT YOU IN THE FIRST PLACE, PERCEPTOR.
FIX IT. BEFORE I SEPARATE THAT ESTEEMED CEREBELLUM FROM ITS CRANIAL CASING AND STRIP-MINE IT!
EXACTLY WHAT I WAS DOING. BEFORE YOU INTERRUPTED ME.
GAAH!
WHAT--

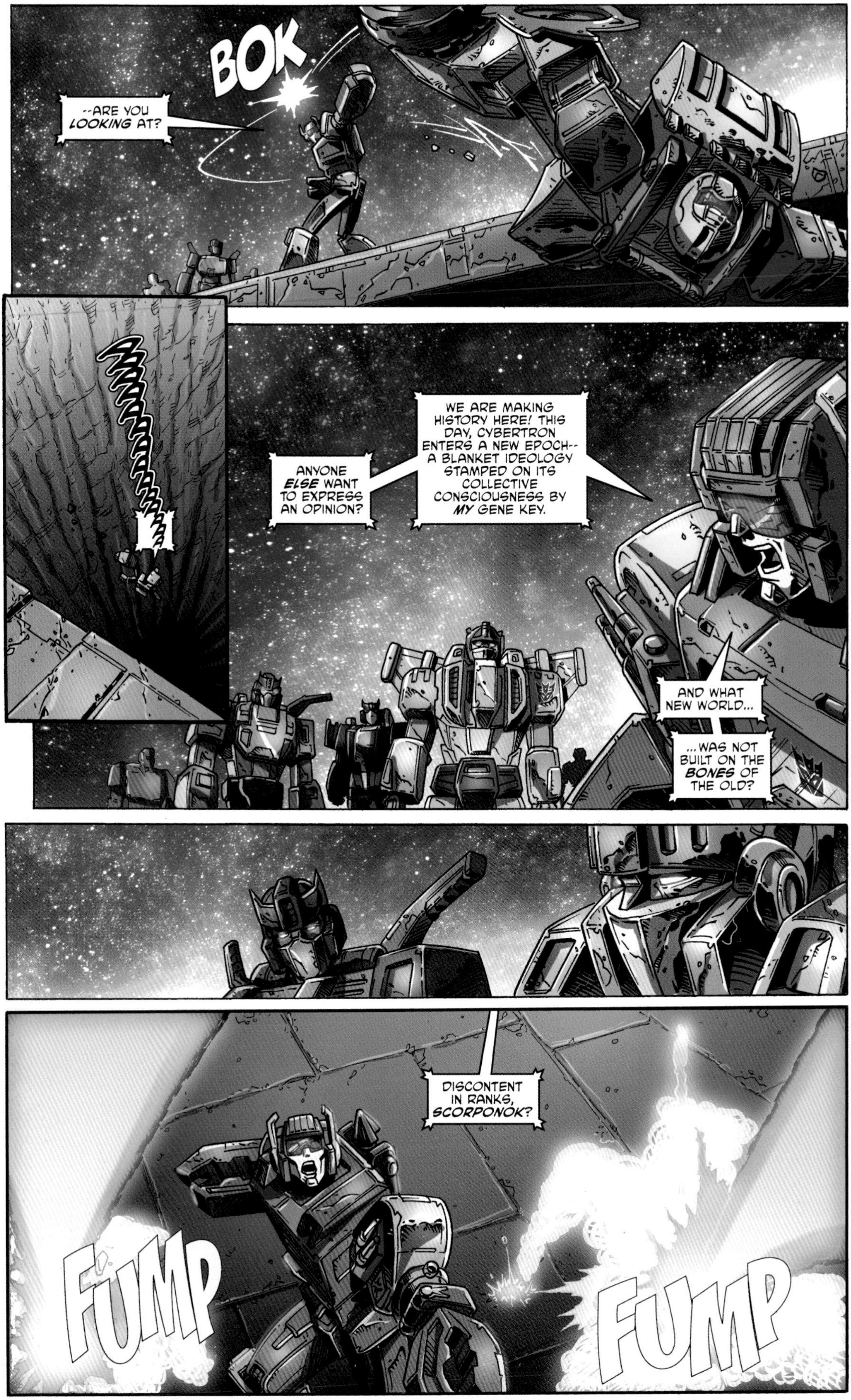
BOK
--ARE YOU LOOKING AT?
ANYONE ELSE WANT TO EXPRESS AN OPINION?
WE ARE MAKING HISTORY HERE! THIS DAY, CYBERTRON ENTERS A NEW EPOCH--A BLANKET IDEOLOGY STAMPED ON ITS COLLECTIVE CONSCIOUSNESS BY MY GENE KEY.
AND WHAT NEW WORLD...
...WAS NOT BUILT ON THE BONES OF THE OLD?
DISCONTENT IN RANKS, SCORPONOK?
FUMP
FUMP

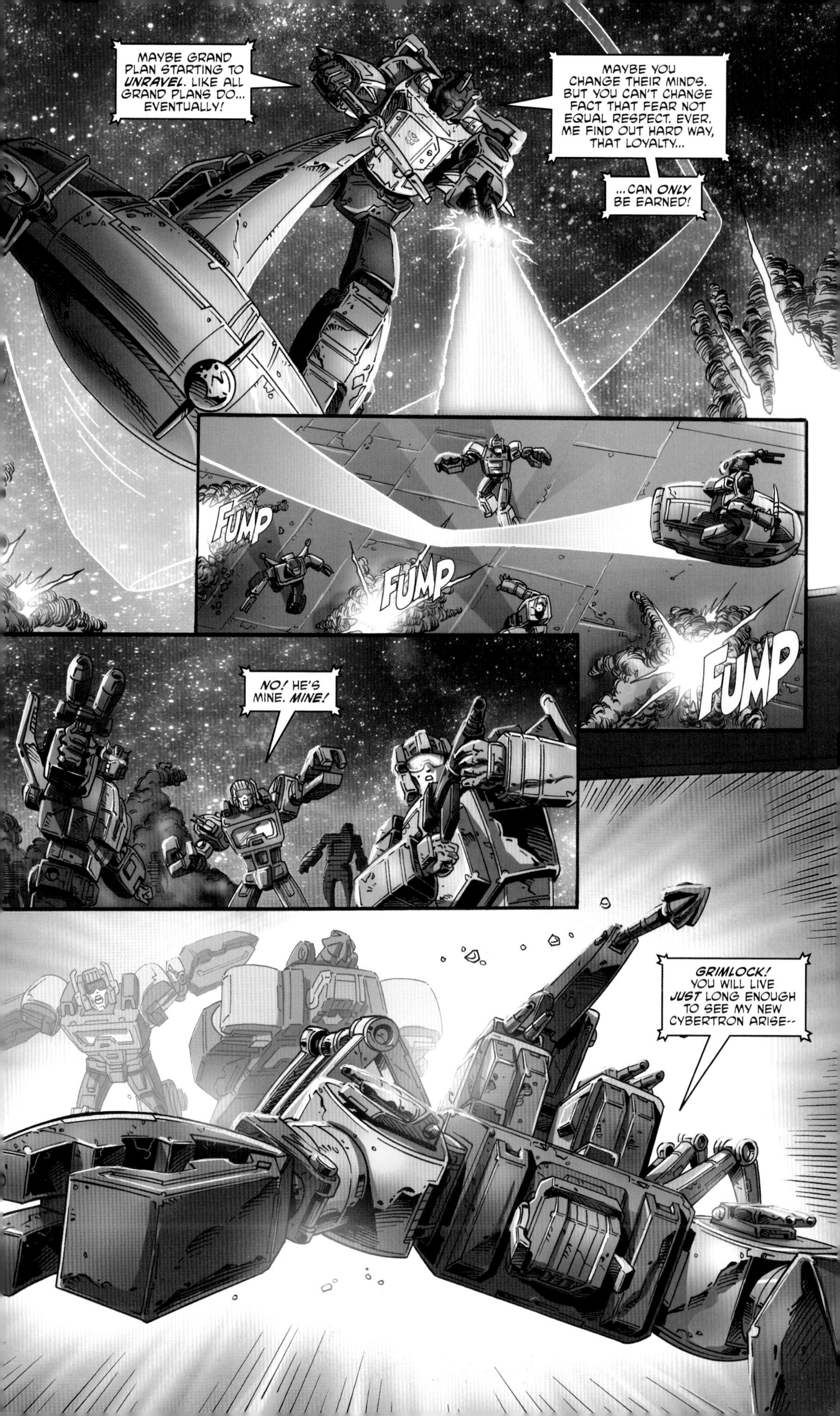
MAYBE GRAND PLAN STARTING TO UNRAVEL. LIKE ALL GRAND PLANS DO... EVENTUALLY!
MAYBE YOU CHANGE THEIR MINDS. BUT YOU CAN'T CHANGE FACT THAT FEAR NOT EQUAL RESPECT. EVER. ME FIND OUT HARD WAY, THAT LOYALTY...
...CAN ONLY BE EARNED!
FUMP
FUMP
FUMP
NO! HE'S MINE. MINE!
GRIMLOCK! YOU WILL LIVE JUST LONG ENOUGH TO SEE MY NEW CYBERTRON ARISE--

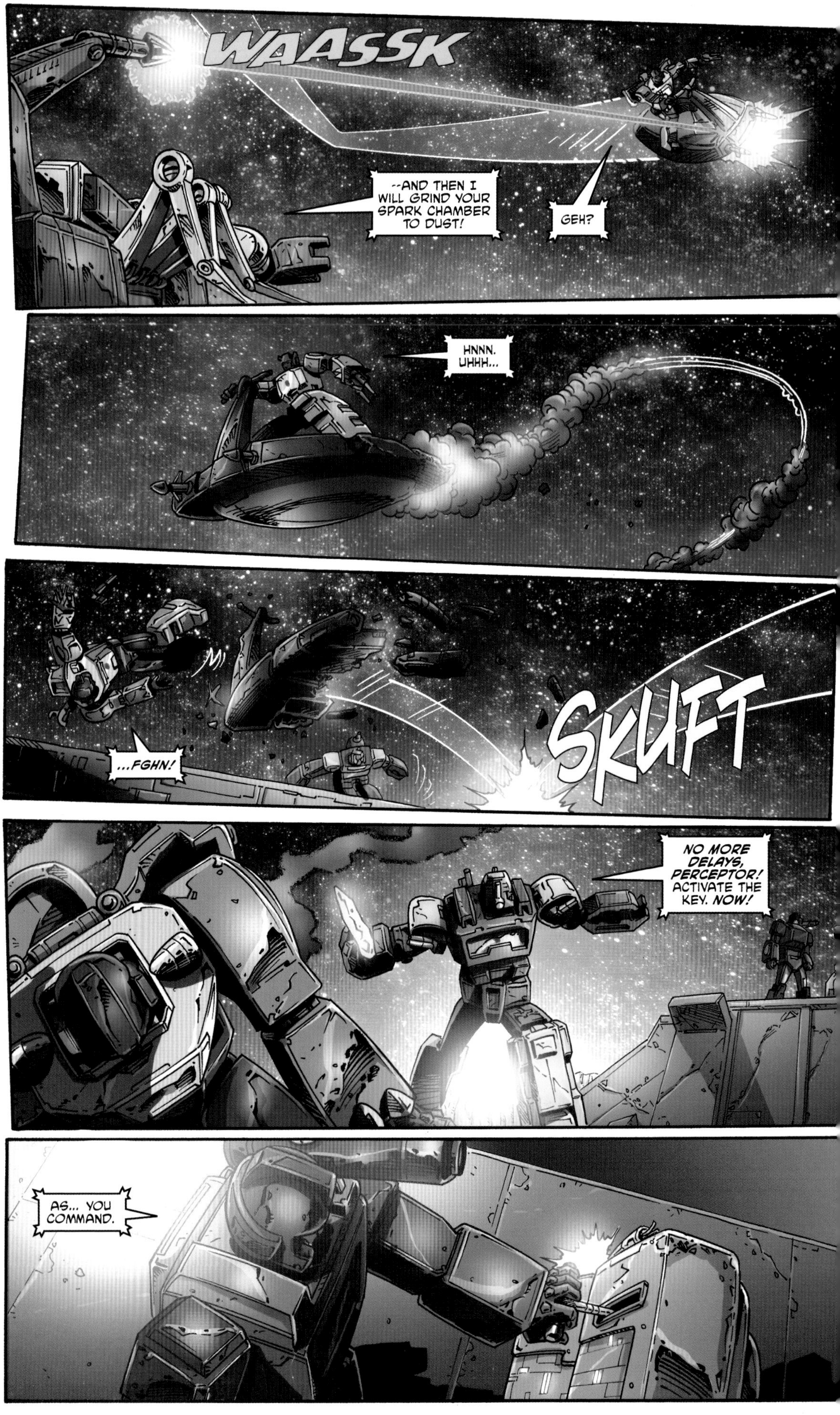
WAASSK
--AND THEN I WILL GRIND YOUR SPARK CHAMBER TO DUST!
GEH?
HNNN. UHHH...
...FGHN!
SKUFT
NO MORE DELAYS, PERCEPTOR! ACTIVATE THE KEY. NOW!
AS... YOU COMMAND.

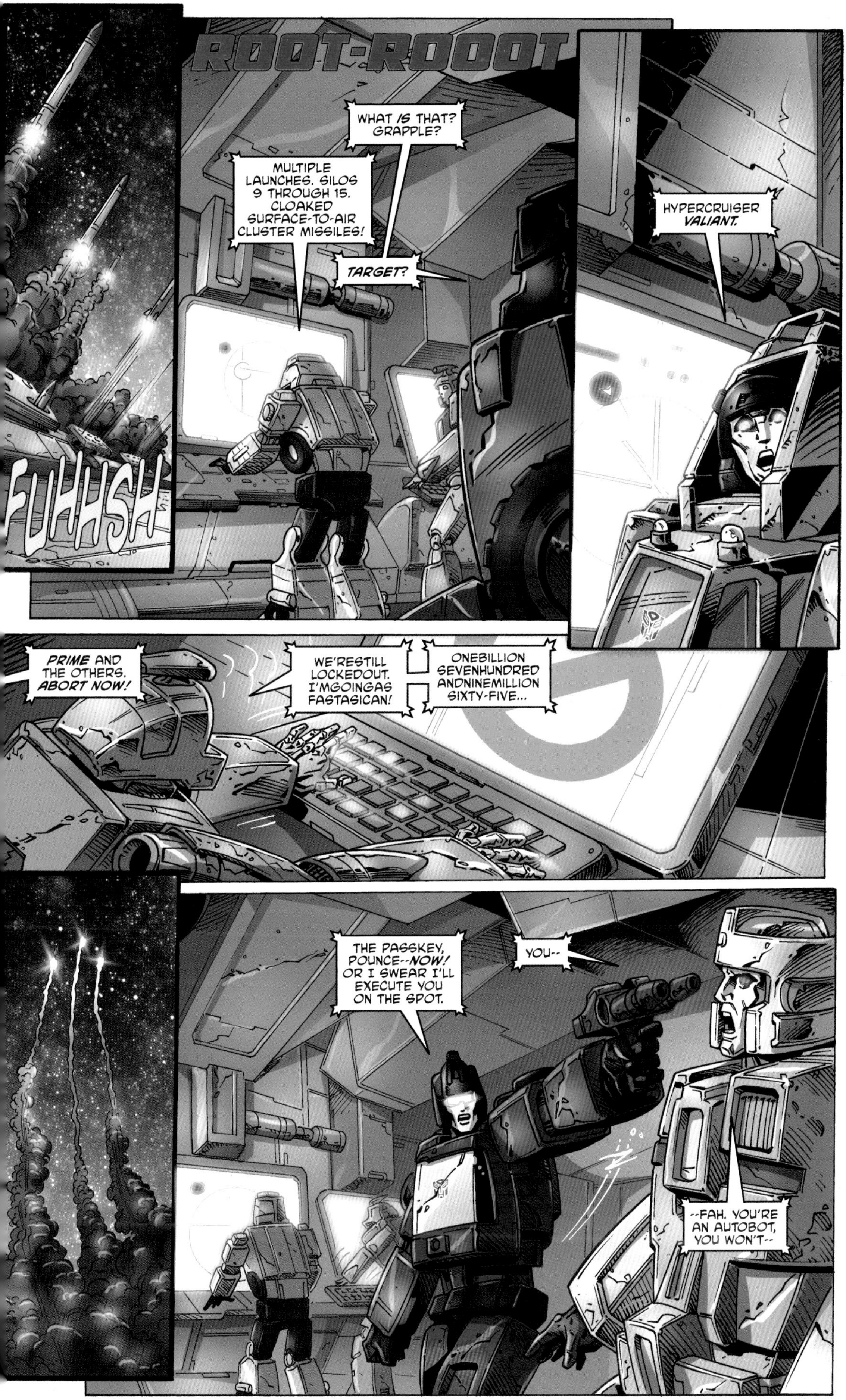
FUHHSH
ROOT-ROOOT
MULTIPLE LAUNCHES. SILOS 9 THROUGH 15. CLOAKED SURFACE-TO-AIR CLUSTER MISSILES!
WHAT *IS* THAT? GRAPPLE?
TARGET?
HYPERCRUISER *VALIANT.*
PRIME AND THE OTHERS. *ABORT NOW!*
WE'RESTILL LOCKEDOUT. I'MGOINGAS FASTASICAN!
ONEBILLION SEVENHUNDRED ANDNINEMILLION SIXTY-FIVE...
THE PASSKEY, POUNCE--*NOW!* OR I SWEAR I'LL EXECUTE YOU ON THE SPOT.
YOU--
--FAH. YOU'RE AN AUTOBOT, YOU WON'T--

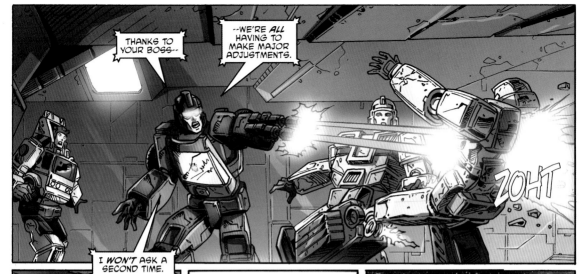

THANKS TO YOUR BOSS--

--WE'RE *ALL* HAVING TO MAKE MAJOR ADJUSTMENTS.

ZOHT

I *WON'T* ASK A SECOND TIME.

J-JUU-KYUU-HACHI-JUUSHI--

--NIJUU-JUU-YON!

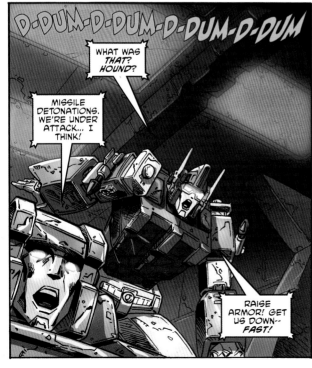

D-DUM-D-DUM-D-DUM-D-DUM

WHAT WAS *THAT?* HOUND?

MISSILE DETONATIONS. WE'RE UNDER ATTACK... I THINK!

RAISE ARMOR! GET US DOWN-- *FAST!*

AUTOBOTS... WRECKERS... PREP FOR *IMMEDIATE* DEPLOYMENT!

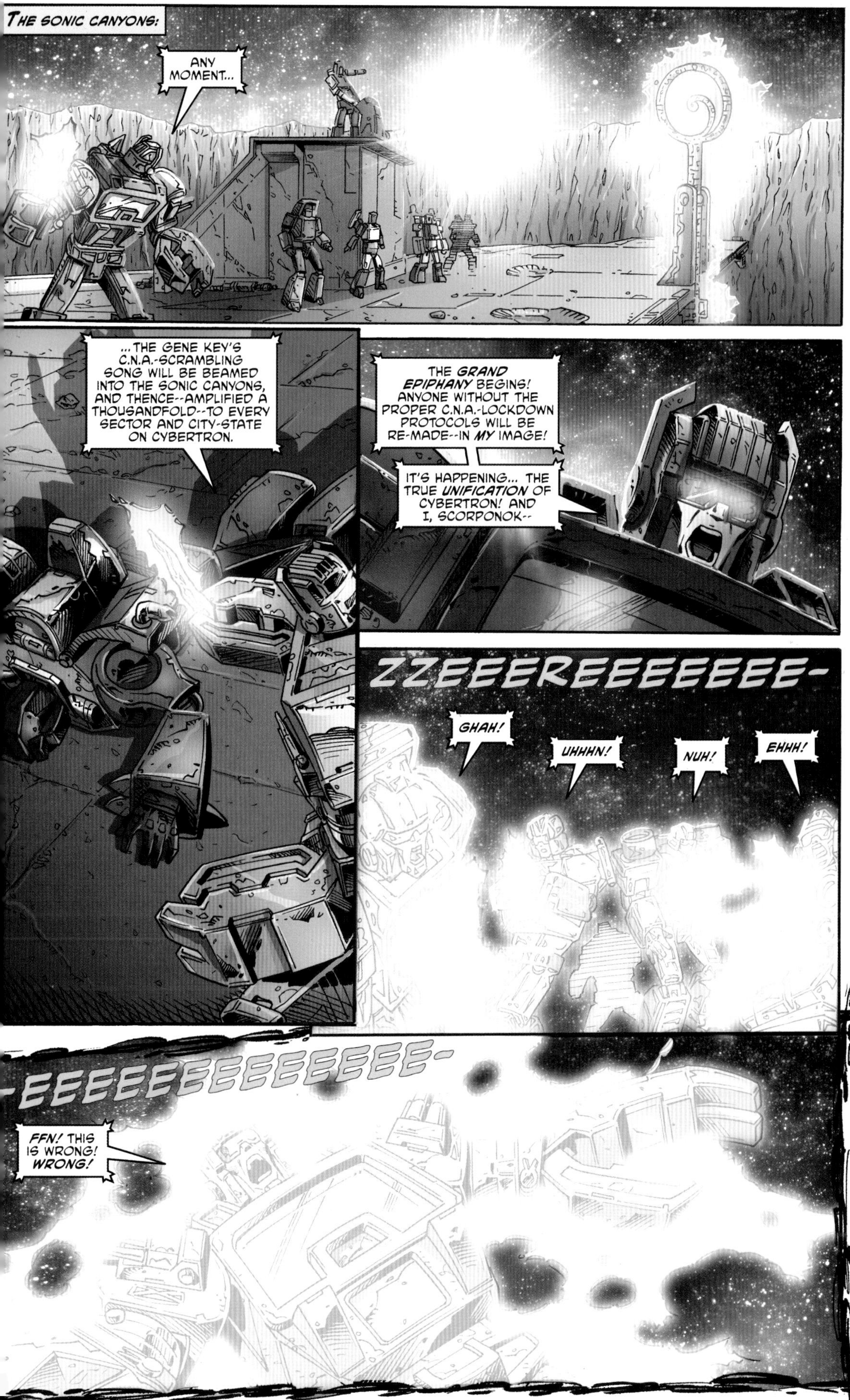
THE SONIC CANYONS:
ANY MOMENT...
...THE GENE KEY'S C.N.A.-SCRAMBLING SONG WILL BE BEAMED INTO THE SONIC CANYONS, AND THENCE--AMPLIFIED A THOUSANDFOLD--TO EVERY SECTOR AND CITY-STATE ON CYBERTRON.
THE GRAND EPIPHANY BEGINS! ANYONE WITHOUT THE PROPER C.N.A.-LOCKDOWN PROTOCOLS WILL BE RE-MADE--IN MY IMAGE!
IT'S HAPPENING... THE TRUE UNIFICATION OF CYBERTRON! AND I, SCORPONOK--
ZZEEEREEEEEEEE-
GHAH!
UHHHN!
NUH!
EHHH!
-EEEEEEEEEEEEEEE-
FFN! THIS IS WRONG! WRONG!

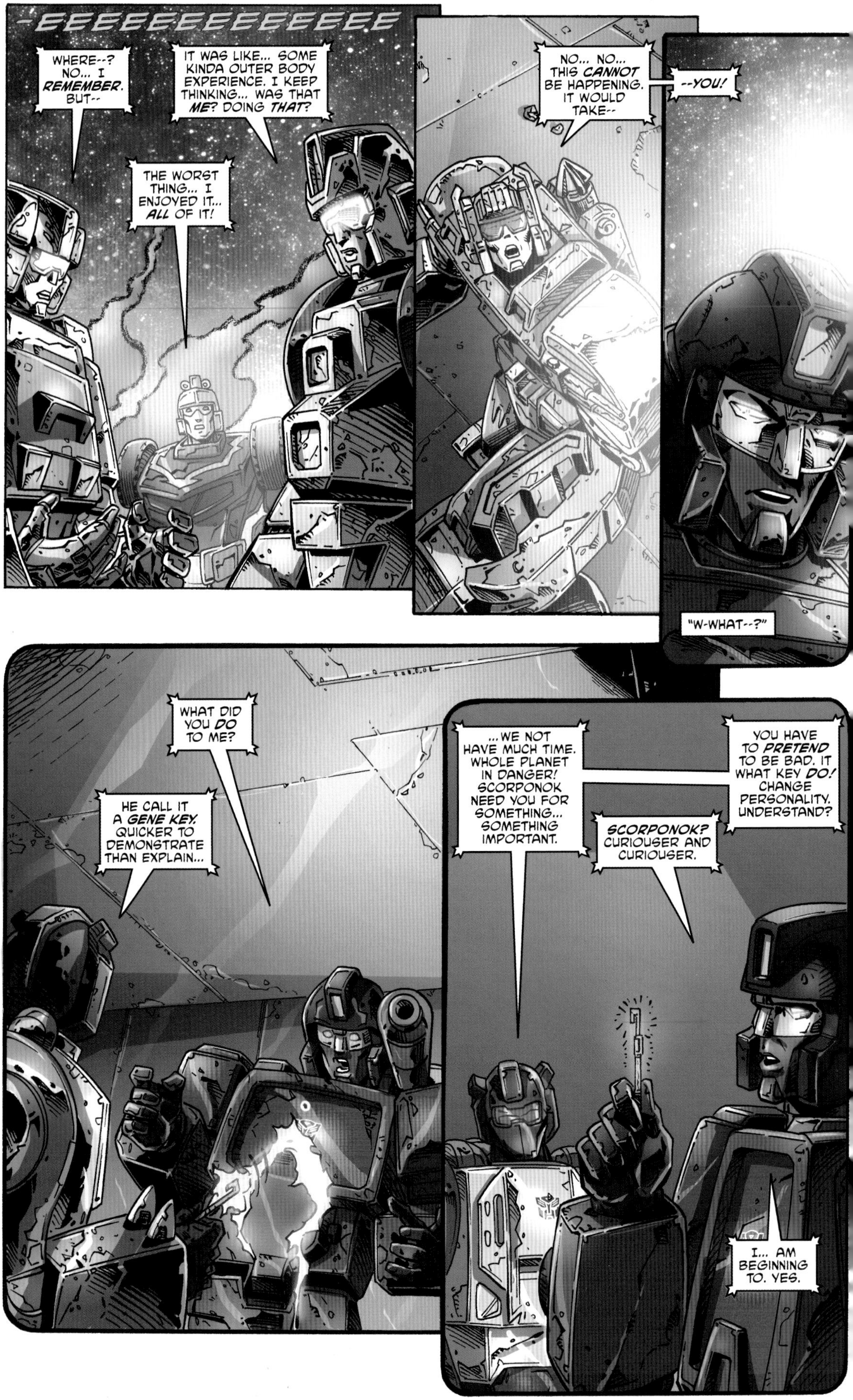
-EEEEEEEEEEEEEE
WHERE--? NO... I REMEMBER. BUT--
IT WAS LIKE... SOME KINDA OUTER BODY EXPERIENCE. I KEEP THINKING... WAS THAT ME? DOING THAT?
THE WORST THING... I ENJOYED IT... ALL OF IT!
NO... NO... THIS CANNOT BE HAPPENING. IT WOULD TAKE--
--YOU!
"W-WHAT--?"
WHAT DID YOU DO TO ME?
HE CALL IT A GENE KEY. QUICKER TO DEMONSTRATE THAN EXPLAIN...
...WE NOT HAVE MUCH TIME. WHOLE PLANET IN DANGER! SCORPONOK NEED YOU FOR SOMETHING... SOMETHING IMPORTANT.
SCORPONOK? CURIOUSER AND CURIOUSER.
YOU HAVE TO PRETEND TO BE BAD. IT WHAT KEY DO! CHANGE PERSONALITY. UNDERSTAND?
I... AM BEGINNING TO. YES.

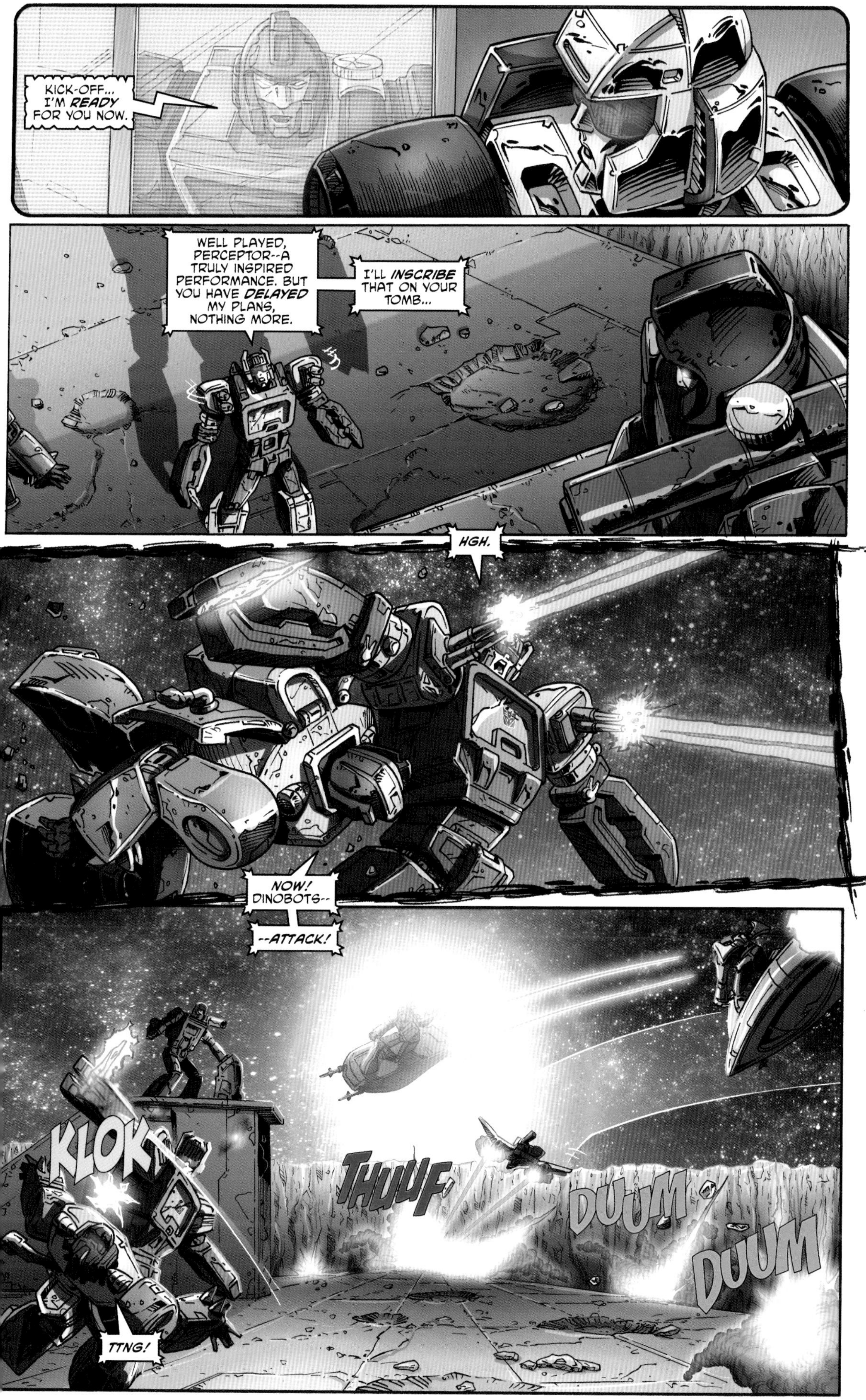
KICK-OFF... I'M READY FOR YOU NOW.
WELL PLAYED, PERCEPTOR--A TRULY INSPIRED PERFORMANCE. BUT YOU HAVE DELAYED MY PLANS, NOTHING MORE.
I'LL INSCRIBE THAT ON YOUR TOMB...
HGH.
NOW! DINOBOTS--
--ATTACK!
KLOK
THUUF
DUUM
DUUM
TTNG!

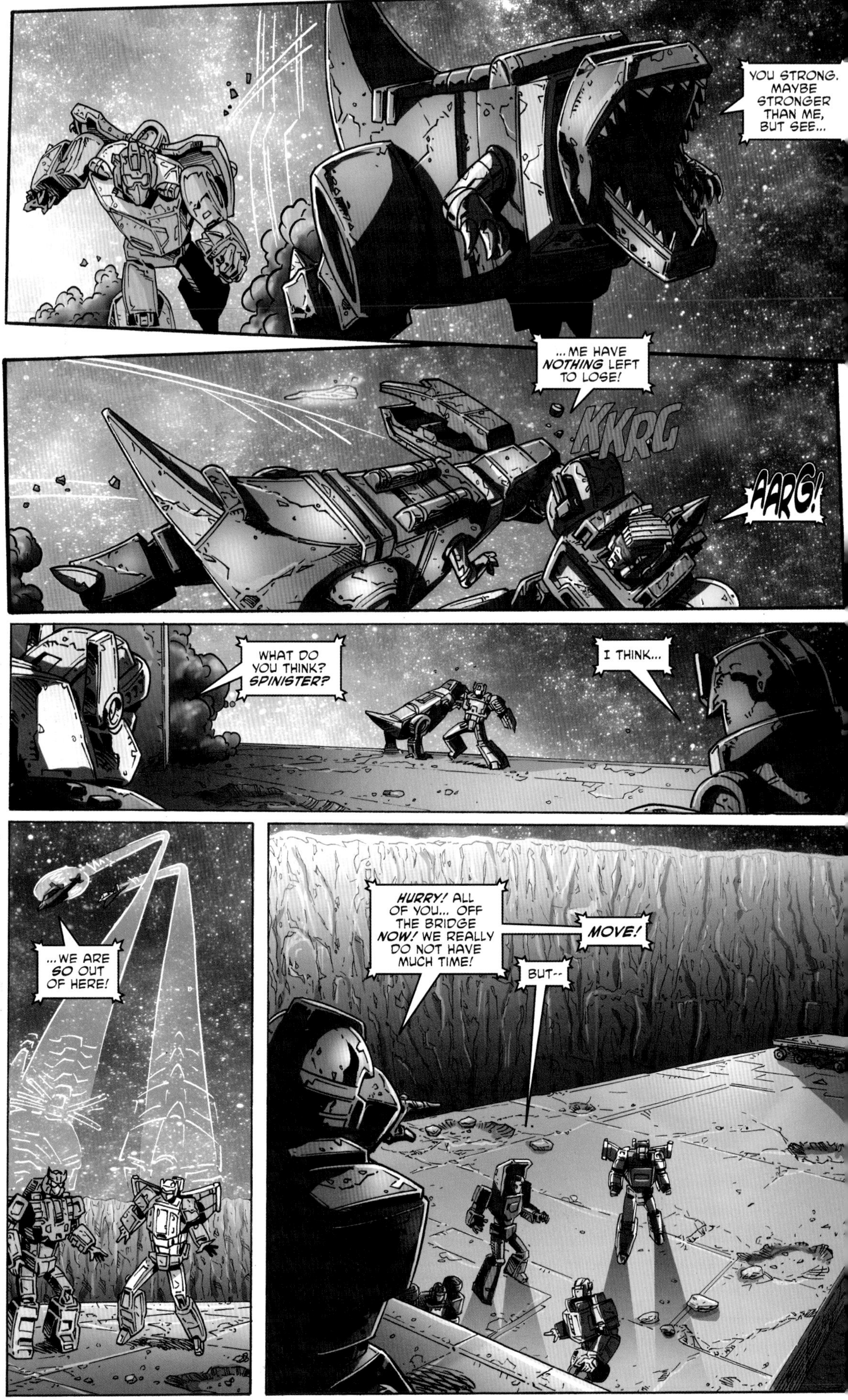

YOU STRONG. MAYBE STRONGER THAN ME, BUT SEE...
...ME HAVE *NOTHING* LEFT TO LOSE!
KKRG
AARG!
WHAT DO YOU THINK? *SPINISTER?*
I THINK...
...WE ARE *SO* OUT OF HERE!
HURRY! ALL OF YOU... OFF THE BRIDGE *NOW!* WE REALLY DO NOT HAVE MUCH TIME!
MOVE!
BUT--

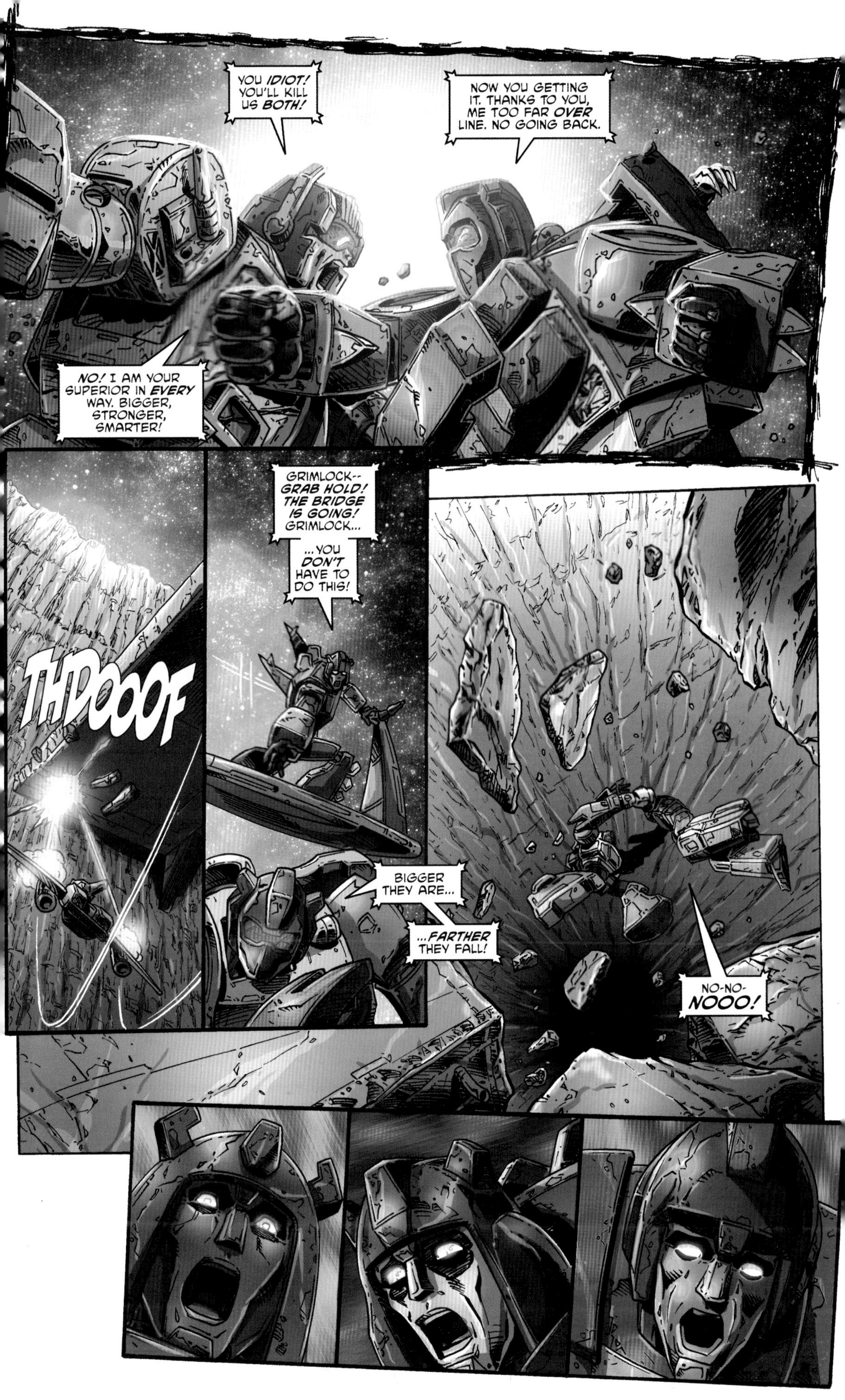
YOU IDIOT! YOU'LL KILL US BOTH!
NOW YOU GETTING IT. THANKS TO YOU, ME TOO FAR OVER LINE. NO GOING BACK.
NO! I AM YOUR SUPERIOR IN EVERY WAY. BIGGER, STRONGER, SMARTER!
THDOOOF
GRIMLOCK-- GRAB HOLD! THE BRIDGE IS GOING! GRIMLOCK...
...YOU DON'T HAVE TO DO THIS!
BIGGER THEY ARE...
...FARTHER THEY FALL!
NO-NO-NOOO!

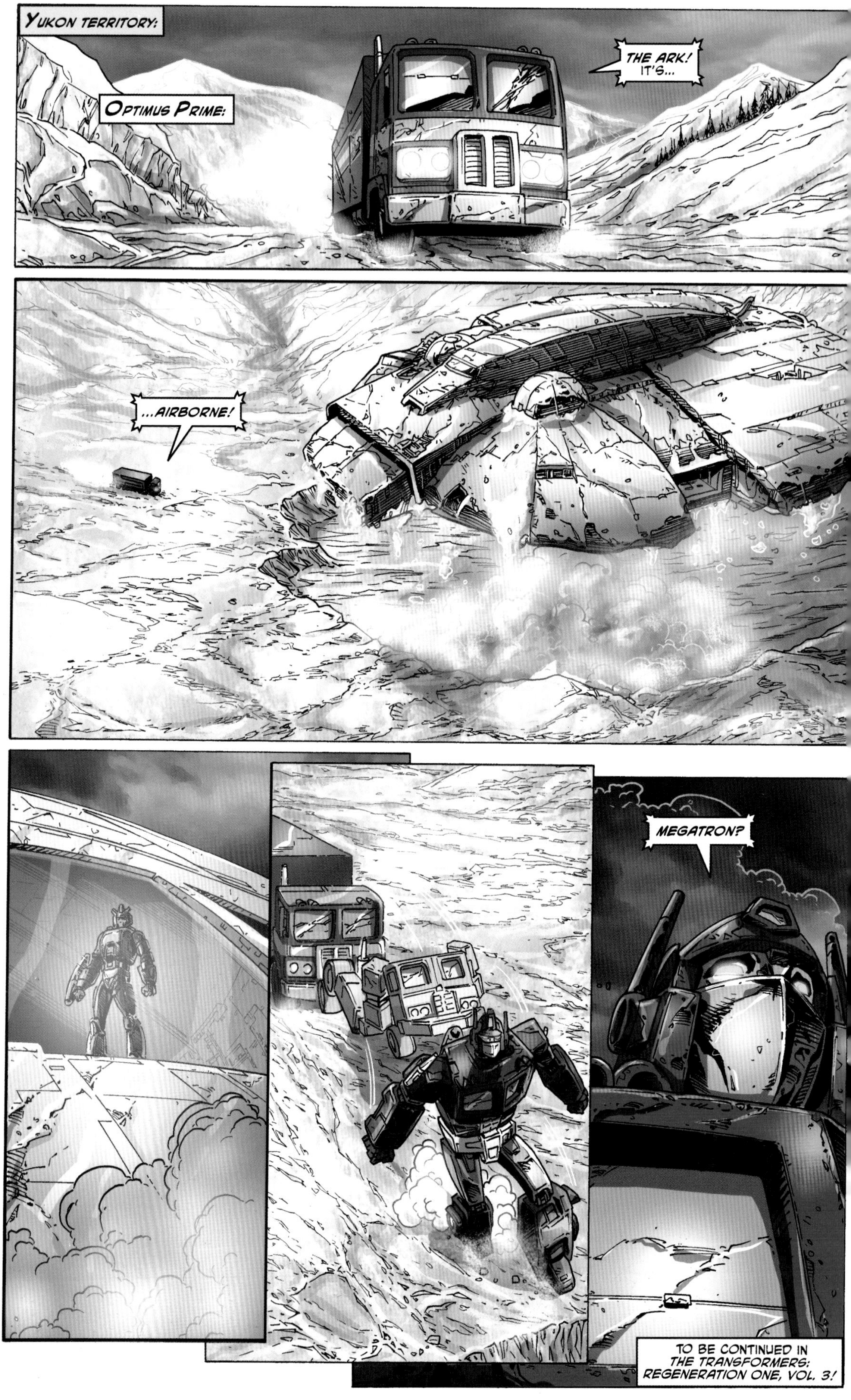
YUKON TERRITORY:
OPTIMUS PRIME:
THE ARK! IT'S...
...AIRBORNE!
MEGATRON?
TO BE CONTINUED IN THE TRANSFORMERS: REGENERATION ONE, VOL. 3!

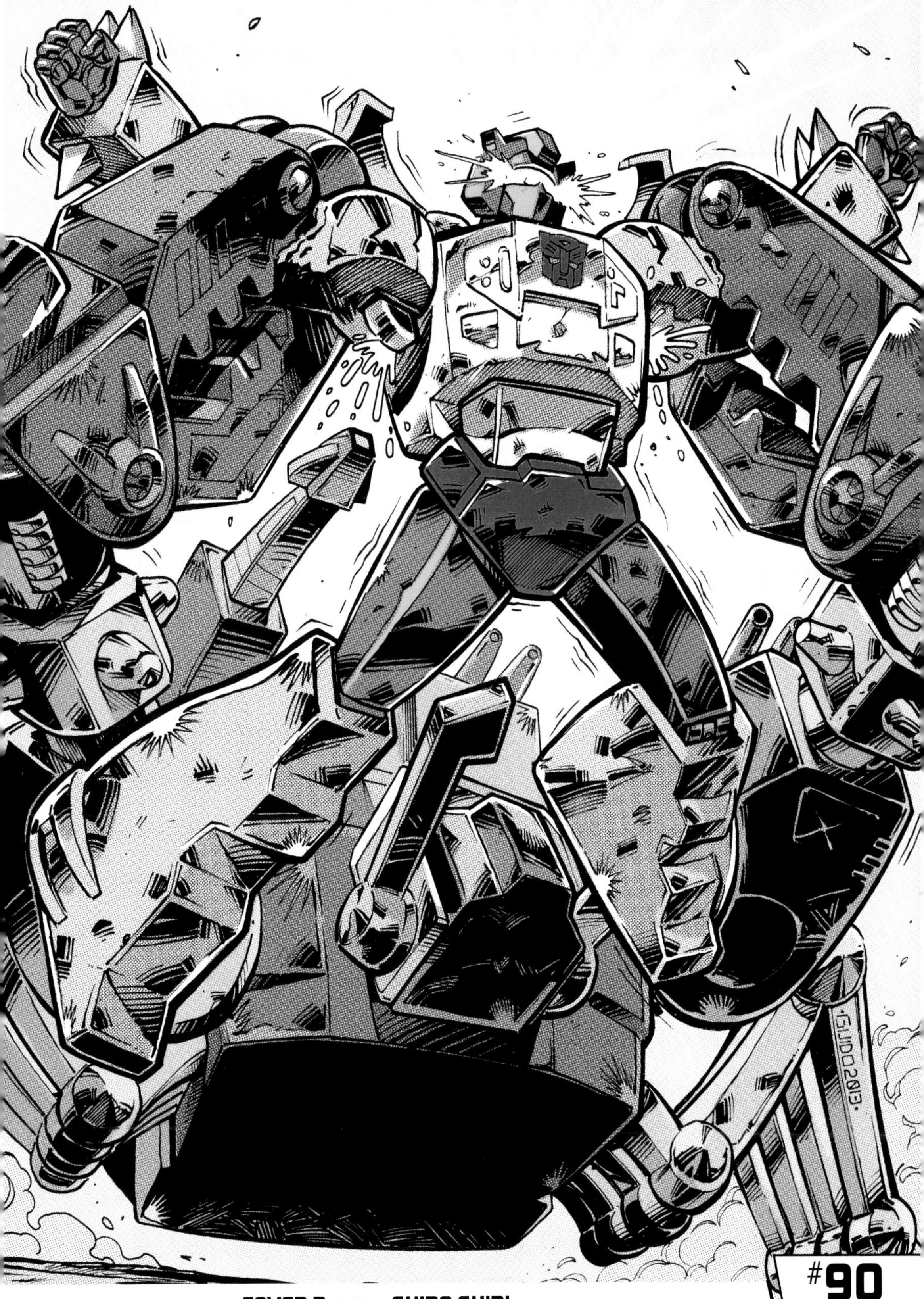

GUIDO 2013
#90

COVER B: Art by GUIDO GUIDI

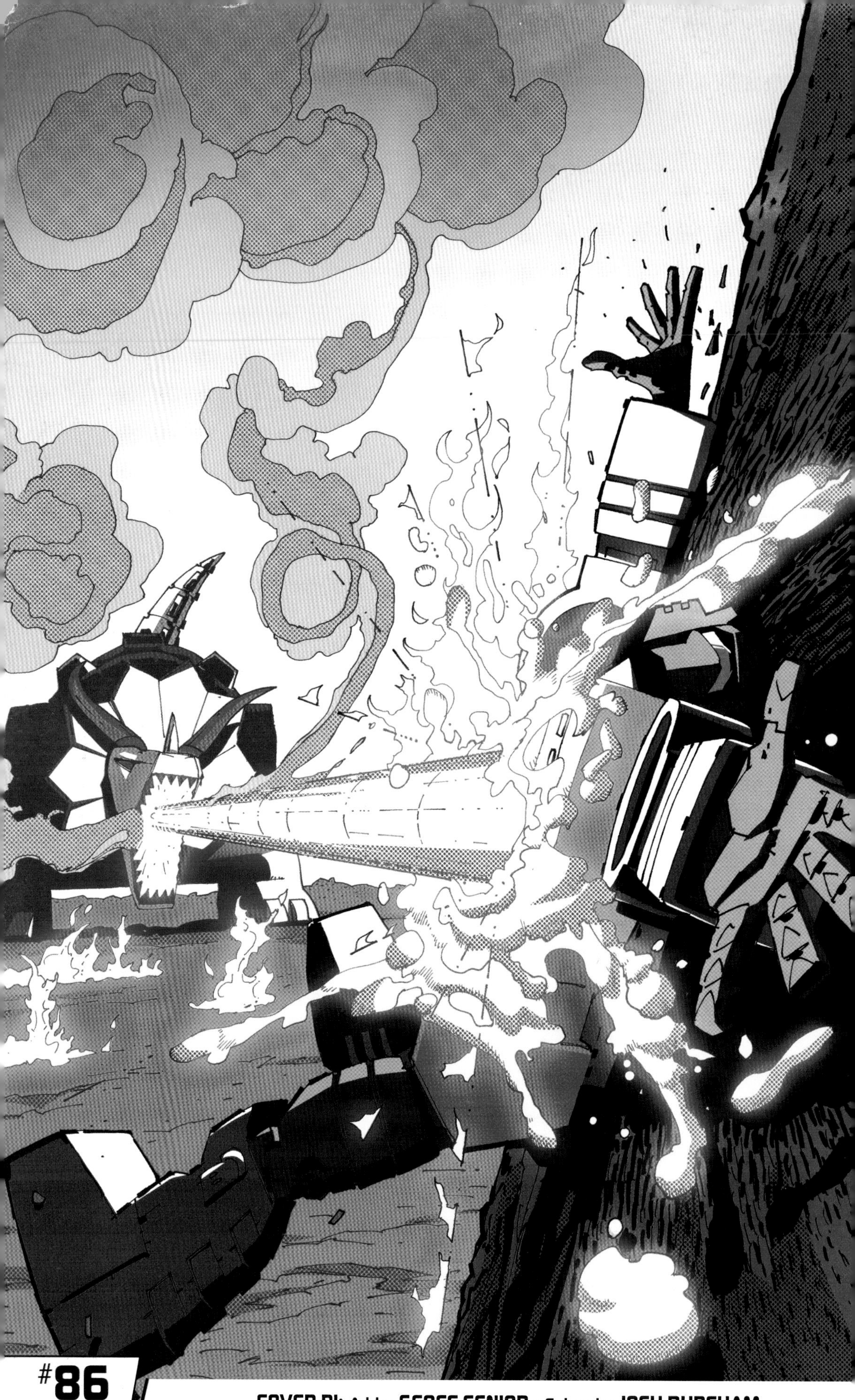

#86

COVER RI: Art by GEOFF SENIOR • Colors by JOSH BURCHAM

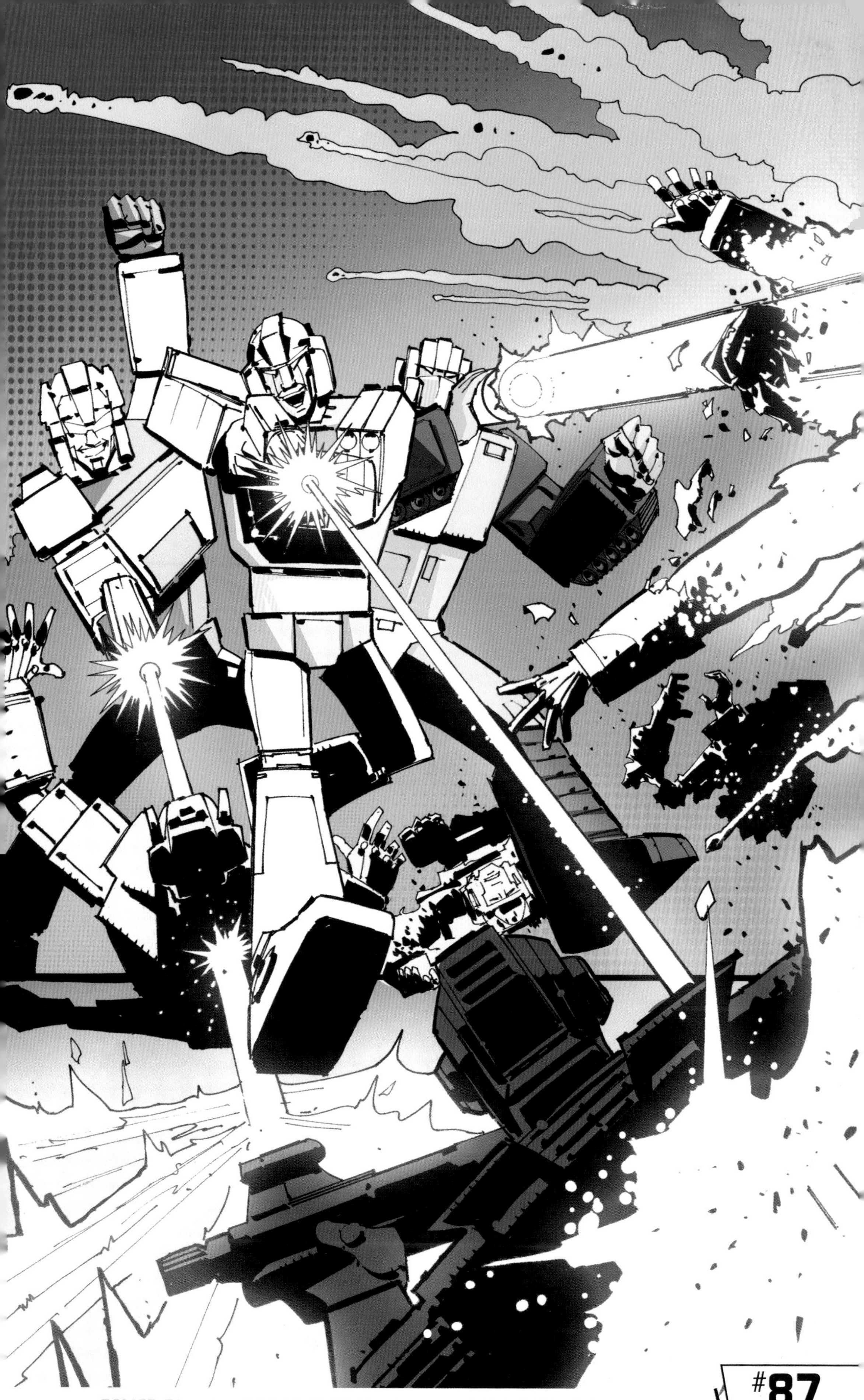

COVER RI: Art by GEOFF SENIOR • Colors by JOSH BURCHAM

#87

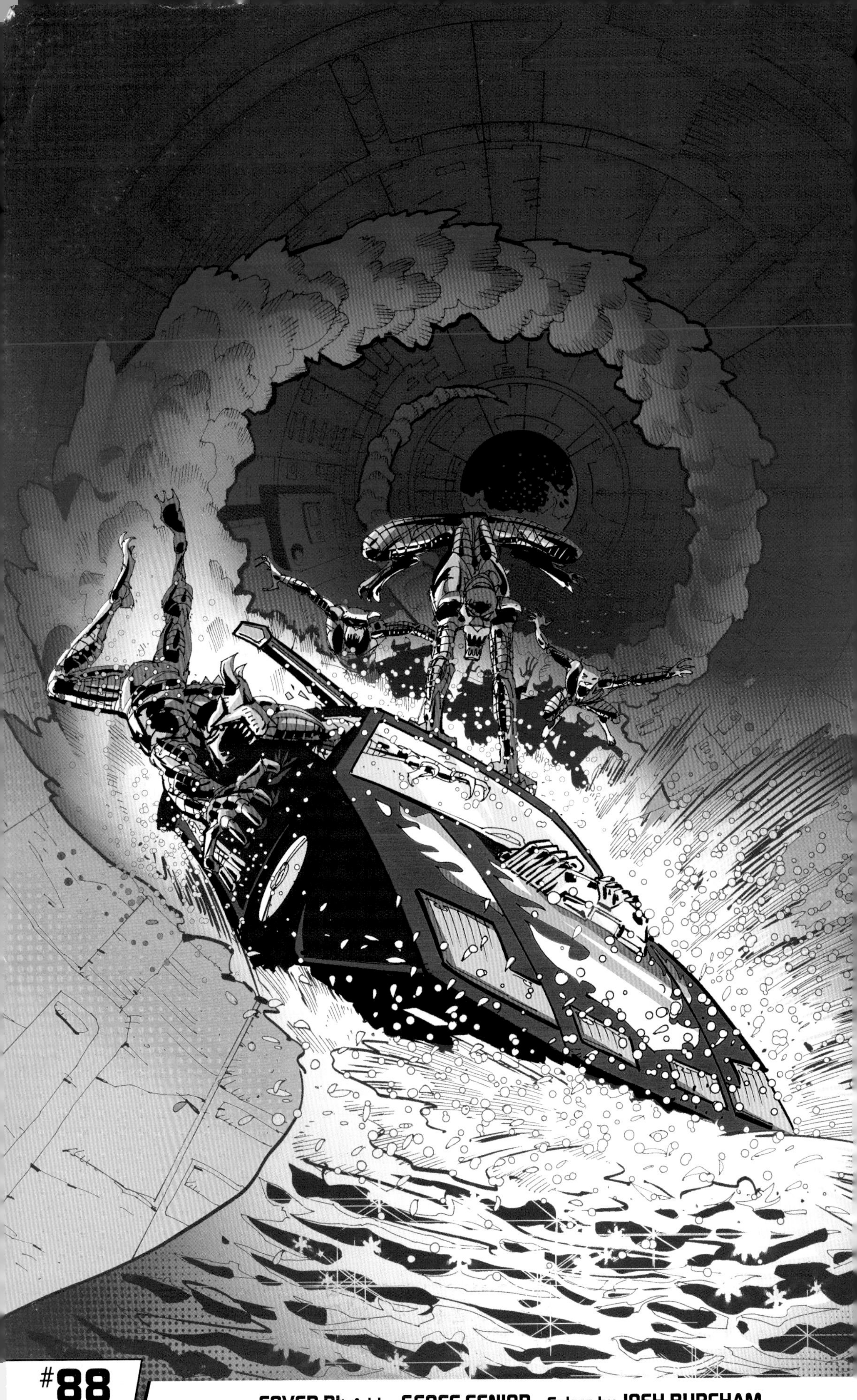

#88

COVER RI: Art by GEOFF SENIOR • Colors by JOSH BURCHAM

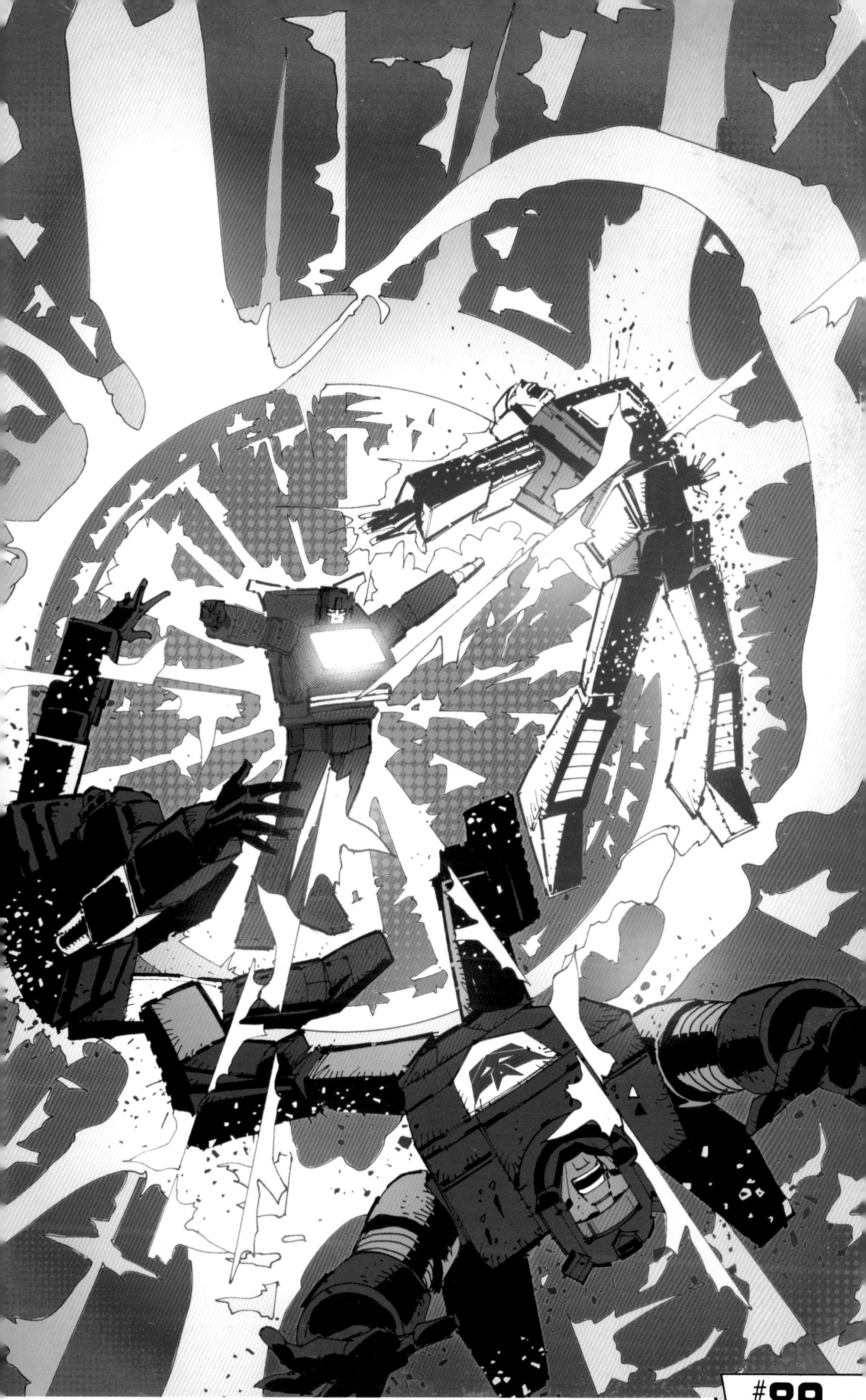

COVER RI: Art by GEOFF SENIOR • Colors by JOSH BURCHAM

#89

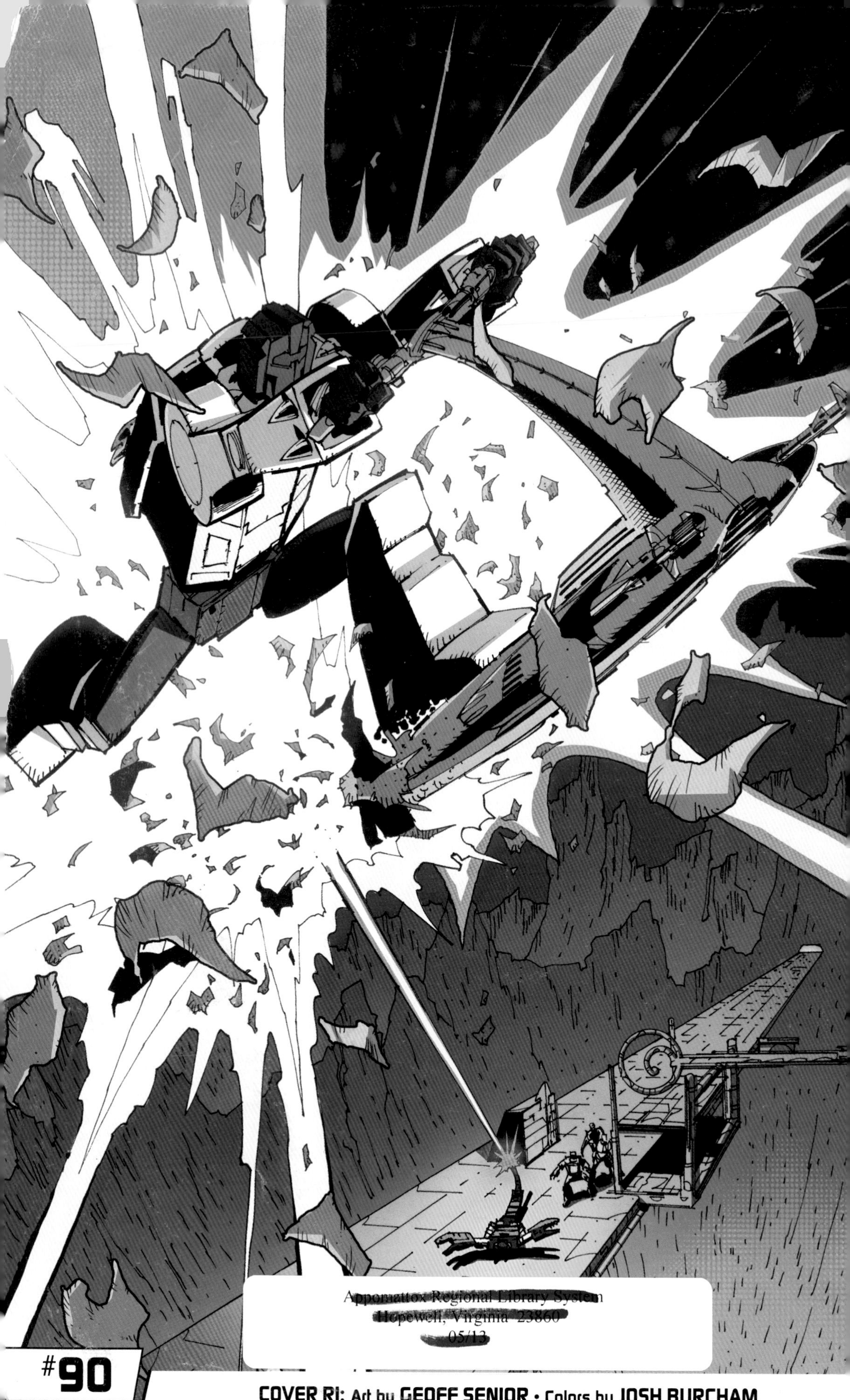

#90

COVER RI: Art by GEOFF SENIOR • Colors by JOSH BURCHAM